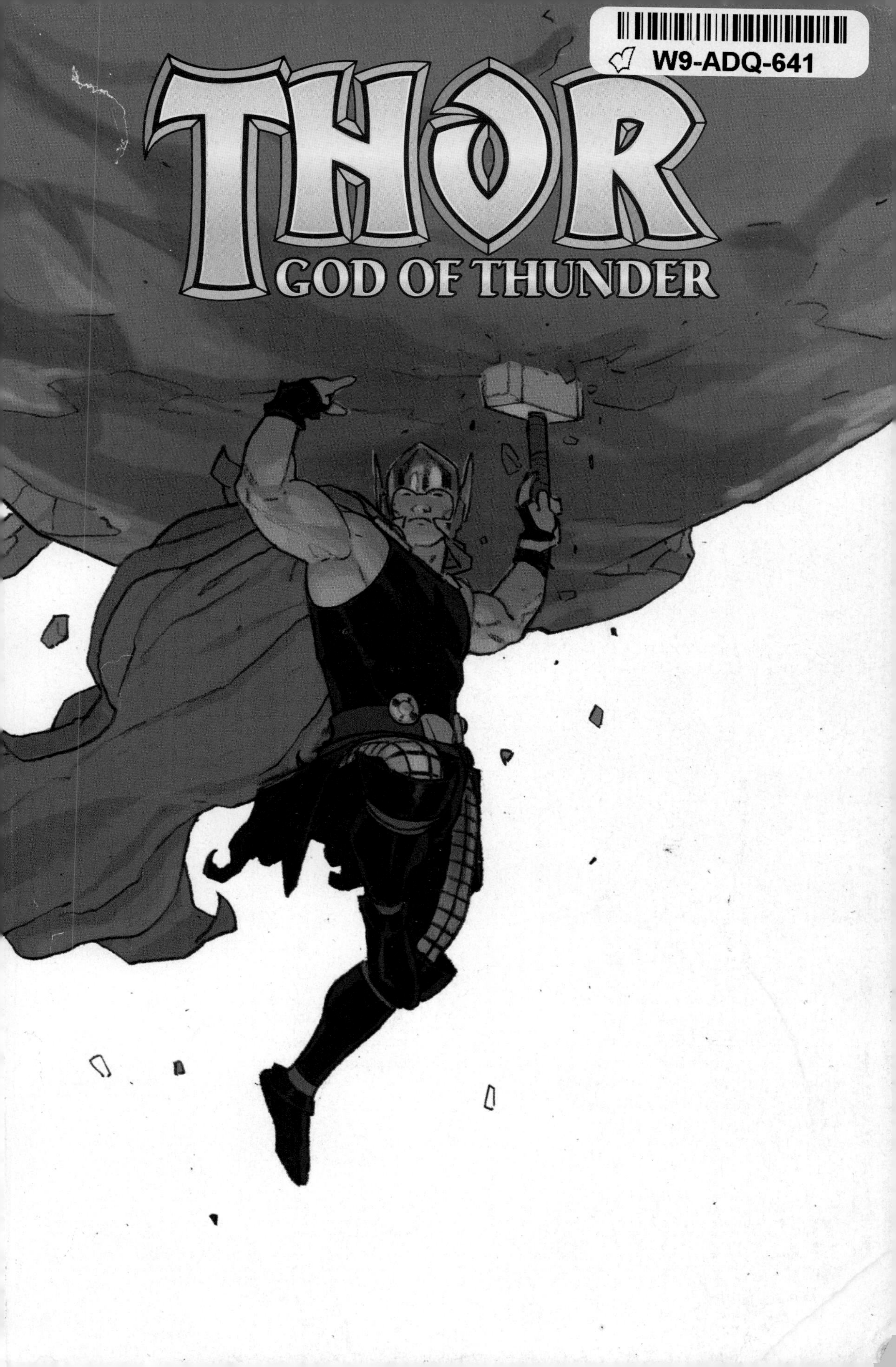
THOR
GOD OF THUNDER

Collection Editor: **Jennifer Grünwald**

Assistant Editor: **Sarah Brunstad**

Associate Managing Editor: **Alex Starbuck**

Editor, Special Projects: **Mark D. Beazley**

Senior Editor, Special Projects: **Jeff Youngquist**

SVP Print, Sales & Marketing: **David Gabriel**

Book Design: **Joe Frontirre**

Editor in Chief: **Axel Alonso**

Chief Creative Officer: **Joe Quesada**

Publisher: **Dan Buckley**

Executive Producer: **Alan Fine**

THOR: GOD OF THUNDER VOL. 4 - THE LAST DAYS OF MIDGARD. Contains material originally published in magazine form as THOR: GOD OF THUNDER #19-25. First printing 2015. ISBN# 978-0-7851-8991-6. Published by MARVEL WORLDWIDE, INC., a subsidiary of MARVEL ENTERTAINMENT, LLC. OFFICE OF PUBLICATION: 135 West 50th Street, New York, NY 10020. Copyright © 2015 MARVEL No similarity between any of the names, characters, persons, and/or institutions in this magazine with those of any living or dead person or institution is intended, and any such similarity which may exist is purely coincidental. **Printed in the U.S.A.** ALAN FINE, President, Marvel Entertainment; DAN BUCKLEY, President, TV, Publishing and Brand Management; JOE QUESADA, Chief Creative Officer; TOM BREVOORT, SVP of Publishing; DAVID BOGART, SVP of Operations & Procurement, Publishing; C.B. CEBULSKI, VP of International Development & Brand Management; DAVID GABRIEL, SVP Print, Sales & Marketing; JIM O'KEEFE, VP of Operations & Logistics; DAN CARR, Executive Director of Publishing Technology; SUSAN CRESPI, Editorial Operations Manager; ALEX MORALES, Publishing Operations Manager; STAN LEE, Chairman Emeritus. For information regarding advertising in Marvel Comics or on Marvel.com, please contact Jonathan Rheingold, VP of Custom Solutions & Ad Sales, at jrheingold@marvel.com. For Marvel subscription inquiries, please call 800-217-9158. **Manufactured between 5/22/2015 and 6/29/2015 by R.R. DONNELLEY, INC., SALEM, VA, USA.**

10 9 8 7 6 5 4 3 2 1

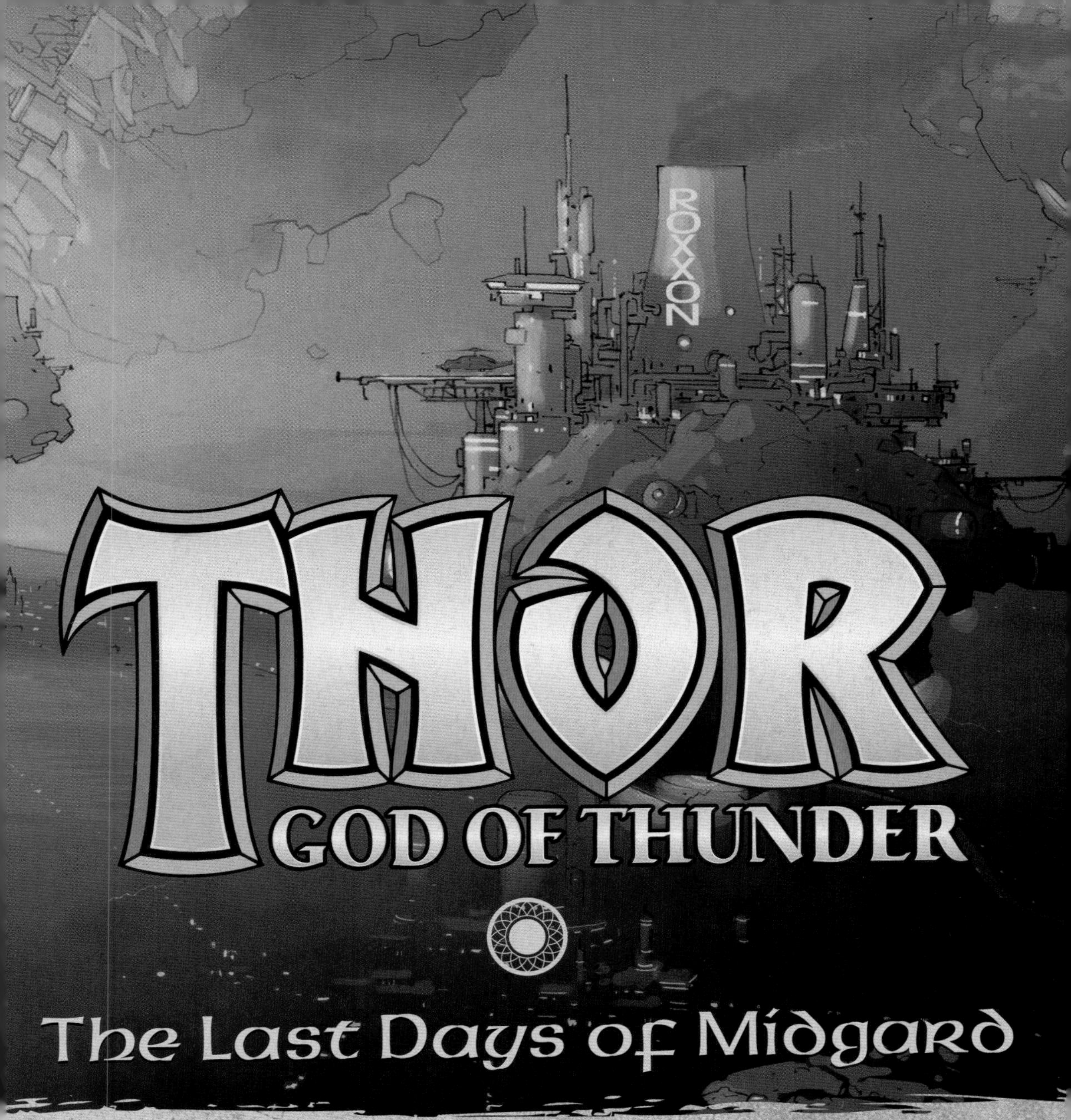
ROXXON

THOR
GOD OF THUNDER
The Last Days of Midgard

WRITER
JASON AARON

ISSUES #19-24
ARTIST
ESAD RIBIC
with **AGUSTIN ALESSIO**
(#24, pp. 1-18)

COLOR ARTIST
IVE SVORCINA
with **AGUSTIN ALESSIO**
(#24, pp. 1-18)

ISSUE #25

"THE 13TH SON OF A 13TH SON"
ARTIST
R.M. GUÉRA
COLOR ARTIST
GIULIA BRUSCO

"BLOOD AND ICE"
ARTIST
SIMON BISLEY

"UNWORTHY"
ARTIST
ESAD RIBIC
COLOR ARTIST
IVE SVORCINA

COVER ART
ESAD RIBIC (#19-21 & #25), **JEE-HYUNG** (#22) and **AGUSTIN ALESSIO** (#23-24)

LETTERER
VC'S JOE SABINO

ASSISTANT EDITOR
JON MOISAN

EDITOR
WIL MOSS

THOR CREATED BY STAN LEE, LARRY LIEBER & JACK KIRBY

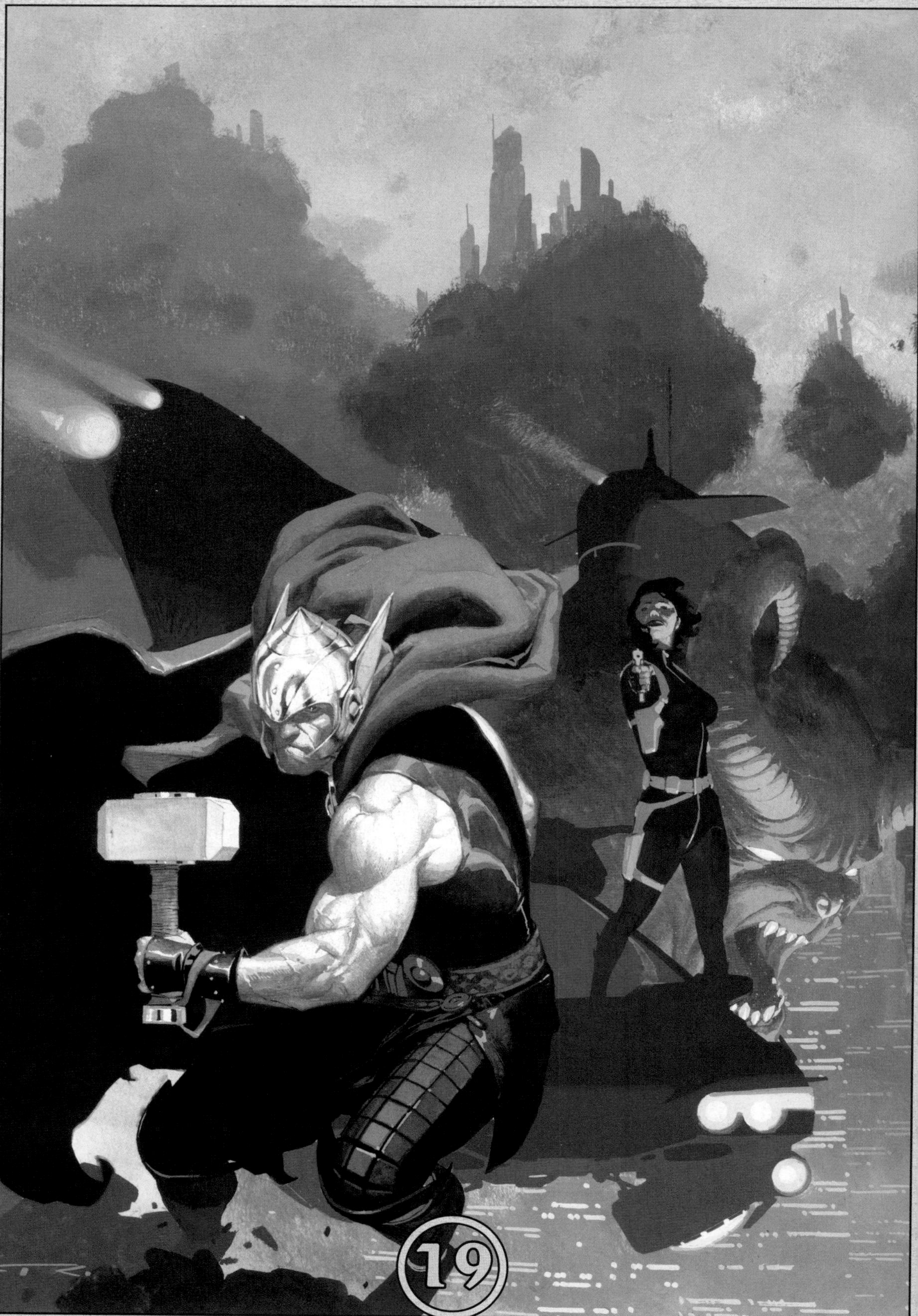
19

The Last Days of Midgard — Part 1: Gods and CEOs

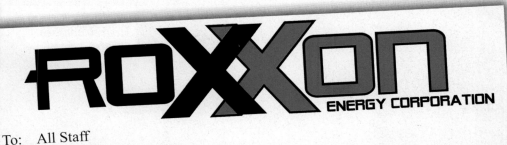

THOR IS THE ASGARDIAN GOD OF THUNDER AND AN AVENGER. AS THE WEILD
MJOLNIR, A MYSTICAL URU HAMMER OF IMMENSE POWER, H
WORLD, MIDGARD, FOR THE REST OF HIS DAYS. WHICH IS
NOW WHEN HE HAS BECOME KING THOR, HE LABORS TO REVIVE THE RUINED PLAN

ROXXON ENERGY CORPORATION

To: All Staff
Date: 02/12/2014
Subject: Public Relations

It has been a hard road, but we are all the stronger for it. ROXXON is its own master once again. As we prepare to take the corporate world by storm, we must guard our good reputation as the world's wealthiest, most powerful super-corporation with all due diligence.

With that in mind, there are a couple pieces of related business to address:

1.) As you may know, recently a S.H.I.E.L.D. environmental investigation team claimed that the unfortunate deaths of some sea life in the Southern Ocean were due to our underwater mining station there. It was a completely fraudulent claim, as was soon proven in a court of law. However, we continue to be dogged by a member of that team, a rookie S.H.I.E.L.D. agent named Roz Solomon. As is our policy, please continue to forward any and all communications from Agent Solomon to our PR team. She will be dealt with accordingly.

2.) On a more positive note, we are about to send out a press release inviting the media tothe grand unveiling of the Pipeline project in Glacier Bay National Park, Alaska. When the public gets their first glimpse of the gift we are bestowing upon them, I believe that the reaction will be "out of this world." But please, do keep the details under wraps until then.

I trust you all understand the importance of these matters. I look forward to working with you in our mission to make the world a better place through ROXXON.

Dario Agger

Dario Agger
CEO

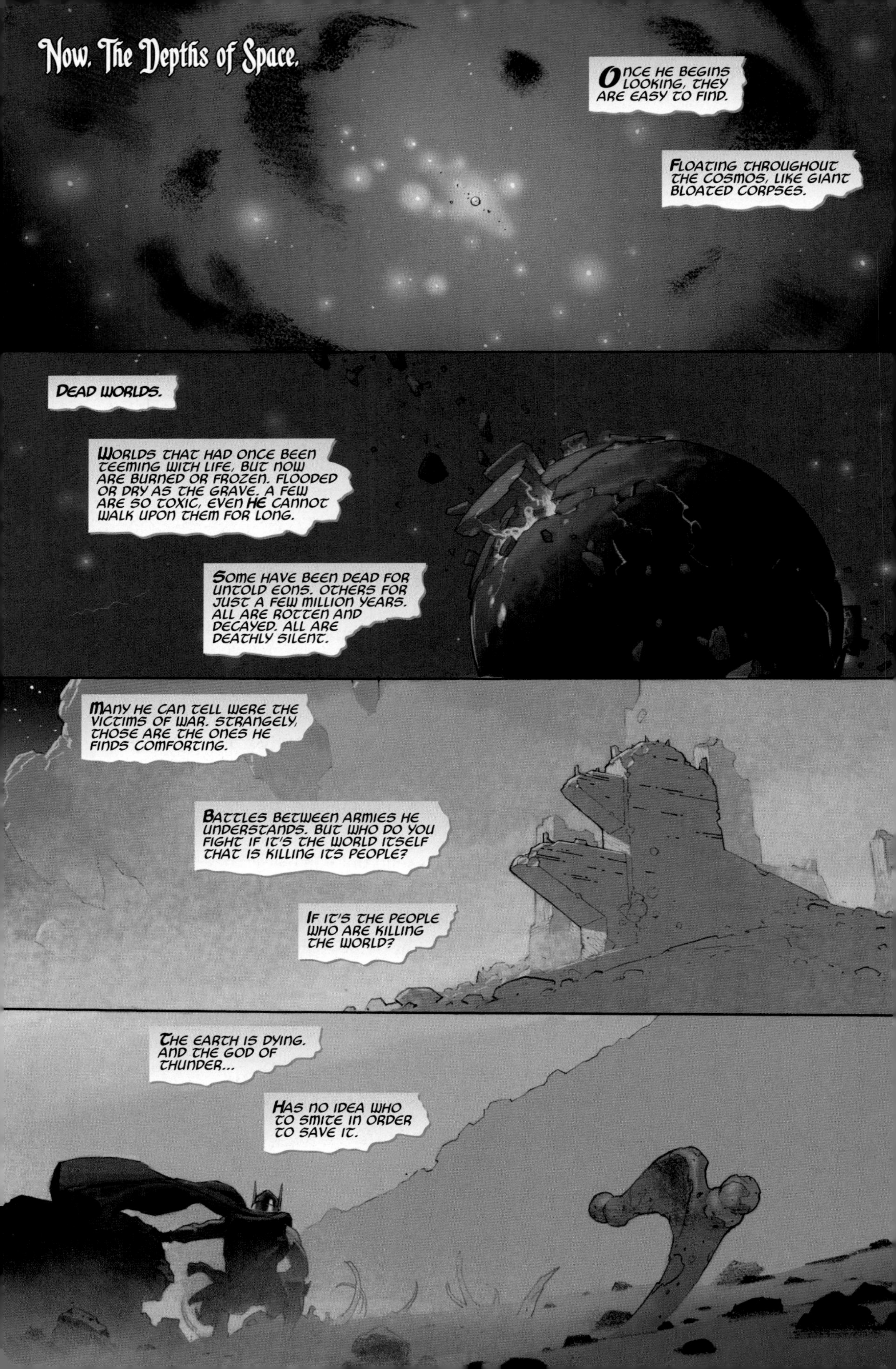
Now, The Depths of Space.
ONCE HE BEGINS LOOKING, THEY ARE EASY TO FIND.
FLOATING THROUGHOUT THE COSMOS, LIKE GIANT BLOATED CORPSES.
DEAD WORLDS.
WORLDS THAT HAD ONCE BEEN TEEMING WITH LIFE, BUT NOW ARE BURNED OR FROZEN. FLOODED OR DRY AS THE GRAVE. A FEW ARE SO TOXIC, EVEN HE CANNOT WALK UPON THEM FOR LONG.
SOME HAVE BEEN DEAD FOR UNTOLD EONS. OTHERS FOR JUST A FEW MILLION YEARS. ALL ARE ROTTEN AND DECAYED. ALL ARE DEATHLY SILENT.
MANY HE CAN TELL WERE THE VICTIMS OF WAR. STRANGELY, THOSE ARE THE ONES HE FINDS COMFORTING.
BATTLES BETWEEN ARMIES HE UNDERSTANDS. BUT WHO DO YOU FIGHT IF IT'S THE WORLD ITSELF THAT IS KILLING ITS PEOPLE?
IF IT'S THE PEOPLE WHO ARE KILLING THE WORLD?
THE EARTH IS DYING. AND THE GOD OF THUNDER...
HAS NO IDEA WHO TO SMITE IN ORDER TO SAVE IT.

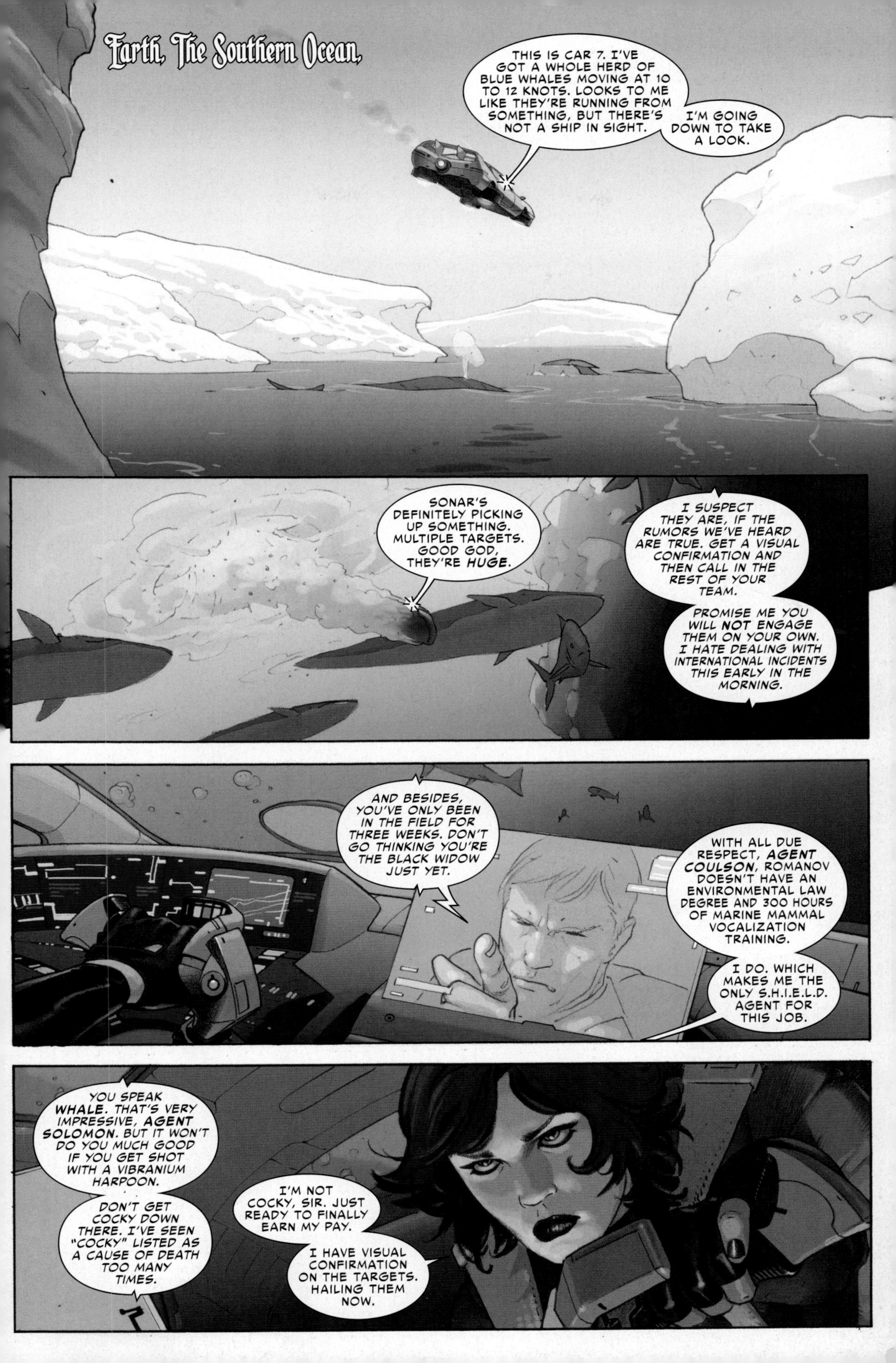
Earth, The Southern Ocean.
THIS IS CAR 7. I'VE GOT A WHOLE HERD OF BLUE WHALES MOVING AT 10 TO 12 KNOTS. LOOKS TO ME LIKE THEY'RE RUNNING FROM SOMETHING, BUT THERE'S NOT A SHIP IN SIGHT.
I'M GOING DOWN TO TAKE A LOOK.
SONAR'S DEFINITELY PICKING UP SOMETHING. MULTIPLE TARGETS. GOOD GOD, THEY'RE HUGE.
I SUSPECT THEY ARE, IF THE RUMORS WE'VE HEARD ARE TRUE. GET A VISUAL CONFIRMATION AND THEN CALL IN THE REST OF YOUR TEAM.
PROMISE ME YOU WILL NOT ENGAGE THEM ON YOUR OWN. I HATE DEALING WITH INTERNATIONAL INCIDENTS THIS EARLY IN THE MORNING.
AND BESIDES, YOU'VE ONLY BEEN IN THE FIELD FOR THREE WEEKS. DON'T GO THINKING YOU'RE THE BLACK WIDOW JUST YET.
WITH ALL DUE RESPECT, AGENT COULSON, ROMANOV DOESN'T HAVE AN ENVIRONMENTAL LAW DEGREE AND 300 HOURS OF MARINE MAMMAL VOCALIZATION TRAINING.
I DO. WHICH MAKES ME THE ONLY S.H.I.E.L.D. AGENT FOR THIS JOB.
YOU SPEAK WHALE. THAT'S VERY IMPRESSIVE, AGENT SOLOMON. BUT IT WON'T DO YOU MUCH GOOD IF YOU GET SHOT WITH A VIBRANIUM HARPOON.
DON'T GET COCKY DOWN THERE. I'VE SEEN "COCKY" LISTED AS A CAUSE OF DEATH TOO MANY TIMES.
I'M NOT COCKY, SIR. JUST READY TO FINALLY EARN MY PAY.
I HAVE VISUAL CONFIRMATION ON THE TARGETS. HAILING THEM NOW.

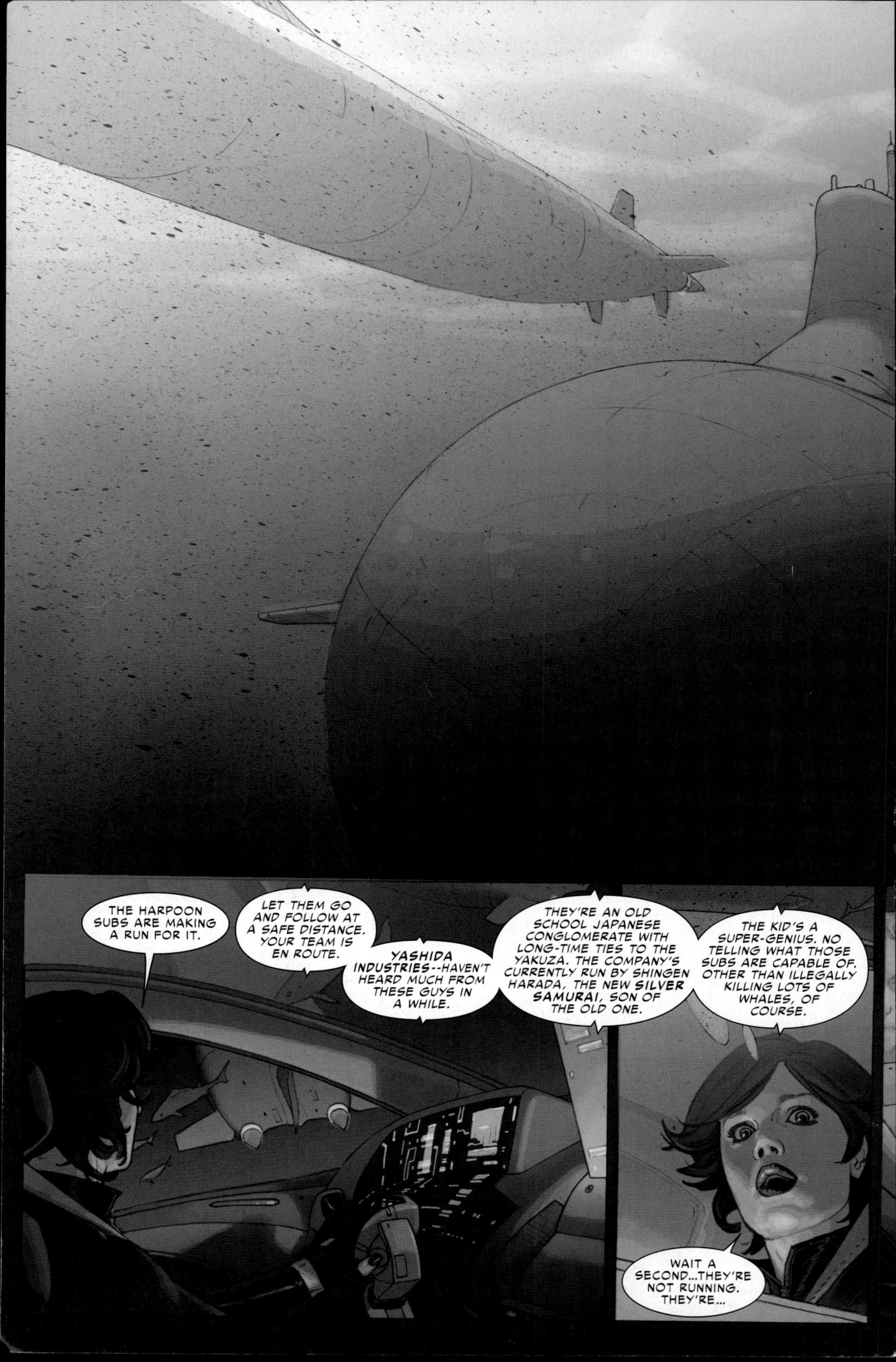
THE HARPOON SUBS ARE MAKING A RUN FOR IT.
LET THEM GO AND FOLLOW AT A SAFE DISTANCE. YOUR TEAM IS EN ROUTE.
YASHIDA INDUSTRIES--HAVEN'T HEARD MUCH FROM THESE GUYS IN A WHILE.
THEY'RE AN OLD SCHOOL JAPANESE CONGLOMERATE WITH LONG-TIME TIES TO THE YAKUZA. THE COMPANY'S CURRENTLY RUN BY SHINGEN HARADA, THE NEW SILVER SAMURAI, SON OF THE OLD ONE.
THE KID'S A SUPER-GENIUS. NO TELLING WHAT THOSE SUBS ARE CAPABLE OF. OTHER THAN ILLEGALLY KILLING LOTS OF WHALES, OF COURSE.
WAIT A SECOND...THEY'RE NOT RUNNING. THEY'RE...

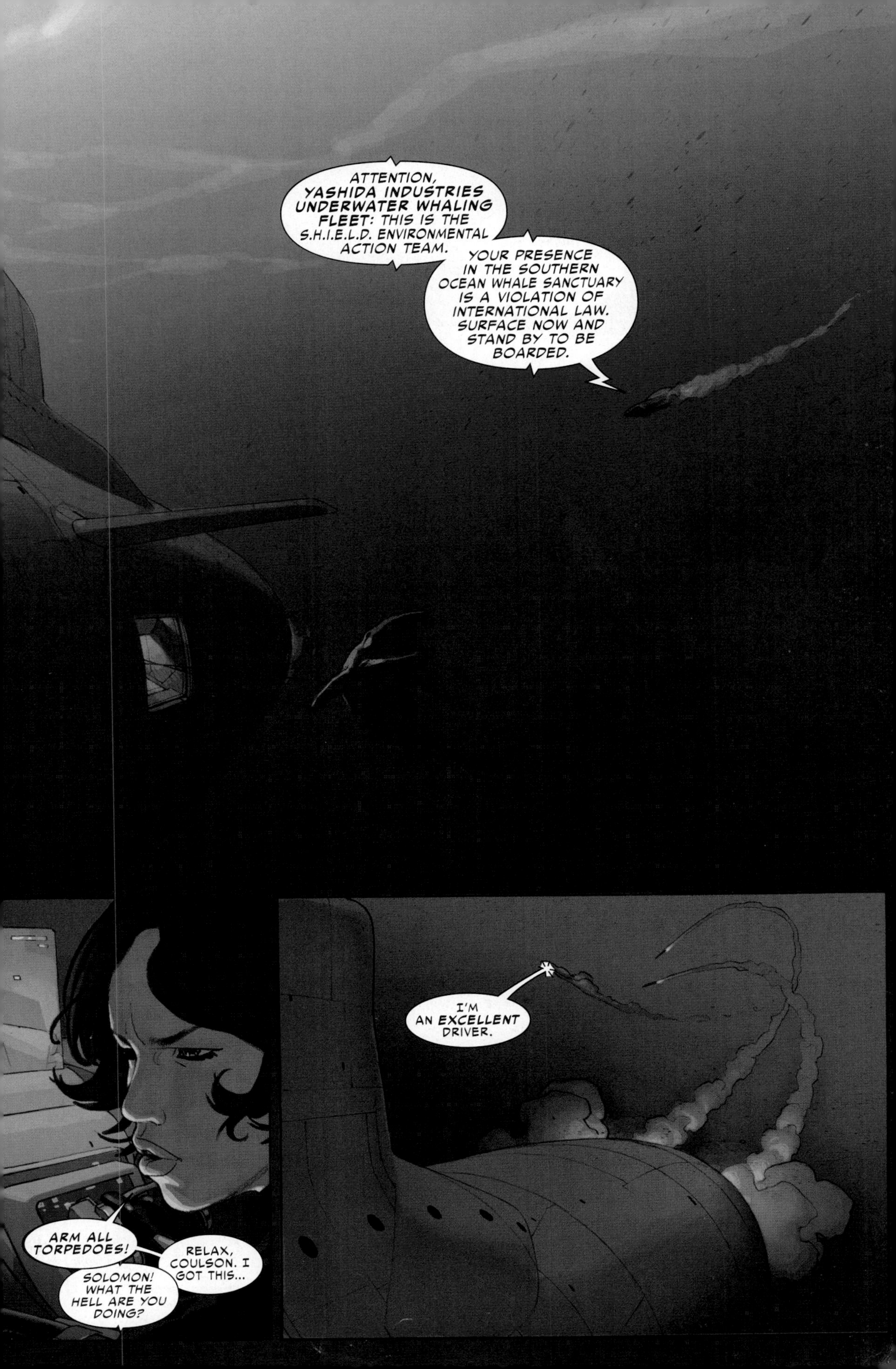
ATTENTION, YASHIDA INDUSTRIES UNDERWATER WHALING FLEET: THIS IS THE S.H.I.E.L.D. ENVIRONMENTAL ACTION TEAM.
YOUR PRESENCE IN THE SOUTHERN OCEAN WHALE SANCTUARY IS A VIOLATION OF INTERNATIONAL LAW. SURFACE NOW AND STAND BY TO BE BOARDED.
ARM ALL TORPEDOES!
SOLOMON! WHAT THE HELL ARE YOU DOING?
RELAX, COULSON. I GOT THIS...
I'M AN EXCELLENT DRIVER.

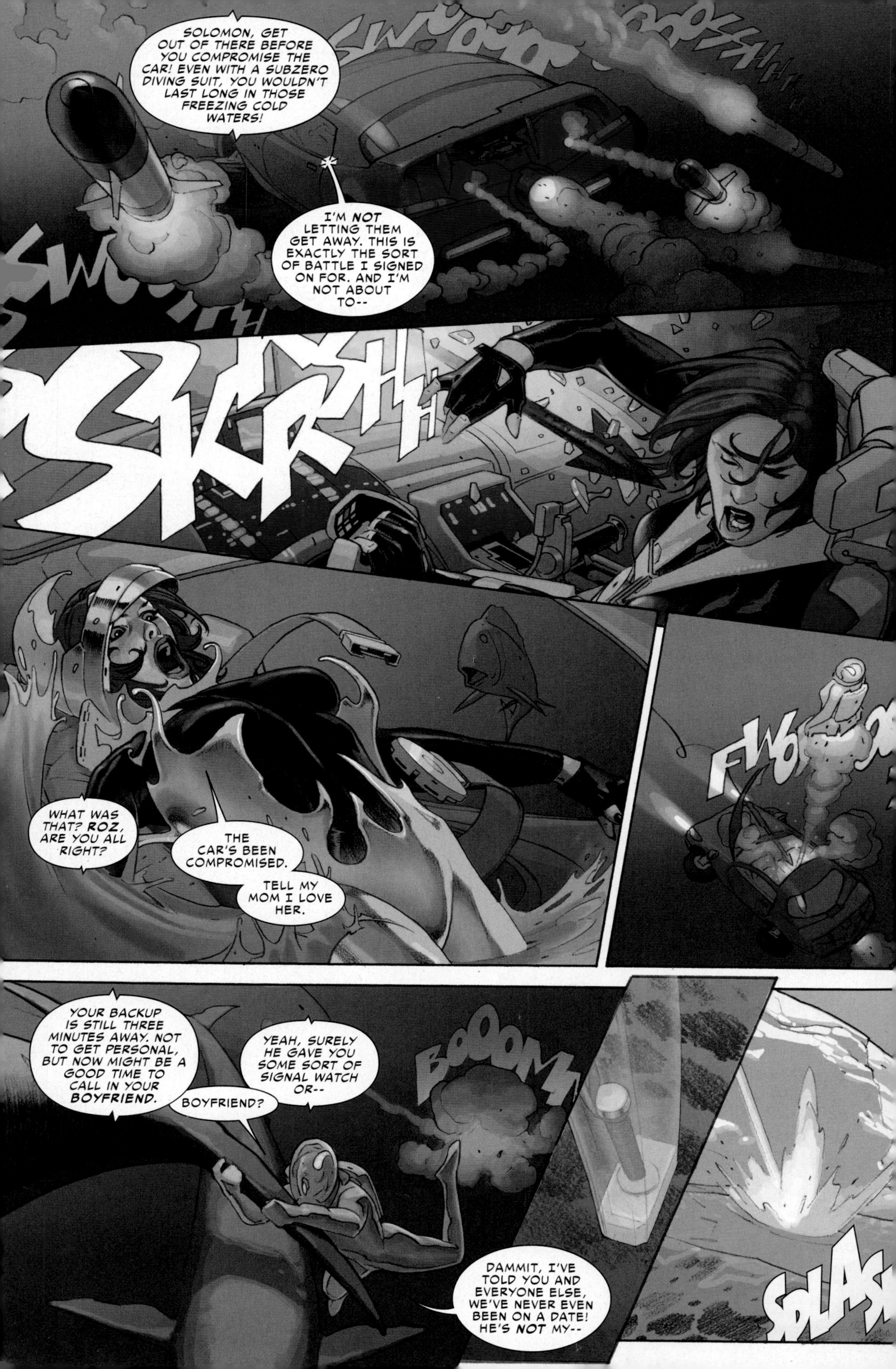
SOLOMON, GET OUT OF THERE BEFORE YOU COMPROMISE THE CAR! EVEN WITH A SUBZERO DIVING SUIT, YOU WOULDN'T LAST LONG IN THOSE FREEZING COLD WATERS!
I'M NOT LETTING THEM GET AWAY. THIS IS EXACTLY THE SORT OF BATTLE I SIGNED ON FOR. AND I'M NOT ABOUT TO--
SKRSHH
WHAT WAS THAT? ROZ, ARE YOU ALL RIGHT?
THE CAR'S BEEN COMPROMISED.
TELL MY MOM I LOVE HER.
YOUR BACKUP IS STILL THREE MINUTES AWAY. NOT TO GET PERSONAL, BUT NOW MIGHT BE A GOOD TIME TO CALL IN YOUR BOYFRIEND.
BOYFRIEND?
YEAH, SURELY HE GAVE YOU SOME SORT OF SIGNAL WATCH OR--
BOOOM
DAMMIT, I'VE TOLD YOU AND EVERYONE ELSE, WE'VE NEVER EVEN BEEN ON A DATE! HE'S NOT MY--

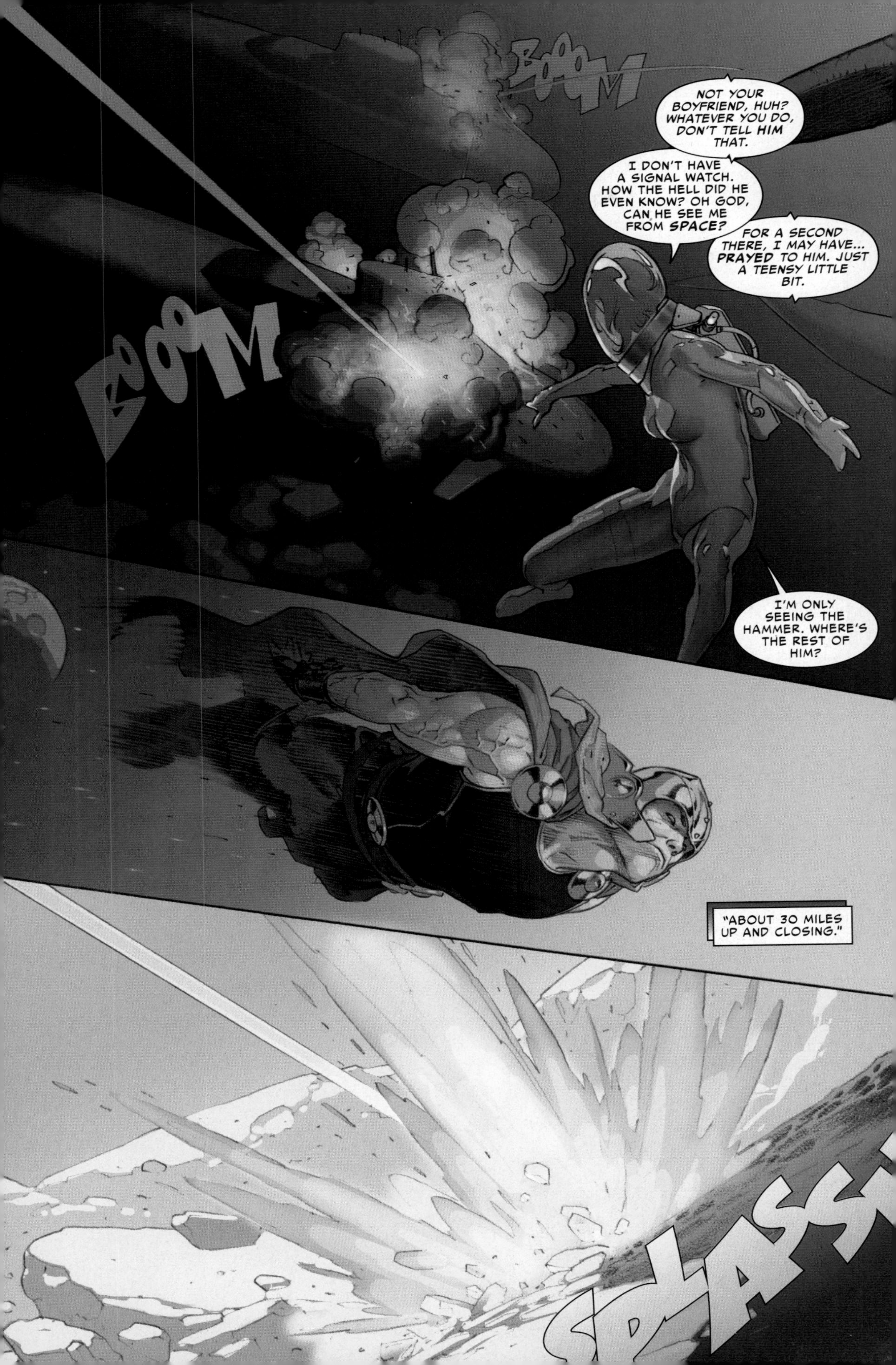
BOOM
NOT YOUR BOYFRIEND, HUH? WHATEVER YOU DO, DON'T TELL HIM THAT.
I DON'T HAVE A SIGNAL WATCH. HOW THE HELL DID HE EVEN KNOW? OH GOD, CAN HE SEE ME FROM SPACE?
FOR A SECOND THERE, I MAY HAVE... PRAYED TO HIM. JUST A TEENSY LITTLE BIT.
BOOM
I'M ONLY SEEING THE HAMMER. WHERE'S THE REST OF HIM?
"ABOUT 30 MILES UP AND CLOSING."

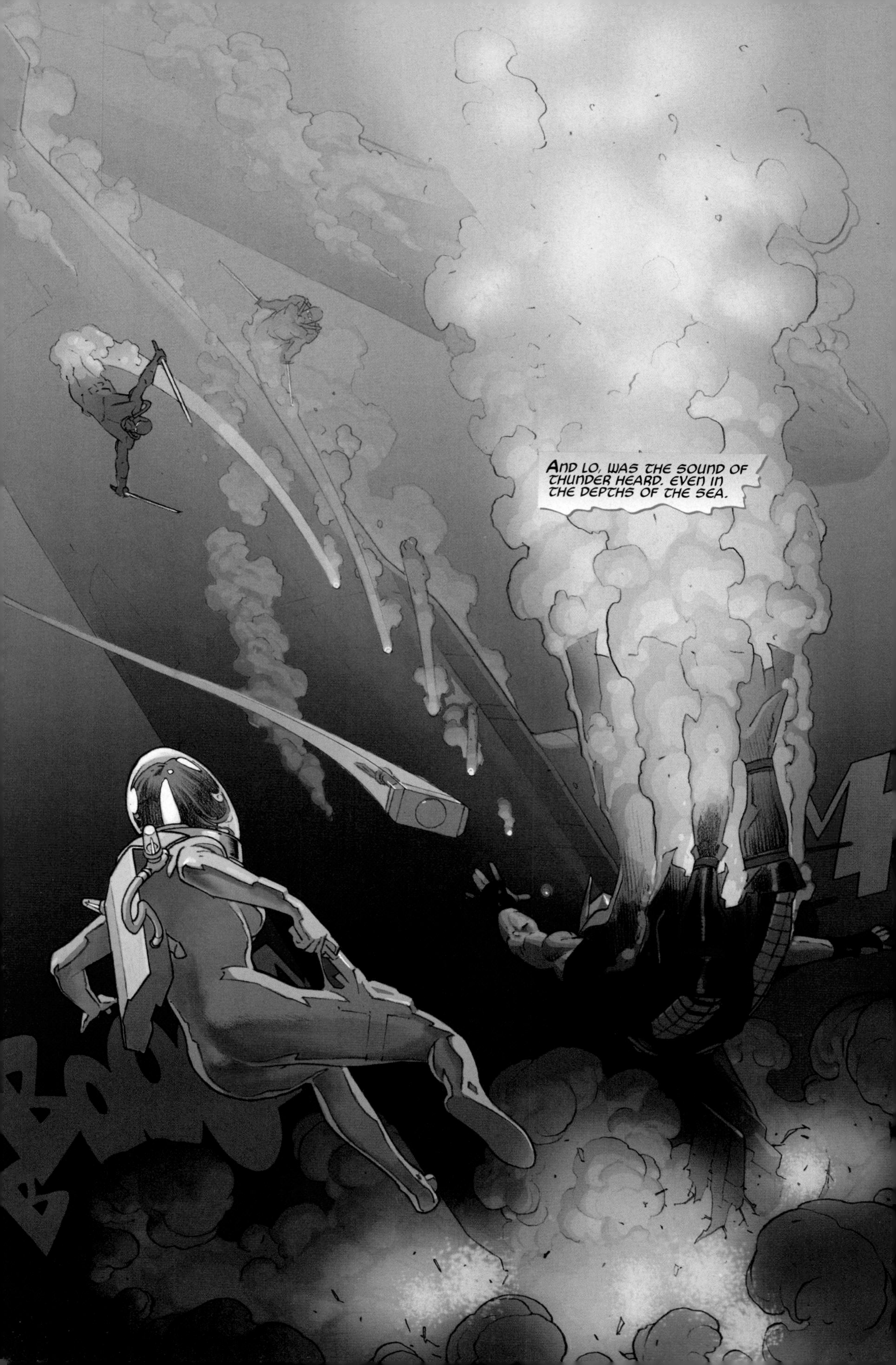
And lo, was the sound of thunder heard. Even in the depths of the sea.

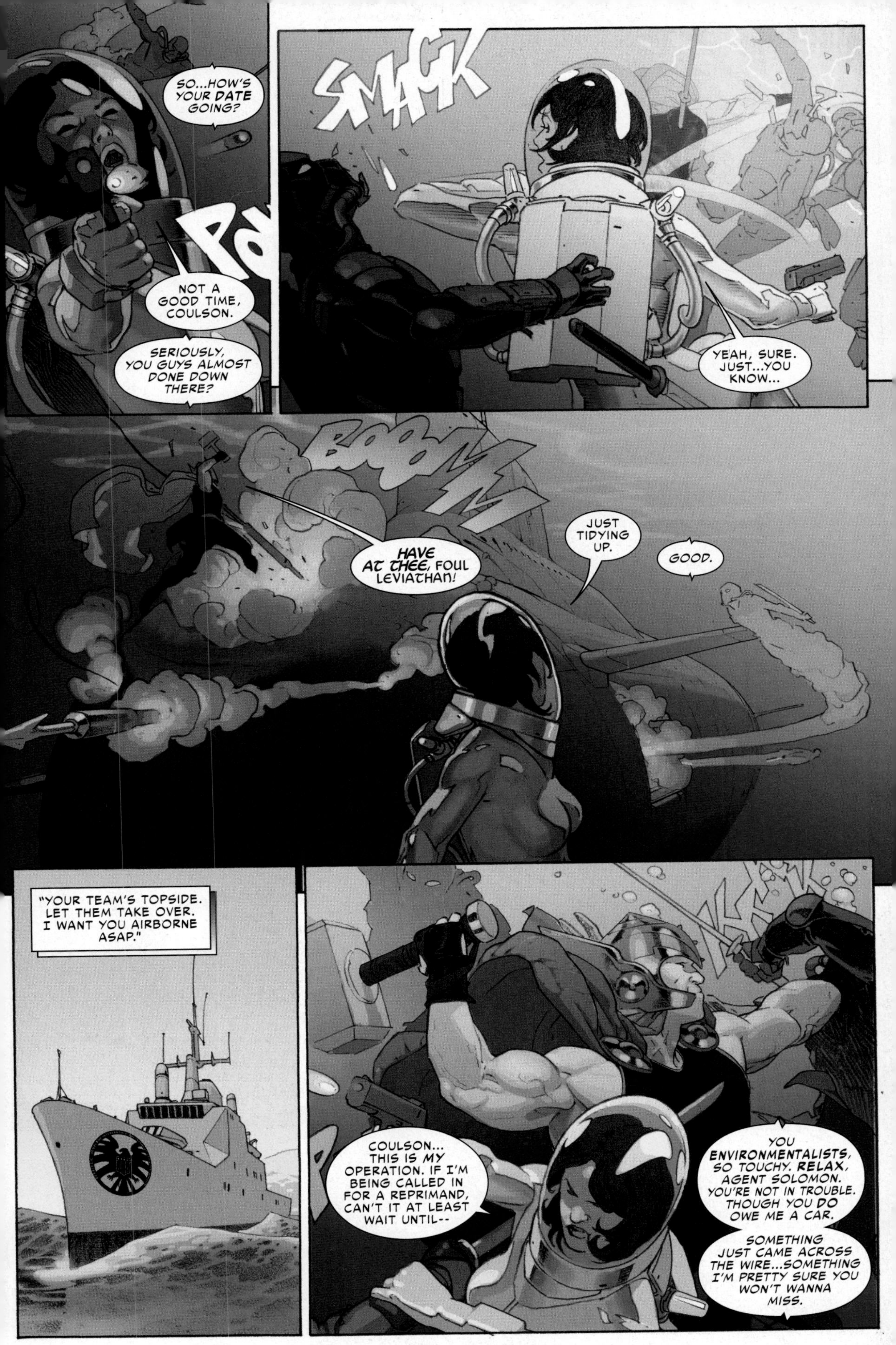
SO...HOW'S YOUR DATE GOING?
PA
NOT A GOOD TIME, COULSON.
SERIOUSLY, YOU GUYS ALMOST DONE DOWN THERE?
SMACK
YEAH, SURE. JUST...YOU KNOW...
BOOM
HAVE AT THEE, FOUL LEVIATHAN!
JUST TIDYING UP.
GOOD.
"YOUR TEAM'S TOPSIDE. LET THEM TAKE OVER. I WANT YOU AIRBORNE ASAP."
COULSON... THIS IS MY OPERATION. IF I'M BEING CALLED IN FOR A REPRIMAND, CAN'T IT AT LEAST WAIT UNTIL--
YOU ENVIRONMENTALISTS, SO TOUCHY. RELAX, AGENT SOLOMON. YOU'RE NOT IN TROUBLE. THOUGH YOU DO OWE ME A CAR.
SOMETHING JUST CAME ACROSS THE WIRE...SOMETHING I'M PRETTY SURE YOU WON'T WANNA MISS.

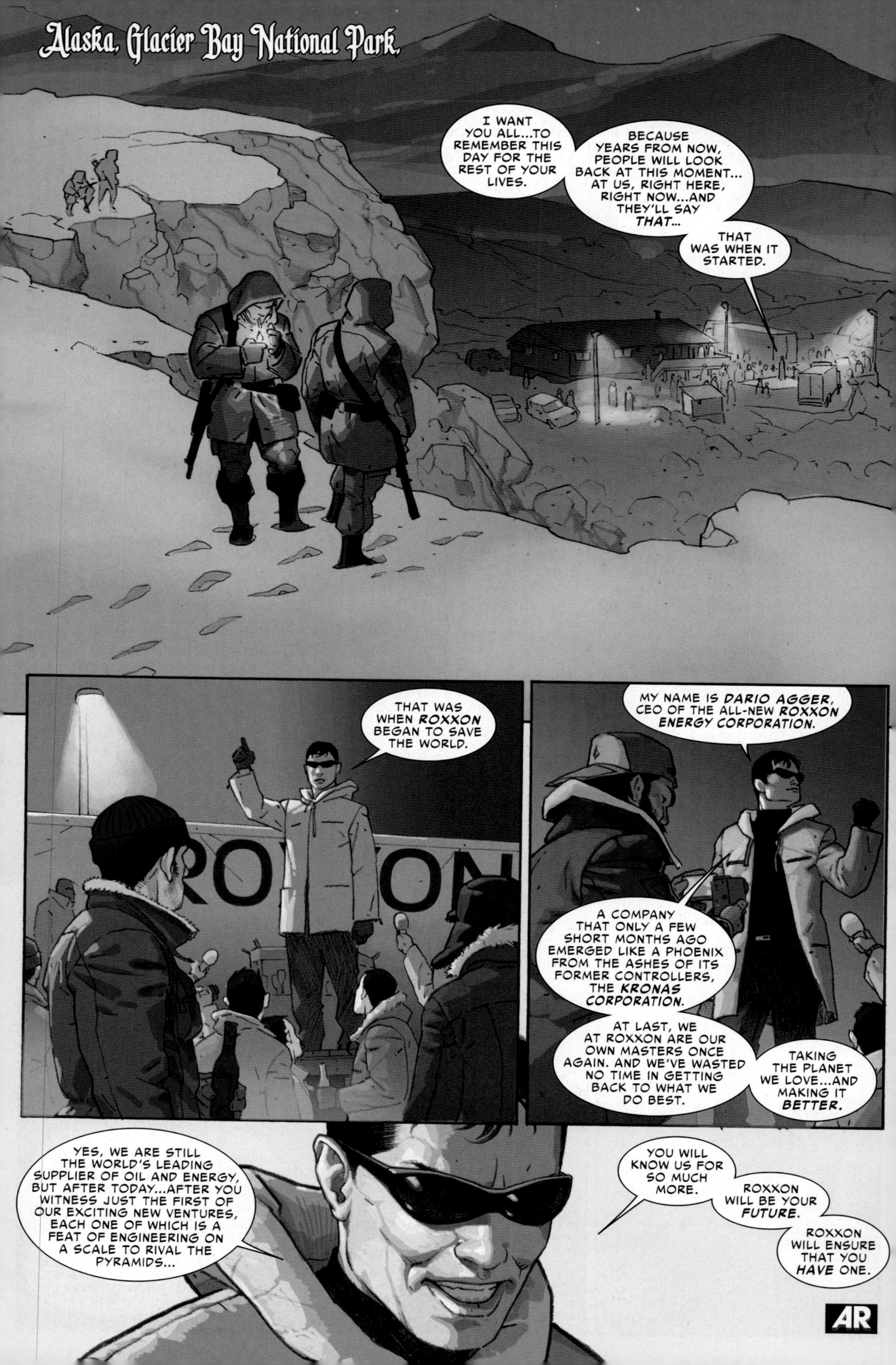
Alaska, Glacier Bay National Park.
I WANT YOU ALL...TO REMEMBER THIS DAY FOR THE REST OF YOUR LIVES.
BECAUSE YEARS FROM NOW, PEOPLE WILL LOOK BACK AT THIS MOMENT... AT US, RIGHT HERE, RIGHT NOW...AND THEY'LL SAY THAT...
THAT WAS WHEN IT STARTED.
THAT WAS WHEN ROXXON BEGAN TO SAVE THE WORLD.
ROXXON
MY NAME IS DARIO AGGER, CEO OF THE ALL-NEW ROXXON ENERGY CORPORATION.
A COMPANY THAT ONLY A FEW SHORT MONTHS AGO EMERGED LIKE A PHOENIX FROM THE ASHES OF ITS FORMER CONTROLLERS, THE KRONAS CORPORATION.
AT LAST, WE AT ROXXON ARE OUR OWN MASTERS ONCE AGAIN. AND WE'VE WASTED NO TIME IN GETTING BACK TO WHAT WE DO BEST.
TAKING THE PLANET WE LOVE...AND MAKING IT BETTER.
YES, WE ARE STILL THE WORLD'S LEADING SUPPLIER OF OIL AND ENERGY, BUT AFTER TODAY...AFTER YOU WITNESS JUST THE FIRST OF OUR EXCITING NEW VENTURES, EACH ONE OF WHICH IS A FEAT OF ENGINEERING ON A SCALE TO RIVAL THE PYRAMIDS...
YOU WILL KNOW US FOR SO MUCH MORE.
ROXXON WILL BE YOUR FUTURE.
ROXXON WILL ENSURE THAT YOU HAVE ONE.
AR

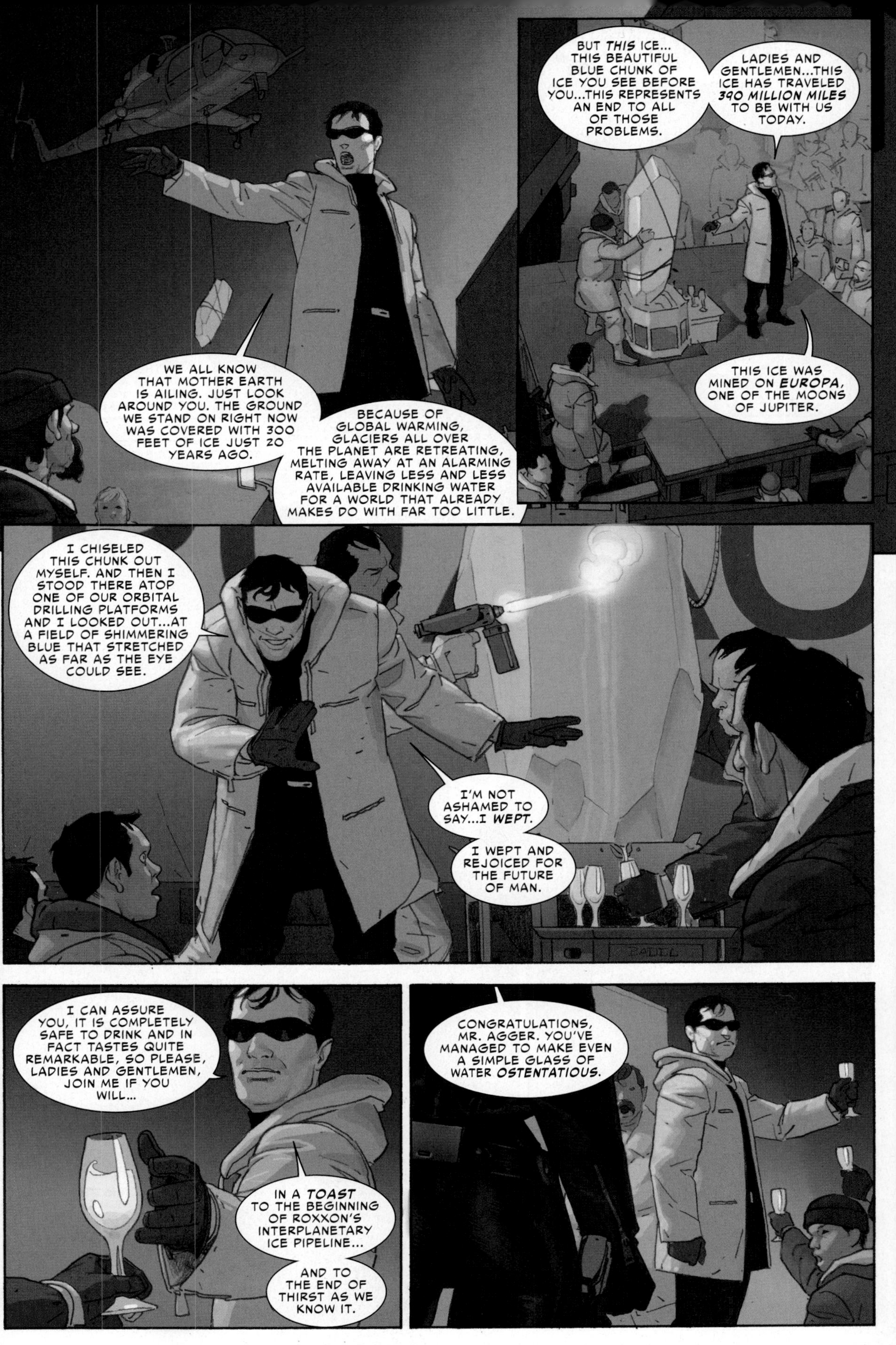
WE ALL KNOW THAT MOTHER EARTH IS AILING. JUST LOOK AROUND YOU. THE GROUND WE STAND ON RIGHT NOW WAS COVERED WITH 300 FEET OF ICE JUST 20 YEARS AGO.
BECAUSE OF GLOBAL WARMING, GLACIERS ALL OVER THE PLANET ARE RETREATING, MELTING AWAY AT AN ALARMING RATE, LEAVING LESS AND LESS AVAILABLE DRINKING WATER FOR A WORLD THAT ALREADY MAKES DO WITH FAR TOO LITTLE.
BUT *THIS* ICE... THIS BEAUTIFUL BLUE CHUNK OF ICE YOU SEE BEFORE YOU...THIS REPRESENTS AN END TO ALL OF THOSE PROBLEMS.
LADIES AND GENTLEMEN...THIS ICE HAS TRAVELED *390 MILLION MILES* TO BE WITH US TODAY.
THIS ICE WAS MINED ON *EUROPA*, ONE OF THE MOONS OF JUPITER.
I CHISELED THIS CHUNK OUT MYSELF. AND THEN I STOOD THERE ATOP ONE OF OUR ORBITAL DRILLING PLATFORMS AND I LOOKED OUT...AT A FIELD OF SHIMMERING BLUE THAT STRETCHED AS FAR AS THE EYE COULD SEE.
I'M NOT ASHAMED TO SAY...I *WEPT*.
I WEPT AND REJOICED FOR THE FUTURE OF MAN.
I CAN ASSURE YOU, IT IS COMPLETELY SAFE TO DRINK AND IN FACT TASTES QUITE REMARKABLE, SO PLEASE, LADIES AND GENTLEMEN, JOIN ME IF YOU WILL...
IN A *TOAST* TO THE BEGINNING OF ROXXON'S INTERPLANETARY ICE PIPELINE...
AND TO THE END OF THIRST AS WE KNOW IT.
CONGRATULATIONS, MR. AGGER. YOU'VE MANAGED TO MAKE EVEN A SIMPLE GLASS OF WATER *OSTENTATIOUS*.

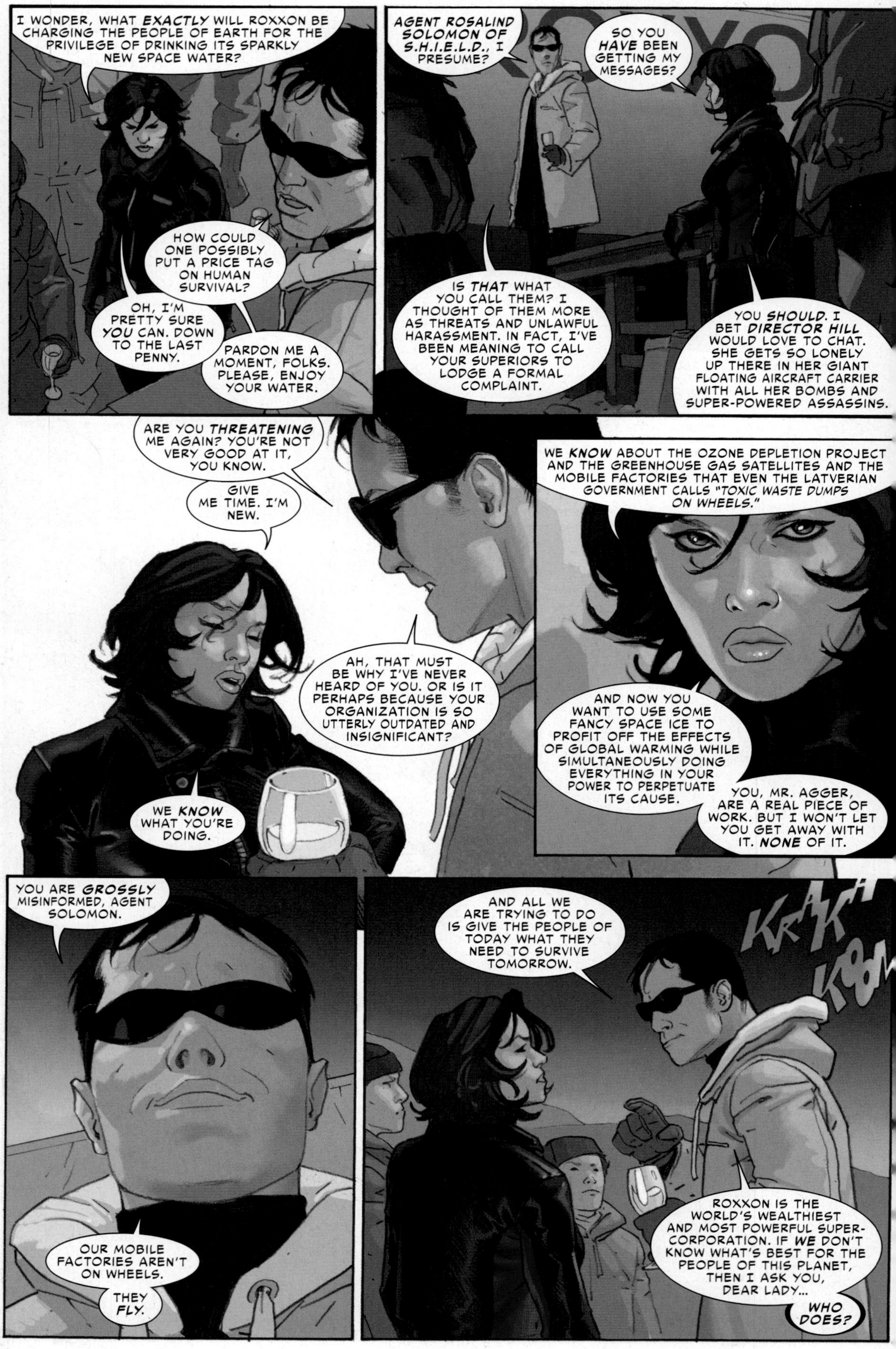
I WONDER, WHAT EXACTLY WILL ROXXON BE CHARGING THE PEOPLE OF EARTH FOR THE PRIVILEGE OF DRINKING ITS SPARKLY NEW SPACE WATER?
HOW COULD ONE POSSIBLY PUT A PRICE TAG ON HUMAN SURVIVAL?
OH, I'M PRETTY SURE YOU CAN. DOWN TO THE LAST PENNY.
PARDON ME A MOMENT, FOLKS. PLEASE, ENJOY YOUR WATER.
AGENT ROSALIND SOLOMON OF S.H.I.E.L.D., I PRESUME?
SO YOU HAVE BEEN GETTING MY MESSAGES?
IS THAT WHAT YOU CALL THEM? I THOUGHT OF THEM MORE AS THREATS AND UNLAWFUL HARASSMENT. IN FACT, I'VE BEEN MEANING TO CALL YOUR SUPERIORS TO LODGE A FORMAL COMPLAINT.
YOU SHOULD. I BET DIRECTOR HILL WOULD LOVE TO CHAT. SHE GETS SO LONELY UP THERE IN HER GIANT FLOATING AIRCRAFT CARRIER WITH ALL HER BOMBS AND SUPER-POWERED ASSASSINS.
ARE YOU THREATENING ME AGAIN? YOU'RE NOT VERY GOOD AT IT, YOU KNOW.
GIVE ME TIME. I'M NEW.
AH, THAT MUST BE WHY I'VE NEVER HEARD OF YOU. OR IS IT PERHAPS BECAUSE YOUR ORGANIZATION IS SO UTTERLY OUTDATED AND INSIGNIFICANT?
WE KNOW WHAT YOU'RE DOING.
WE KNOW ABOUT THE OZONE DEPLETION PROJECT AND THE GREENHOUSE GAS SATELLITES AND THE MOBILE FACTORIES THAT EVEN THE LATVERIAN GOVERNMENT CALLS "TOXIC WASTE DUMPS ON WHEELS."
AND NOW YOU WANT TO USE SOME FANCY SPACE ICE TO PROFIT OFF THE EFFECTS OF GLOBAL WARMING WHILE SIMULTANEOUSLY DOING EVERYTHING IN YOUR POWER TO PERPETUATE ITS CAUSE.
YOU, MR. AGGER, ARE A REAL PIECE OF WORK. BUT I WON'T LET YOU GET AWAY WITH IT. NONE OF IT.
YOU ARE GROSSLY MISINFORMED, AGENT SOLOMON.
OUR MOBILE FACTORIES AREN'T ON WHEELS.
THEY FLY.
AND ALL WE ARE TRYING TO DO IS GIVE THE PEOPLE OF TODAY WHAT THEY NEED TO SURVIVE TOMORROW.
ROXXON IS THE WORLD'S WEALTHIEST AND MOST POWERFUL SUPER-CORPORATION. IF WE DON'T KNOW WHAT'S BEST FOR THE PEOPLE OF THIS PLANET, THEN I ASK YOU, DEAR LADY...
WHO DOES?

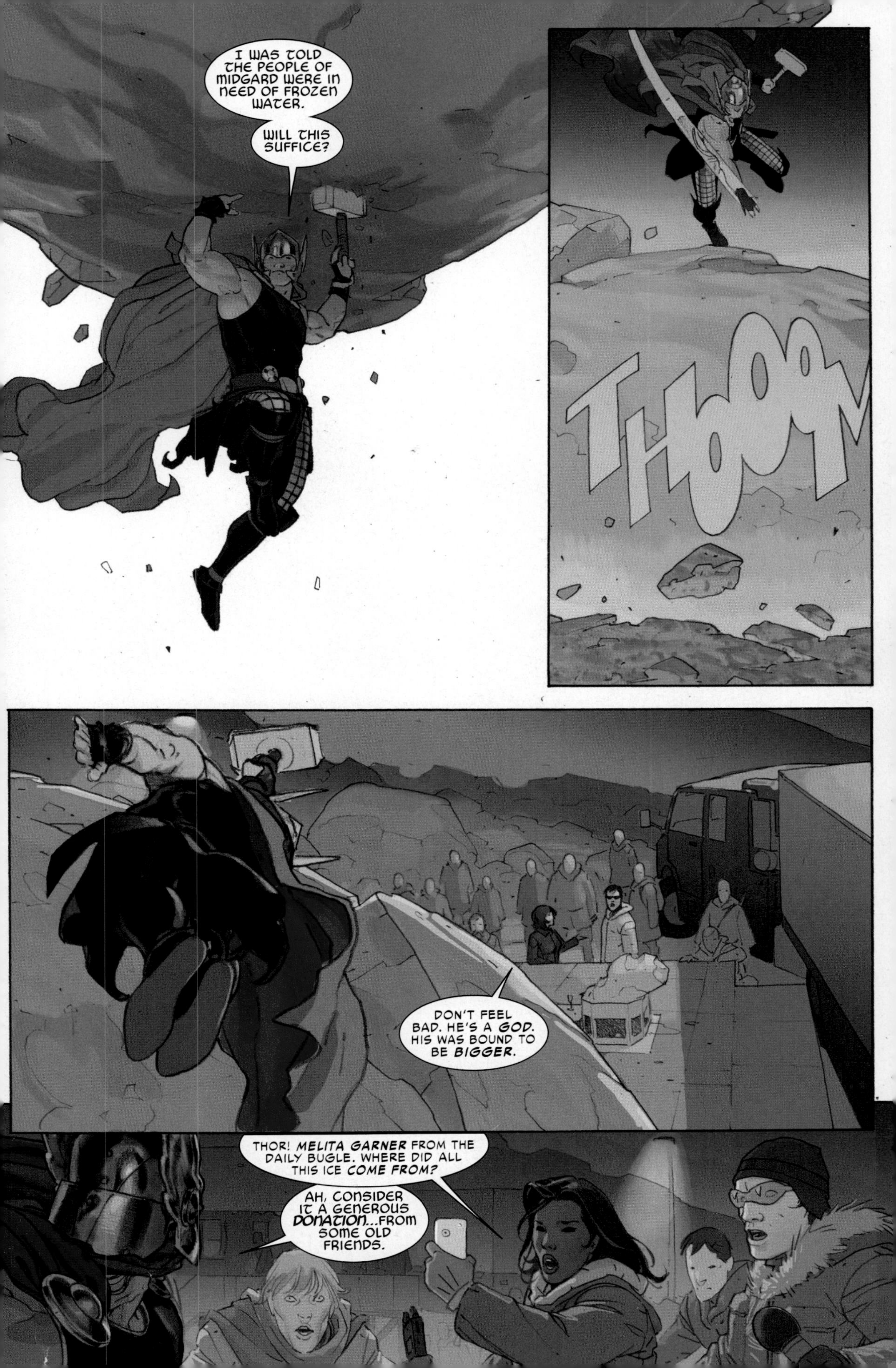
I WAS TOLD THE PEOPLE OF MIDGARD WERE IN NEED OF FROZEN WATER.
WILL THIS SUFFICE?
THOOOM
DON'T FEEL BAD. HE'S A *GOD*. HIS WAS BOUND TO BE *BIGGER*.
THOR! *MELITA GARNER* FROM THE DAILY BUGLE. WHERE DID ALL THIS ICE *COME FROM?*
AH, CONSIDER IT A GENEROUS *DONATION*...FROM SOME OLD FRIENDS.

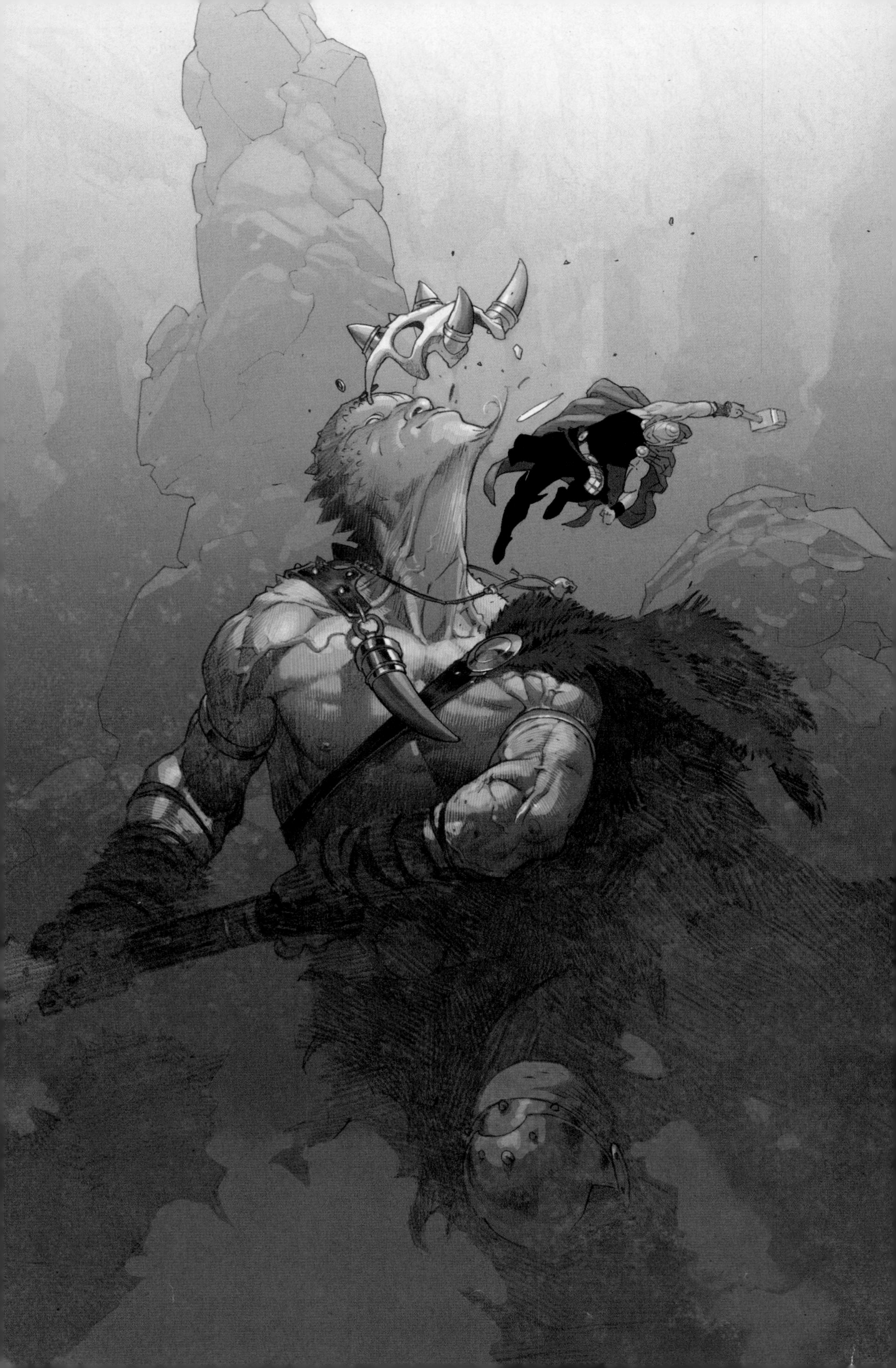

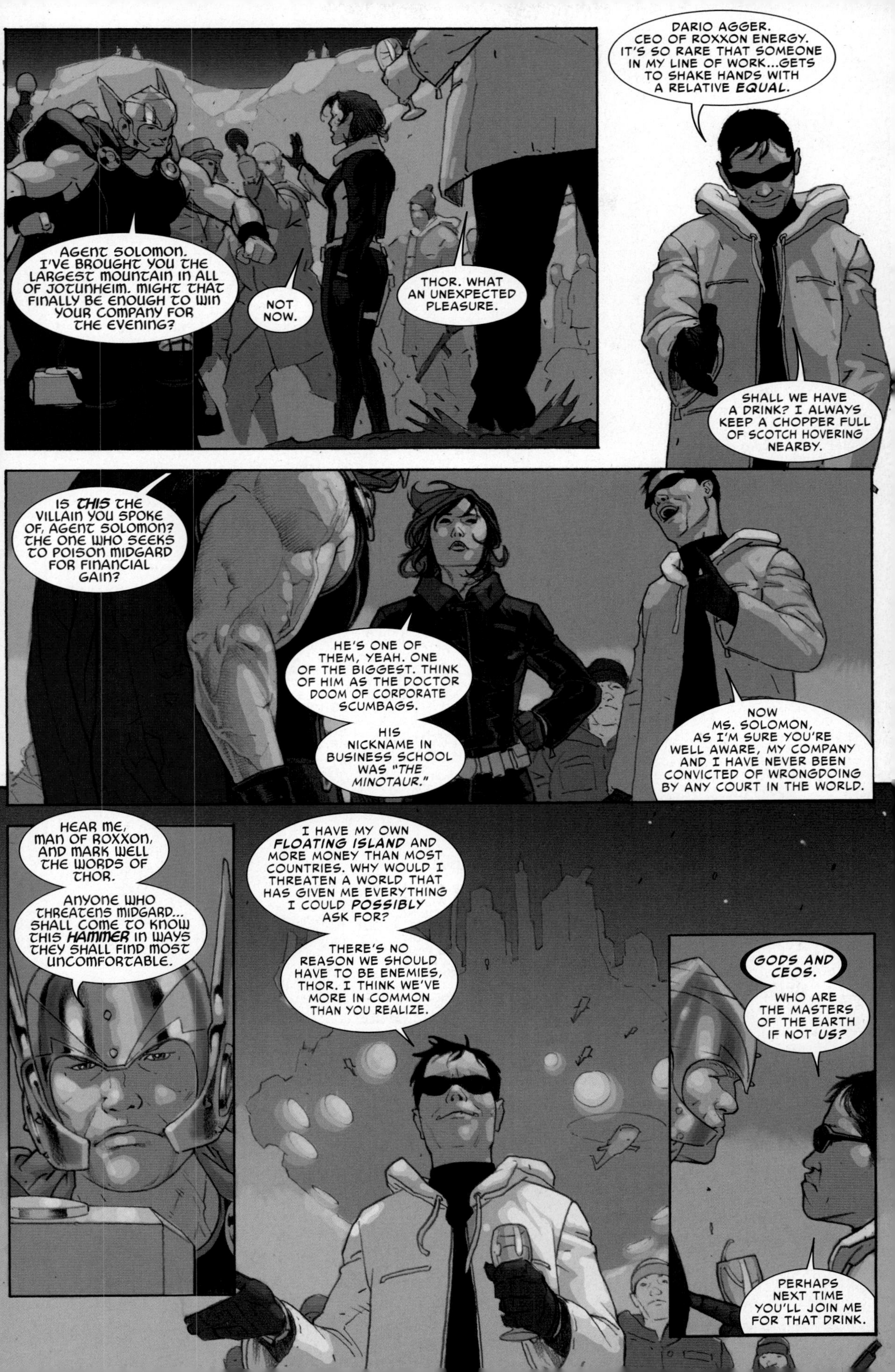
DARIO AGGER. CEO OF ROXXON ENERGY. IT'S SO RARE THAT SOMEONE IN MY LINE OF WORK...GETS TO SHAKE HANDS WITH A RELATIVE EQUAL.
AGENT SOLOMON. I'VE BROUGHT YOU THE LARGEST MOUNTAIN IN ALL OF JOTUNHEIM. MIGHT THAT FINALLY BE ENOUGH TO WIN YOUR COMPANY FOR THE EVENING?
NOT NOW.
THOR. WHAT AN UNEXPECTED PLEASURE.
SHALL WE HAVE A DRINK? I ALWAYS KEEP A CHOPPER FULL OF SCOTCH HOVERING NEARBY.
IS THIS THE VILLAIN YOU SPOKE OF, AGENT SOLOMON? THE ONE WHO SEEKS TO POISON MIDGARD FOR FINANCIAL GAIN?
HE'S ONE OF THEM, YEAH. ONE OF THE BIGGEST. THINK OF HIM AS THE DOCTOR DOOM OF CORPORATE SCUMBAGS.
HIS NICKNAME IN BUSINESS SCHOOL WAS "THE MINOTAUR."
NOW MS. SOLOMON, AS I'M SURE YOU'RE WELL AWARE, MY COMPANY AND I HAVE NEVER BEEN CONVICTED OF WRONGDOING BY ANY COURT IN THE WORLD.
HEAR ME, MAN OF ROXXON, AND MARK WELL THE WORDS OF THOR.
ANYONE WHO THREATENS MIDGARD... SHALL COME TO KNOW THIS HAMMER IN WAYS THEY SHALL FIND MOST UNCOMFORTABLE.
I HAVE MY OWN FLOATING ISLAND AND MORE MONEY THAN MOST COUNTRIES. WHY WOULD I THREATEN A WORLD THAT HAS GIVEN ME EVERYTHING I COULD POSSIBLY ASK FOR?
THERE'S NO REASON WE SHOULD HAVE TO BE ENEMIES, THOR. I THINK WE'VE MORE IN COMMON THAN YOU REALIZE.
GODS AND CEOS.
WHO ARE THE MASTERS OF THE EARTH IF NOT US?
PERHAPS NEXT TIME YOU'LL JOIN ME FOR THAT DRINK.

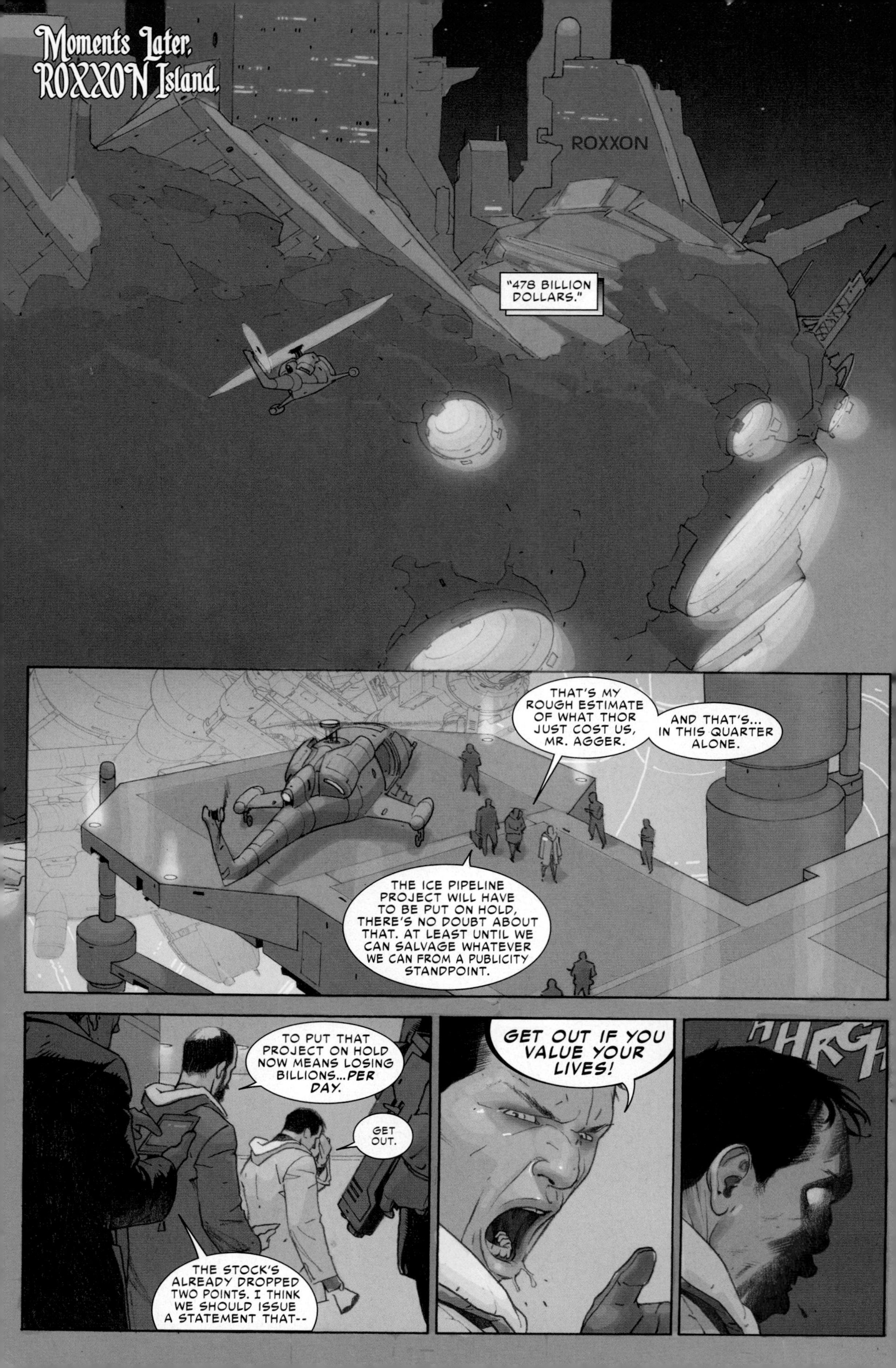
Moments Later, ROXXON Island.
ROXXON
"478 BILLION DOLLARS."
THAT'S MY ROUGH ESTIMATE OF WHAT THOR JUST COST US, MR. AGGER.
AND THAT'S... IN THIS QUARTER ALONE.
THE ICE PIPELINE PROJECT WILL HAVE TO BE PUT ON HOLD, THERE'S NO DOUBT ABOUT THAT. AT LEAST UNTIL WE CAN SALVAGE WHATEVER WE CAN FROM A PUBLICITY STANDPOINT.
TO PUT THAT PROJECT ON HOLD NOW MEANS LOSING BILLIONS...PER DAY.
GET OUT.
THE STOCK'S ALREADY DROPPED TWO POINTS. I THINK WE SHOULD ISSUE A STATEMENT THAT--
GET OUT IF YOU VALUE YOUR LIVES!
HHRGH

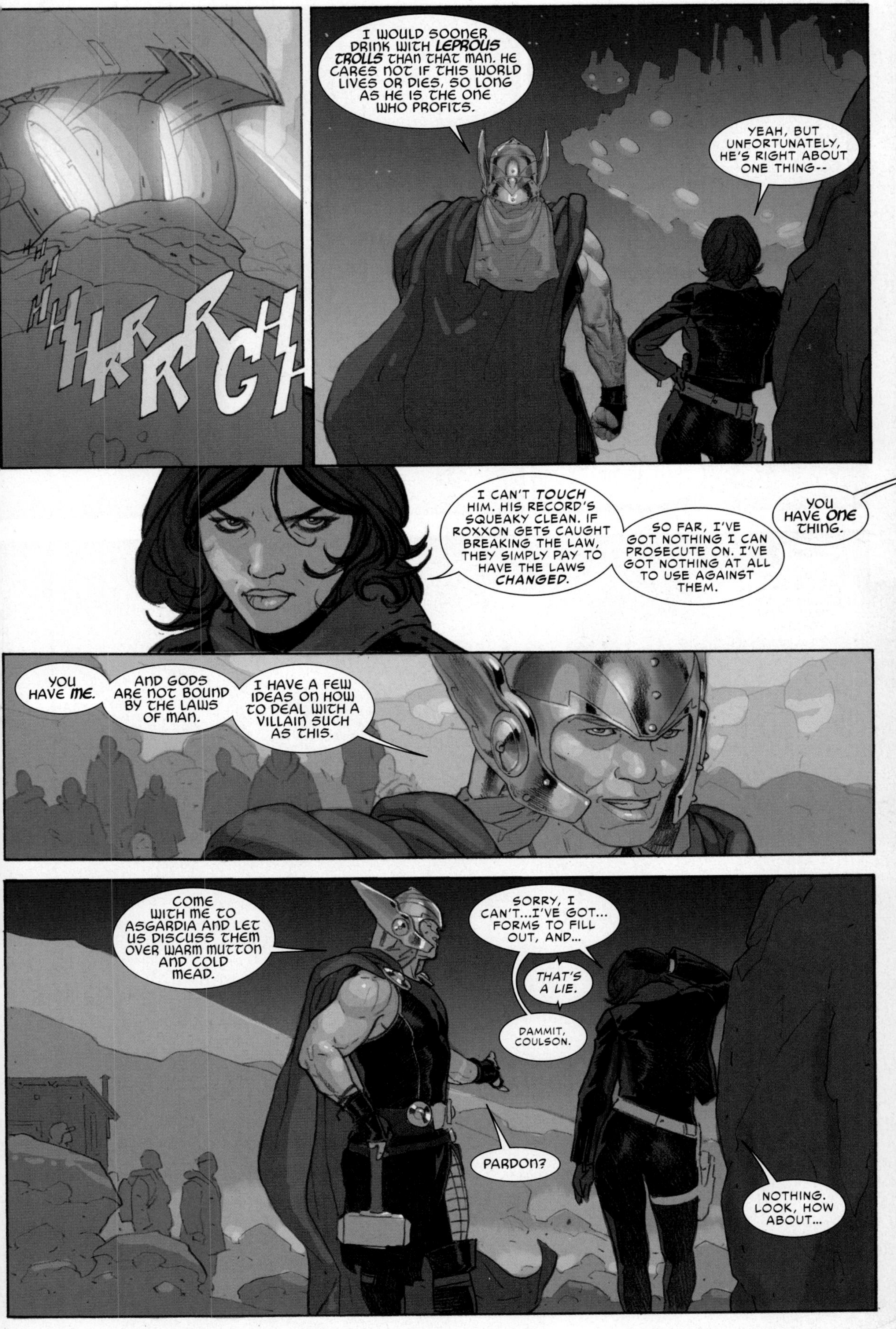
HHHHRRRRRGH
I WOULD SOONER DRINK WITH LEPROUS TROLLS THAN THAT MAN. HE CARES NOT IF THIS WORLD LIVES OR DIES, SO LONG AS HE IS THE ONE WHO PROFITS.
YEAH, BUT UNFORTUNATELY, HE'S RIGHT ABOUT ONE THING--
I CAN'T TOUCH HIM. HIS RECORD'S SQUEAKY CLEAN. IF ROXXON GETS CAUGHT BREAKING THE LAW, THEY SIMPLY PAY TO HAVE THE LAWS CHANGED.
SO FAR, I'VE GOT NOTHING I CAN PROSECUTE ON. I'VE GOT NOTHING AT ALL TO USE AGAINST THEM.
YOU HAVE ONE THING.
YOU HAVE ME.
AND GODS ARE NOT BOUND BY THE LAWS OF MAN.
I HAVE A FEW IDEAS ON HOW TO DEAL WITH A VILLAIN SUCH AS THIS.
COME WITH ME TO ASGARDIA AND LET US DISCUSS THEM OVER WARM MUTTON AND COLD MEAD.
SORRY, I CAN'T...I'VE GOT... FORMS TO FILL OUT, AND...
THAT'S A LIE.
DAMMIT, COULSON.
PARDON?
NOTHING. LOOK, HOW ABOUT...

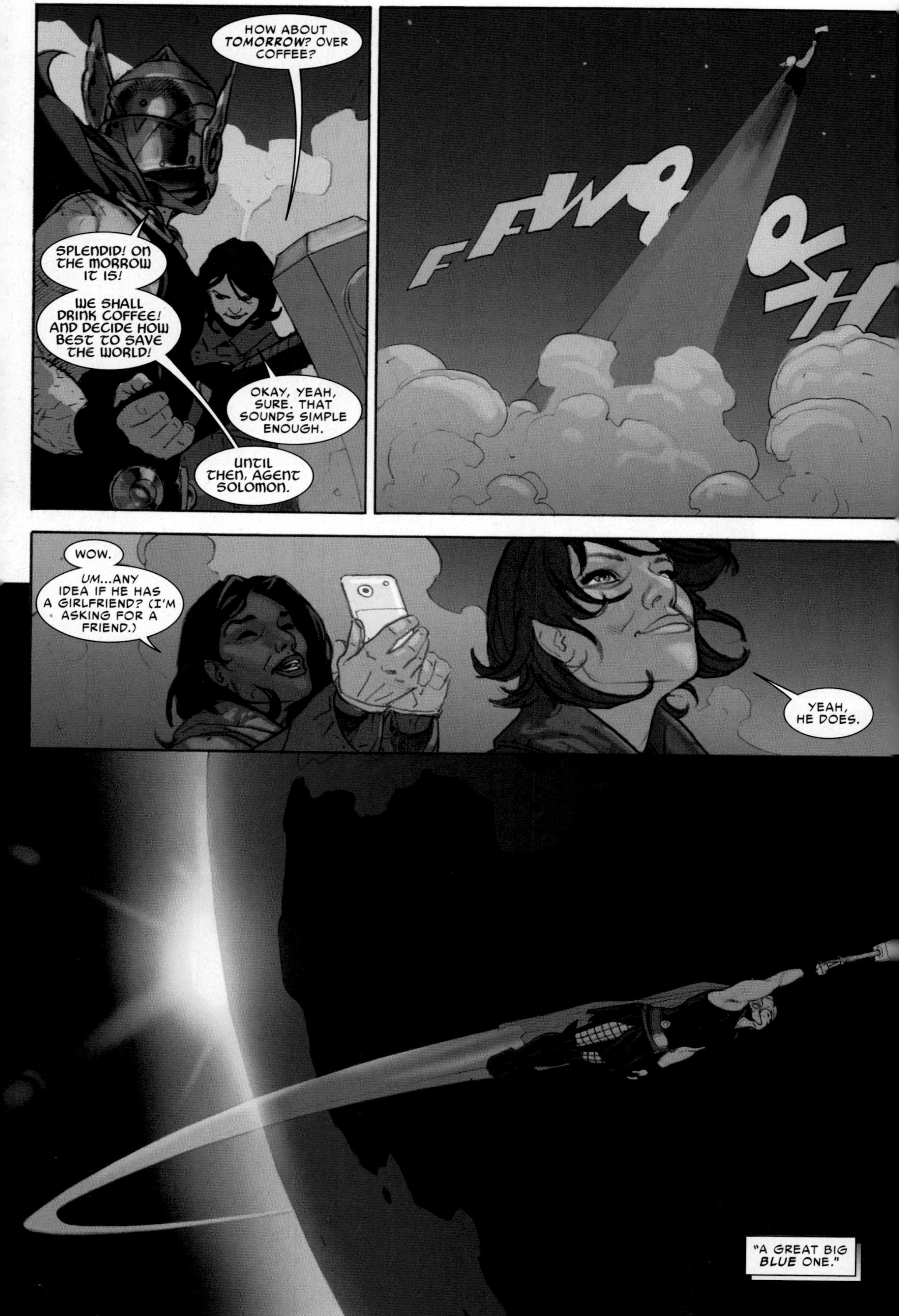
HOW ABOUT TOMORROW? OVER COFFEE?
SPLENDID! ON THE MORROW IT IS!
WE SHALL DRINK COFFEE! AND DECIDE HOW BEST TO SAVE THE WORLD!
OKAY, YEAH, SURE. THAT SOUNDS SIMPLE ENOUGH.
UNTIL THEN, AGENT SOLOMON.
FFWOOOSH
WOW.
UM...ANY IDEA IF HE HAS A GIRLFRIEND? (I'M ASKING FOR A FRIEND.)
YEAH, HE DOES.
"A GREAT BIG BLUE ONE."

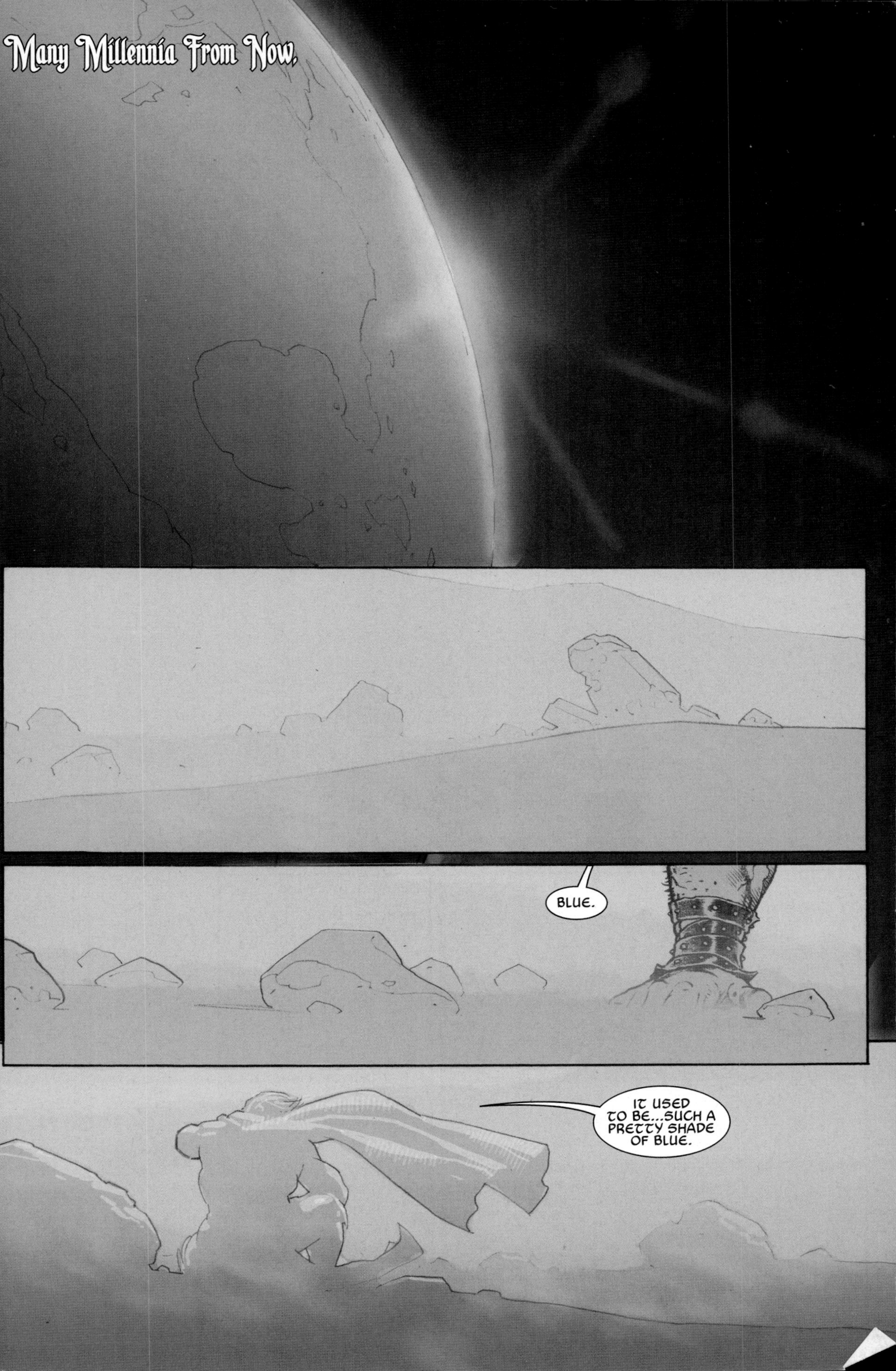
Many Millennia From Now,
BLUE.
IT USED TO BE...SUCH A PRETTY SHADE OF BLUE.

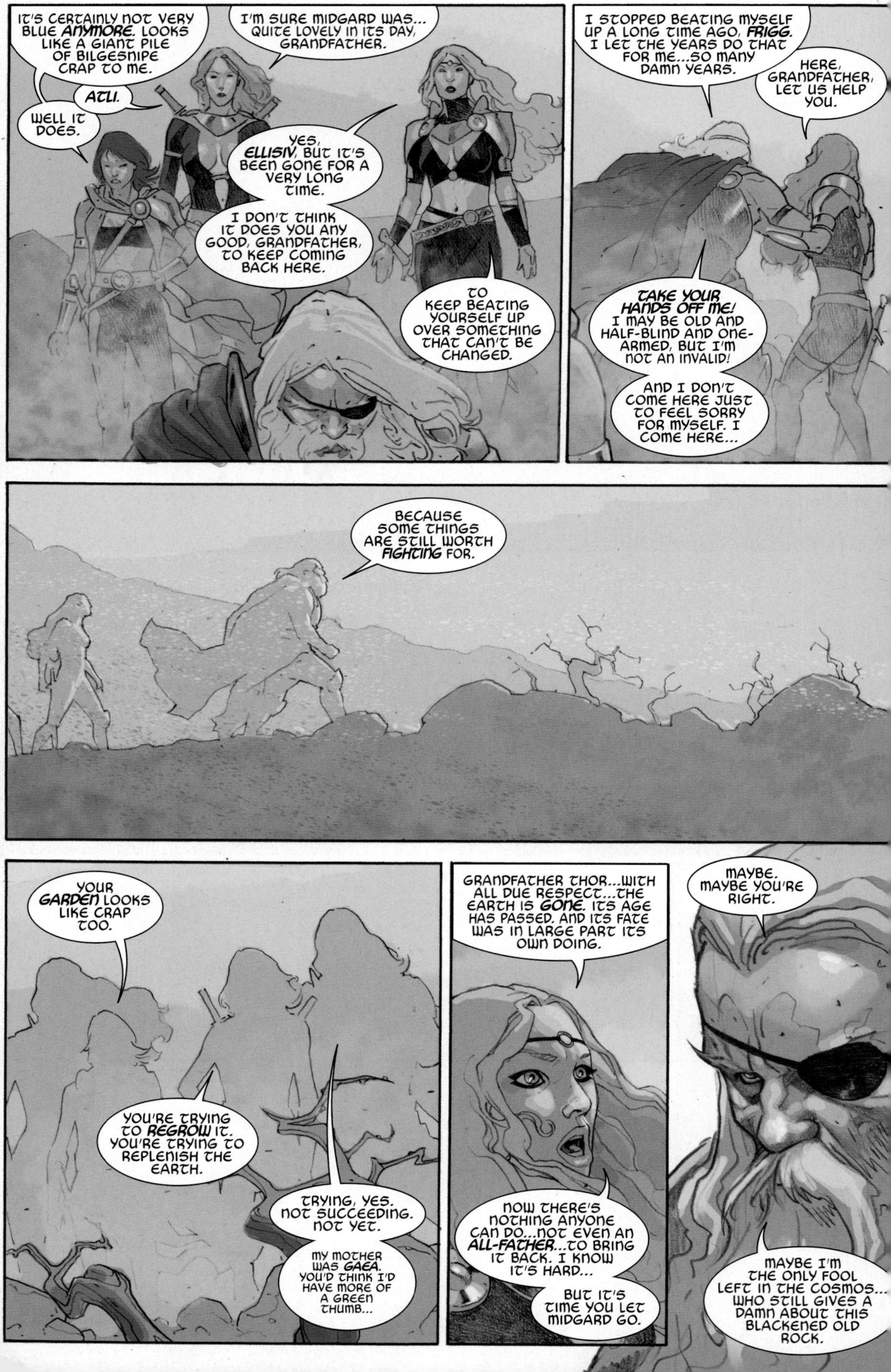
IT'S CERTAINLY NOT VERY BLUE ANYMORE. LOOKS LIKE A GIANT PILE OF BILGESNIPE CRAP TO ME.
I'M SURE MIDGARD WAS... QUITE LOVELY IN ITS DAY, GRANDFATHER.
ATLI.
WELL IT DOES.
YES, ELLISIV, BUT IT'S BEEN GONE FOR A VERY LONG TIME.
I DON'T THINK IT DOES YOU ANY GOOD, GRANDFATHER, TO KEEP COMING BACK HERE.
TO KEEP BEATING YOURSELF UP OVER SOMETHING THAT CAN'T BE CHANGED.
I STOPPED BEATING MYSELF UP A LONG TIME AGO, FRIGG. I LET THE YEARS DO THAT FOR ME...SO MANY DAMN YEARS.
HERE, GRANDFATHER, LET US HELP YOU.
TAKE YOUR HANDS OFF ME! I MAY BE OLD AND HALF-BLIND AND ONE-ARMED, BUT I'M NOT AN INVALID!
AND I DON'T COME HERE JUST TO FEEL SORRY FOR MYSELF. I COME HERE...
BECAUSE SOME THINGS ARE STILL WORTH FIGHTING FOR.
YOUR GARDEN LOOKS LIKE CRAP TOO.
YOU'RE TRYING TO REGROW IT. YOU'RE TRYING TO REPLENISH THE EARTH.
TRYING, YES. NOT SUCCEEDING. NOT YET.
MY MOTHER WAS GAEA. YOU'D THINK I'D HAVE MORE OF A GREEN THUMB...
GRANDFATHER THOR...WITH ALL DUE RESPECT...THE EARTH IS GONE. ITS AGE HAS PASSED. AND ITS FATE WAS IN LARGE PART ITS OWN DOING.
NOW THERE'S NOTHING ANYONE CAN DO...NOT EVEN AN ALL-FATHER...TO BRING IT BACK. I KNOW IT'S HARD...
BUT IT'S TIME YOU LET MIDGARD GO.
MAYBE. MAYBE YOU'RE RIGHT.
MAYBE I'M THE ONLY FOOL LEFT IN THE COSMOS... WHO STILL GIVES A DAMN ABOUT THIS BLACKENED OLD ROCK.

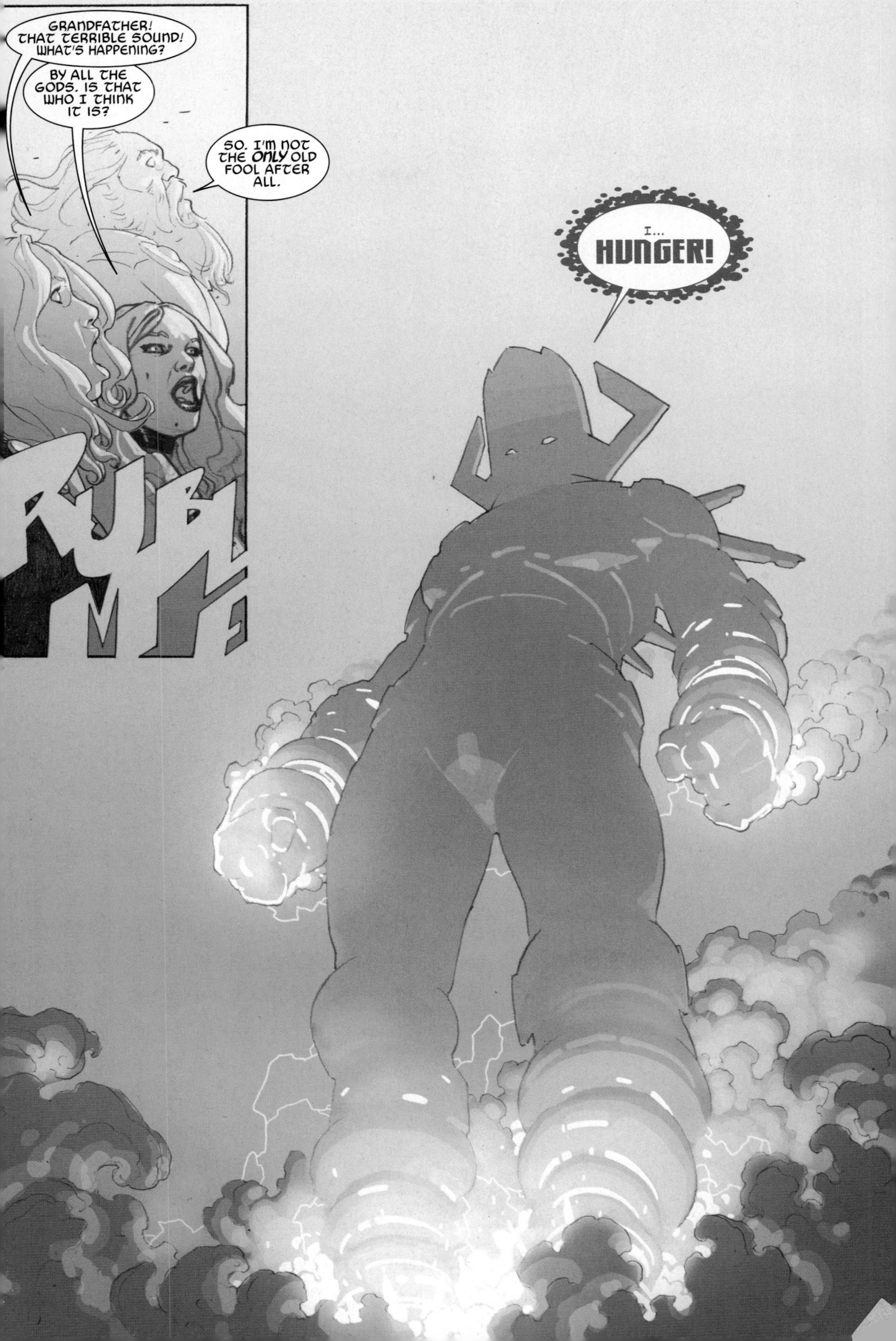
GRANDFATHER! THAT TERRIBLE SOUND! WHAT'S HAPPENING?
BY ALL THE GODS. IS THAT WHO I THINK IT IS?
SO. I'M NOT THE ONLY OLD FOOL AFTER ALL.
I... HUNGER!

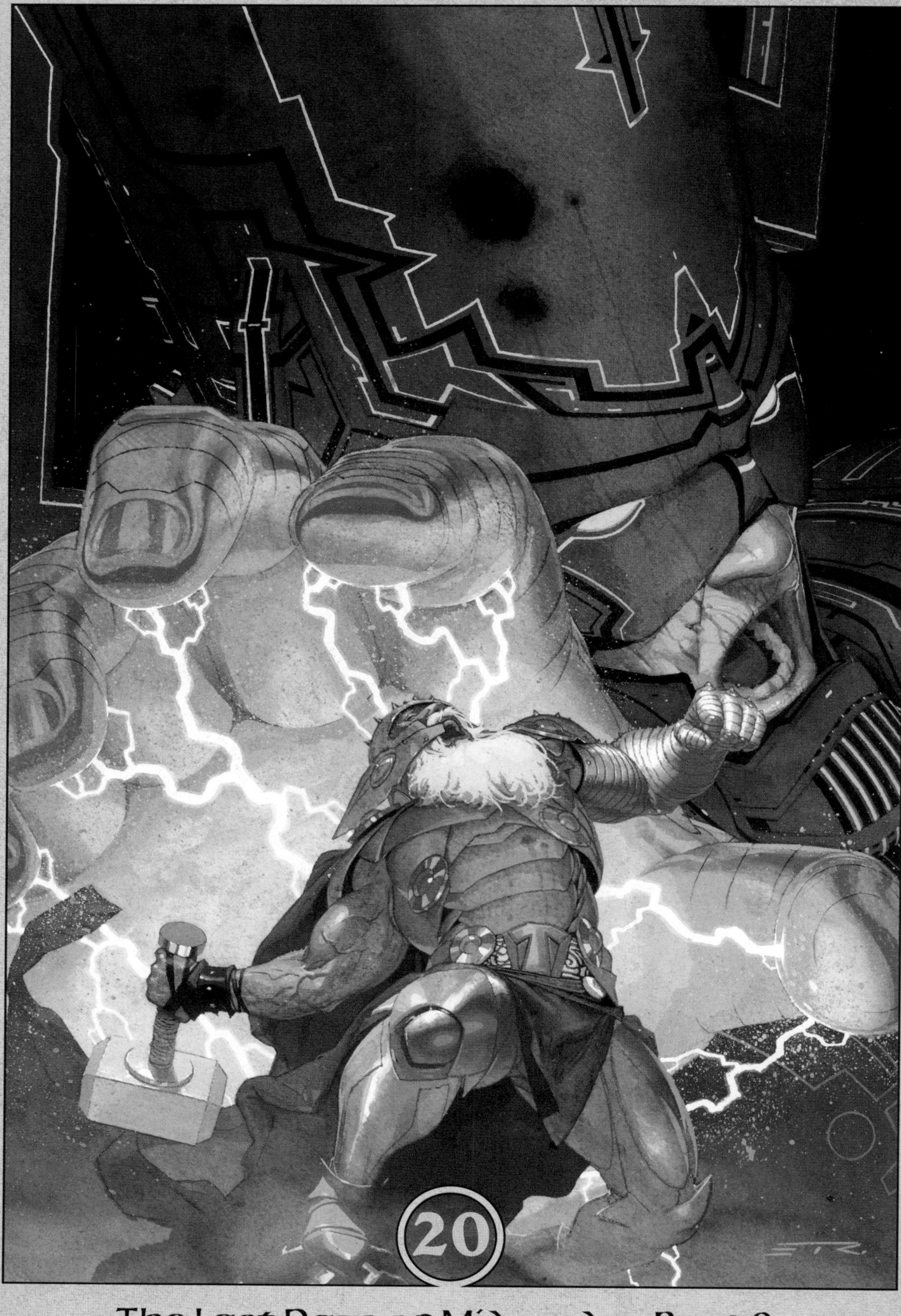
20

The Last Days of Midgard — Part 2:
All Worlds Must Die

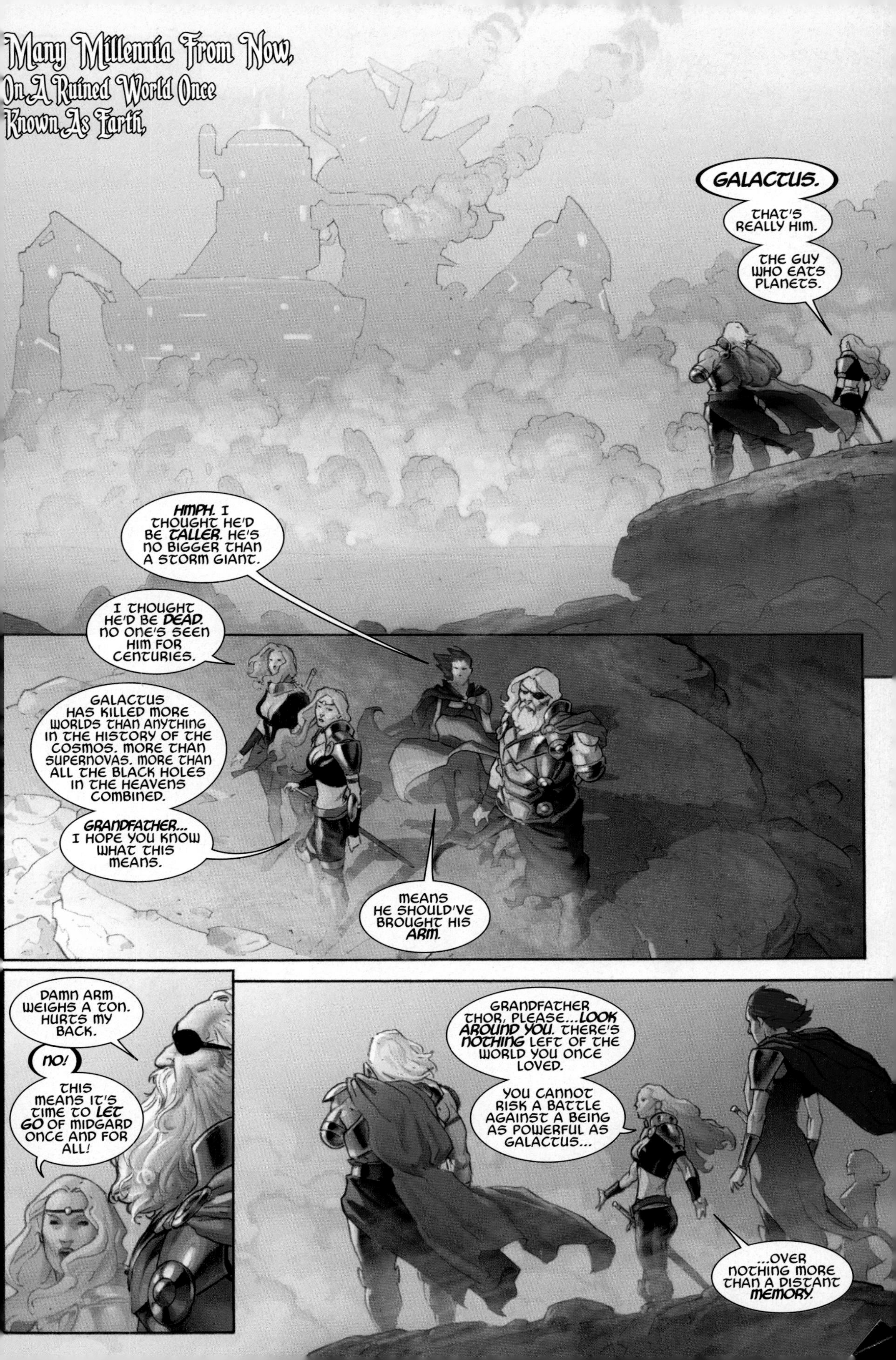
Many Millennia From Now, On A Ruined World Once Known As Earth,
GALACTUS.
THAT'S REALLY HIM.
THE GUY WHO EATS PLANETS.
HMPH. I THOUGHT HE'D BE TALLER. HE'S NO BIGGER THAN A STORM GIANT.
I THOUGHT HE'D BE DEAD. NO ONE'S SEEN HIM FOR CENTURIES.
GALACTUS HAS KILLED MORE WORLDS THAN ANYTHING IN THE HISTORY OF THE COSMOS. MORE THAN SUPERNOVAS. MORE THAN ALL THE BLACK HOLES IN THE HEAVENS COMBINED.
GRANDFATHER... I HOPE YOU KNOW WHAT THIS MEANS.
MEANS HE SHOULD'VE BROUGHT HIS ARM.
DAMN ARM WEIGHS A TON. HURTS MY BACK.
NO!
THIS MEANS IT'S TIME TO LET GO OF MIDGARD ONCE AND FOR ALL!
GRANDFATHER THOR, PLEASE...LOOK AROUND YOU. THERE'S NOTHING LEFT OF THE WORLD YOU ONCE LOVED.
YOU CANNOT RISK A BATTLE AGAINST A BEING AS POWERFUL AS GALACTUS...
...OVER NOTHING MORE THAN A DISTANT MEMORY.

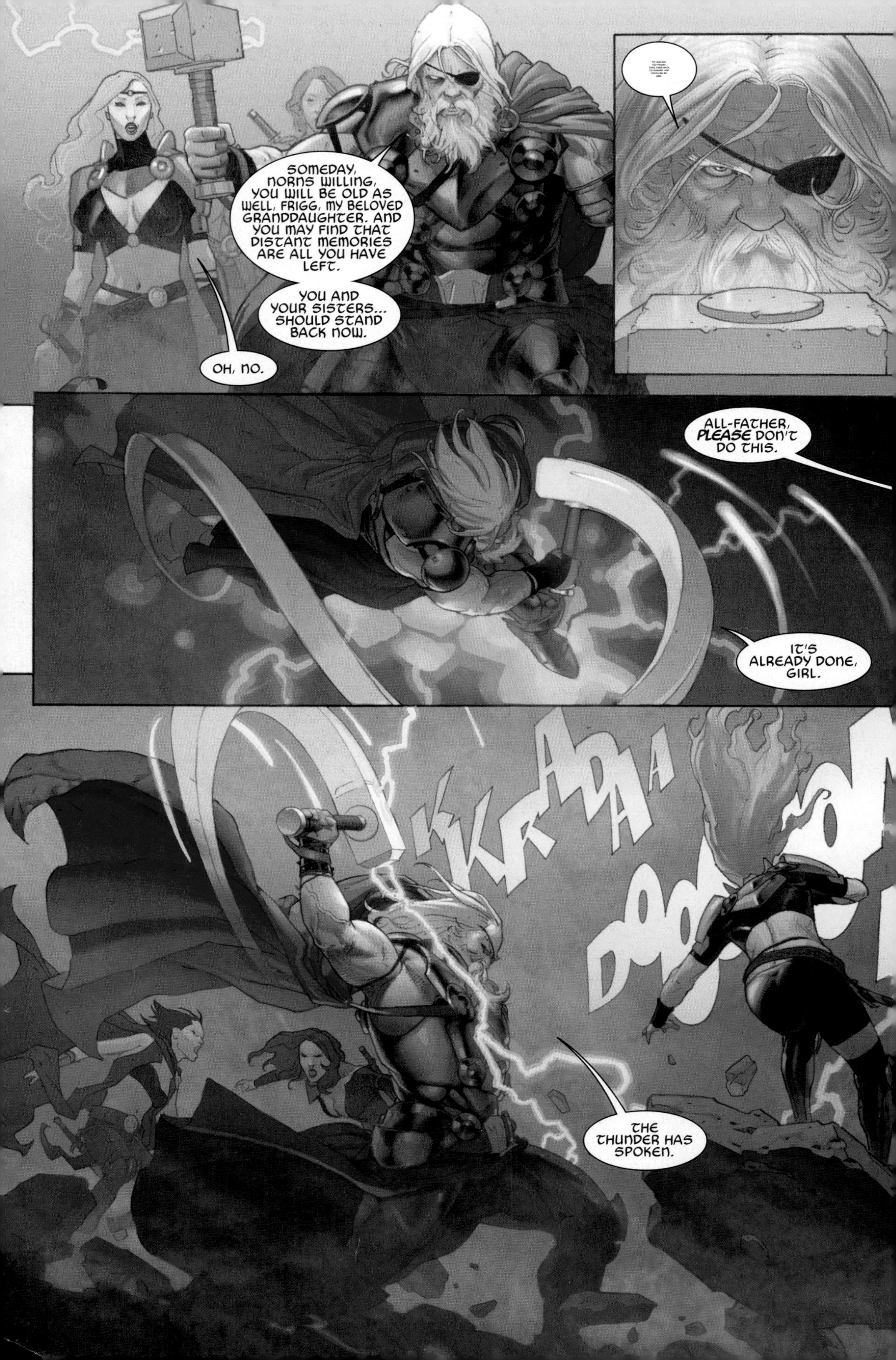
SOMEDAY, NORNS WILLING, YOU WILL BE OLD AS WELL, FRIGG, MY BELOVED GRANDDAUGHTER. AND YOU MAY FIND THAT DISTANT MEMORIES ARE ALL YOU HAVE LEFT.
YOU AND YOUR SISTERS... SHOULD STAND BACK NOW.
OH, NO.
ALL-FATHER, PLEASE DON'T DO THIS.
IT'S ALREADY DONE, GIRL.
THE THUNDER HAS SPOKEN.

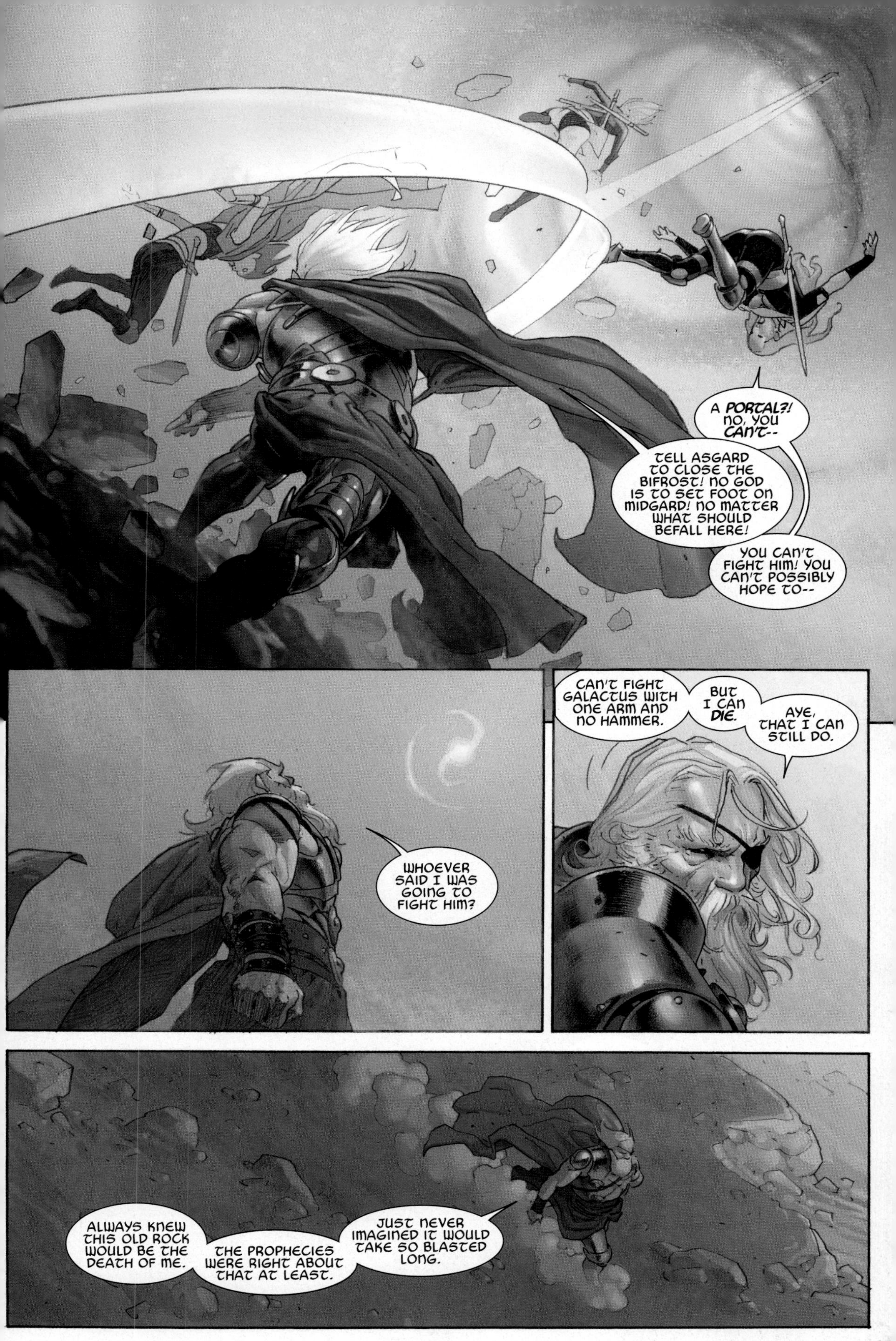
A PORTAL?! NO, YOU CAN'T--
TELL ASGARD TO CLOSE THE BIFROST! NO GOD IS TO SET FOOT ON MIDGARD! NO MATTER WHAT SHOULD BEFALL HERE!
YOU CAN'T FIGHT HIM! YOU CAN'T POSSIBLY HOPE TO--
WHOEVER SAID I WAS GOING TO FIGHT HIM?
CAN'T FIGHT GALACTUS WITH ONE ARM AND NO HAMMER.
BUT I CAN DIE.
AYE, THAT I CAN STILL DO.
ALWAYS KNEW THIS OLD ROCK WOULD BE THE DEATH OF ME.
THE PROPHECIES WERE RIGHT ABOUT THAT AT LEAST.
JUST NEVER IMAGINED IT WOULD TAKE SO BLASTED LONG.

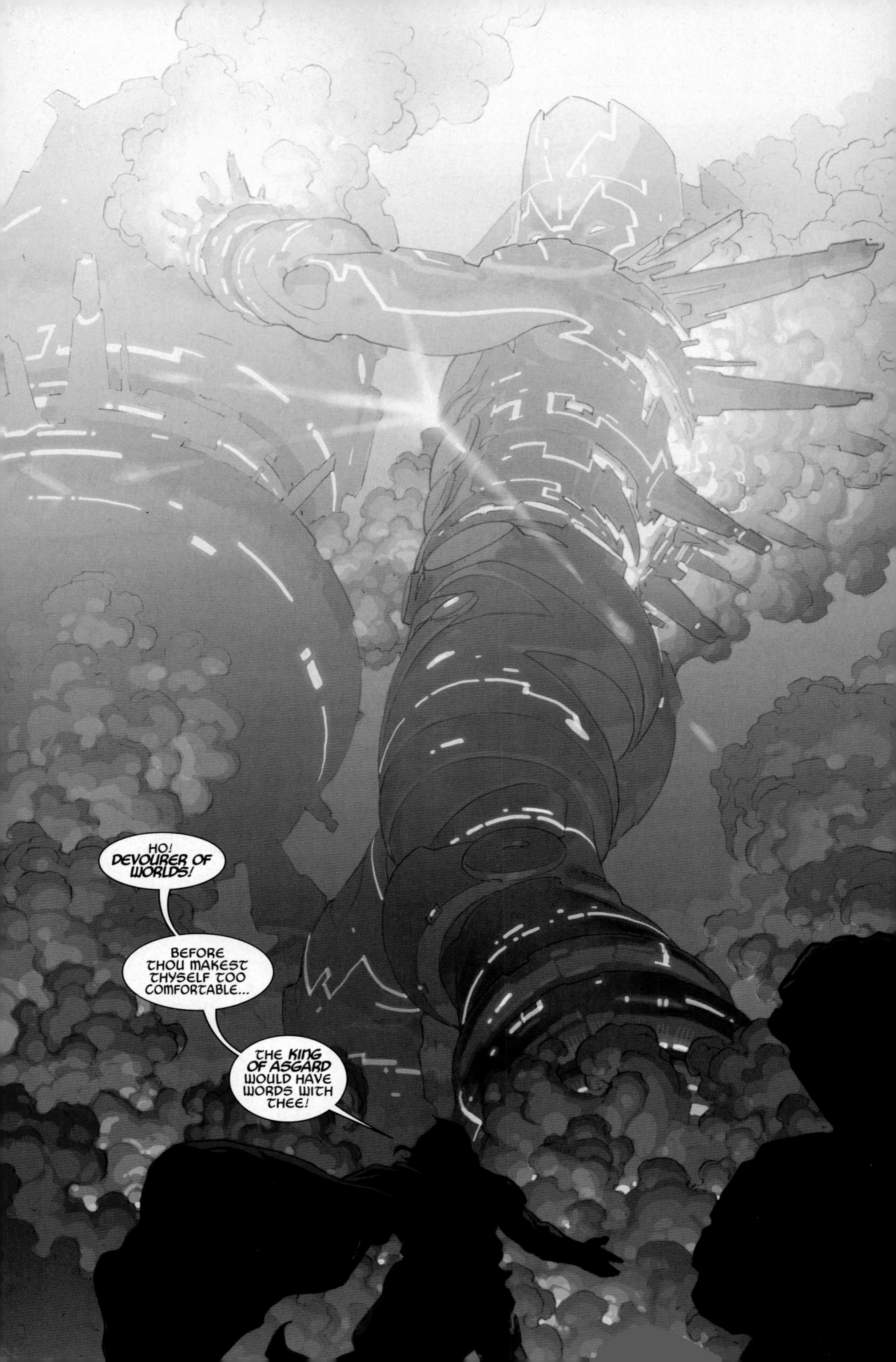
HO! DEVOURER OF WORLDS!
BEFORE THOU MAKEST THYSELF TOO COMFORTABLE...
THE KING OF ASGARD WOULD HAVE WORDS WITH THEE!

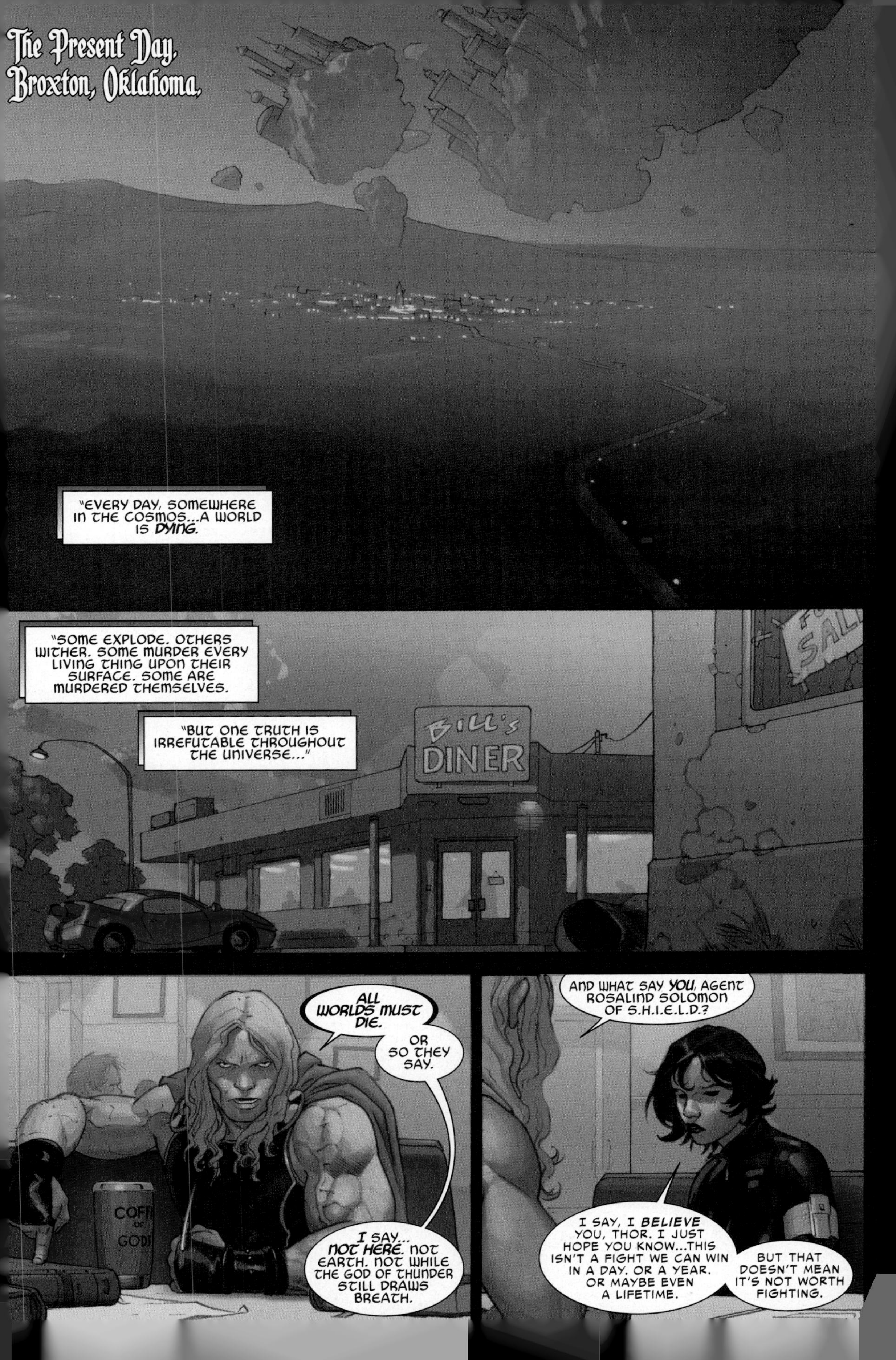
The Present Day,
Broxton, Oklahoma,
"EVERY DAY, SOMEWHERE IN THE COSMOS...A WORLD IS *DYING*.
"SOME EXPLODE. OTHERS WITHER. SOME MURDER EVERY LIVING THING UPON THEIR SURFACE. SOME ARE MURDERED THEMSELVES.
"BUT ONE TRUTH IS IRREFUTABLE THROUGHOUT THE UNIVERSE..."
BILL'S DINER
ALL WORLDS MUST DIE.
OR SO THEY SAY.
*I SAY... **NOT HERE.*** NOT EARTH. NOT WHILE THE GOD OF THUNDER STILL DRAWS BREATH.
AND WHAT SAY ***YOU***, AGENT ROSALIND SOLOMON OF S.H.I.E.L.D.?
I SAY, I ***BELIEVE*** YOU, THOR. I JUST HOPE YOU KNOW...THIS ISN'T A FIGHT WE CAN WIN IN A DAY. OR A YEAR. OR MAYBE EVEN A LIFETIME.
BUT THAT DOESN'T MEAN IT'S NOT WORTH FIGHTING.

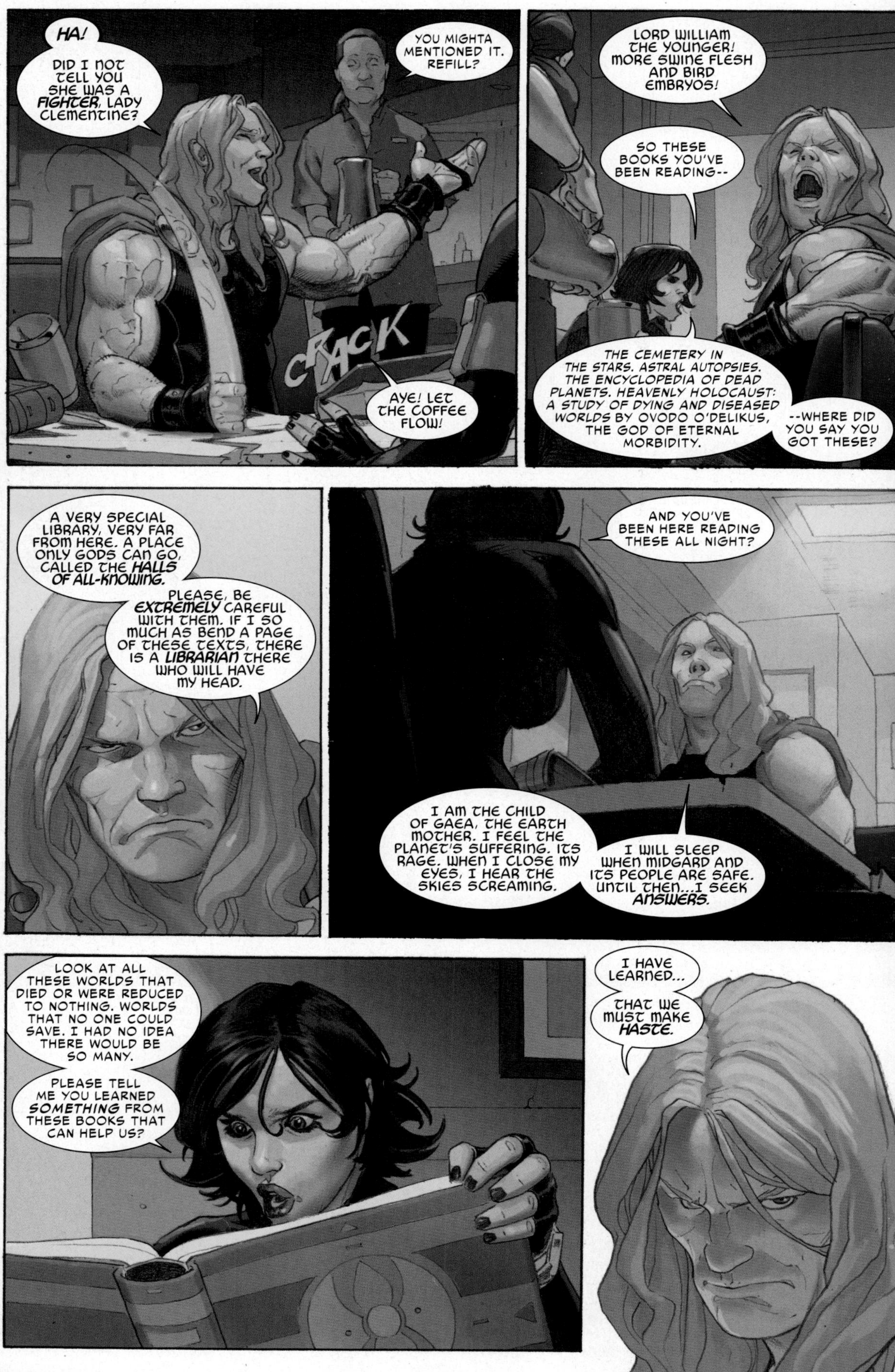
HA!
DID I NOT TELL YOU SHE WAS A FIGHTER, LADY CLEMENTINE?
YOU MIGHTA MENTIONED IT. REFILL?
CRACK
AYE! LET THE COFFEE FLOW!
LORD WILLIAM THE YOUNGER! MORE SWINE FLESH AND BIRD EMBRYOS!
SO THESE BOOKS YOU'VE BEEN READING--
THE CEMETERY IN THE STARS. ASTRAL AUTOPSIES. THE ENCYCLOPEDIA OF DEAD PLANETS. HEAVENLY HOLOCAUST: A STUDY OF DYING AND DISEASED WORLDS BY OVODO O'DELIKUS, THE GOD OF ETERNAL MORBIDITY.
--WHERE DID YOU SAY YOU GOT THESE?
A VERY SPECIAL LIBRARY, VERY FAR FROM HERE. A PLACE ONLY GODS CAN GO, CALLED THE HALLS OF ALL-KNOWING.
PLEASE, BE EXTREMELY CAREFUL WITH THEM. IF I SO MUCH AS BEND A PAGE OF THESE TEXTS, THERE IS A LIBRARIAN THERE WHO WILL HAVE MY HEAD.
AND YOU'VE BEEN HERE READING THESE ALL NIGHT?
I AM THE CHILD OF GAEA, THE EARTH MOTHER. I FEEL THE PLANET'S SUFFERING. ITS RAGE. WHEN I CLOSE MY EYES, I HEAR THE SKIES SCREAMING.
I WILL SLEEP WHEN MIDGARD AND ITS PEOPLE ARE SAFE. UNTIL THEN...I SEEK ANSWERS.
LOOK AT ALL THESE WORLDS THAT DIED OR WERE REDUCED TO NOTHING. WORLDS THAT NO ONE COULD SAVE. I HAD NO IDEA THERE WOULD BE SO MANY.
PLEASE TELL ME YOU LEARNED SOMETHING FROM THESE BOOKS THAT CAN HELP US?
I HAVE LEARNED...
THAT WE MUST MAKE HASTE.

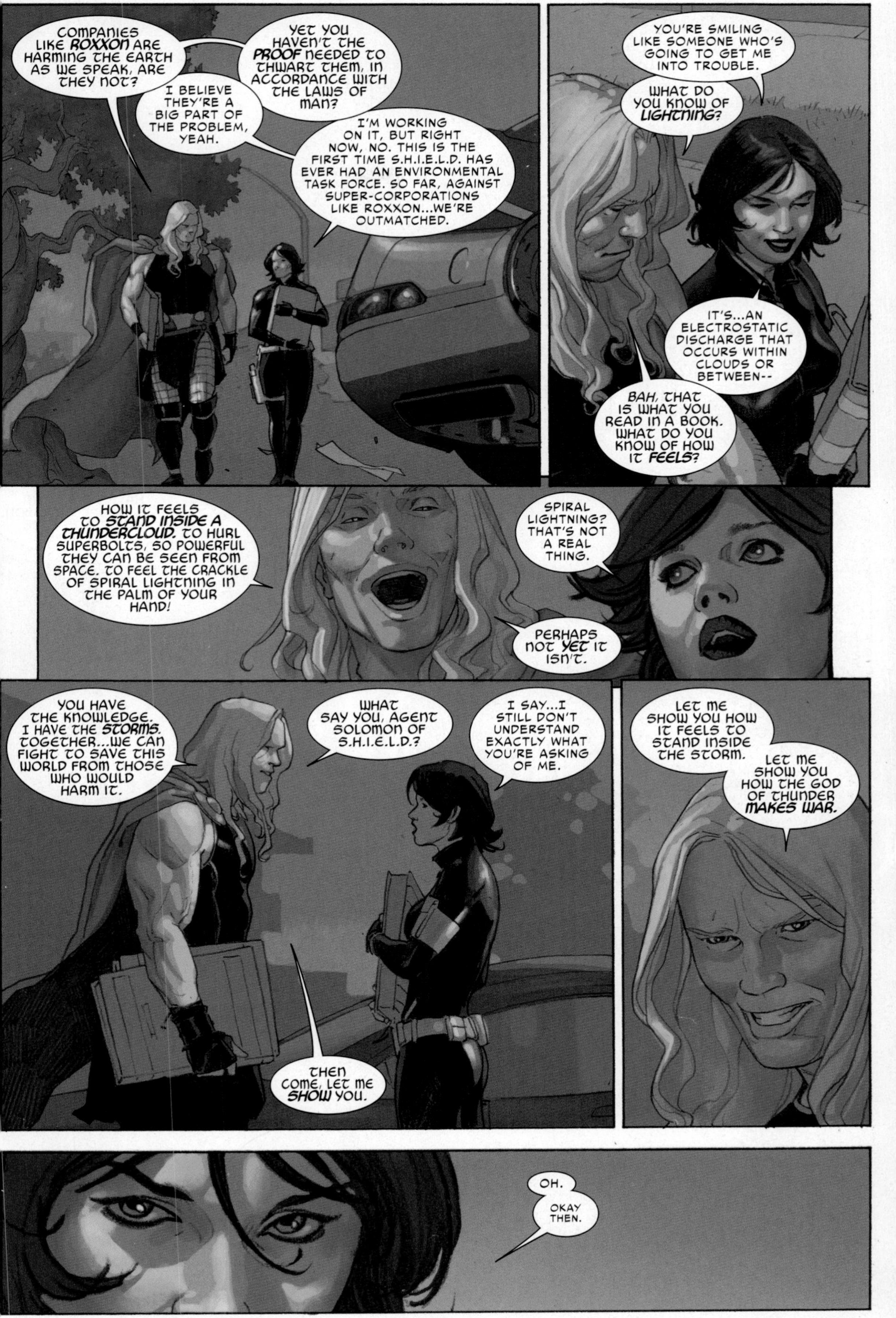
COMPANIES LIKE ROXXON ARE HARMING THE EARTH AS WE SPEAK, ARE THEY NOT?
I BELIEVE THEY'RE A BIG PART OF THE PROBLEM, YEAH.
YET YOU HAVEN'T THE PROOF NEEDED TO THWART THEM, IN ACCORDANCE WITH THE LAWS OF MAN?
I'M WORKING ON IT, BUT RIGHT NOW, NO. THIS IS THE FIRST TIME S.H.I.E.L.D. HAS EVER HAD AN ENVIRONMENTAL TASK FORCE. SO FAR, AGAINST SUPER-CORPORATIONS LIKE ROXXON...WE'RE OUTMATCHED.
YOU'RE SMILING LIKE SOMEONE WHO'S GOING TO GET ME INTO TROUBLE.
WHAT DO YOU KNOW OF LIGHTNING?
IT'S...AN ELECTROSTATIC DISCHARGE THAT OCCURS WITHIN CLOUDS OR BETWEEN--
BAH, THAT IS WHAT YOU READ IN A BOOK. WHAT DO YOU KNOW OF HOW IT FEELS?
HOW IT FEELS TO STAND INSIDE A THUNDERCLOUD. TO HURL SUPERBOLTS, SO POWERFUL THEY CAN BE SEEN FROM SPACE. TO FEEL THE CRACKLE OF SPIRAL LIGHTNING IN THE PALM OF YOUR HAND!
SPIRAL LIGHTNING? THAT'S NOT A REAL THING.
PERHAPS NOT YET IT ISN'T.
YOU HAVE THE KNOWLEDGE. I HAVE THE STORMS. TOGETHER...WE CAN FIGHT TO SAVE THIS WORLD FROM THOSE WHO WOULD HARM IT.
WHAT SAY YOU, AGENT SOLOMON OF S.H.I.E.L.D.?
I SAY...I STILL DON'T UNDERSTAND EXACTLY WHAT YOU'RE ASKING OF ME.
THEN COME, LET ME SHOW YOU.
LET ME SHOW YOU HOW IT FEELS TO STAND INSIDE THE STORM.
LET ME SHOW YOU HOW THE GOD OF THUNDER MAKES WAR.
OH.
OKAY THEN.

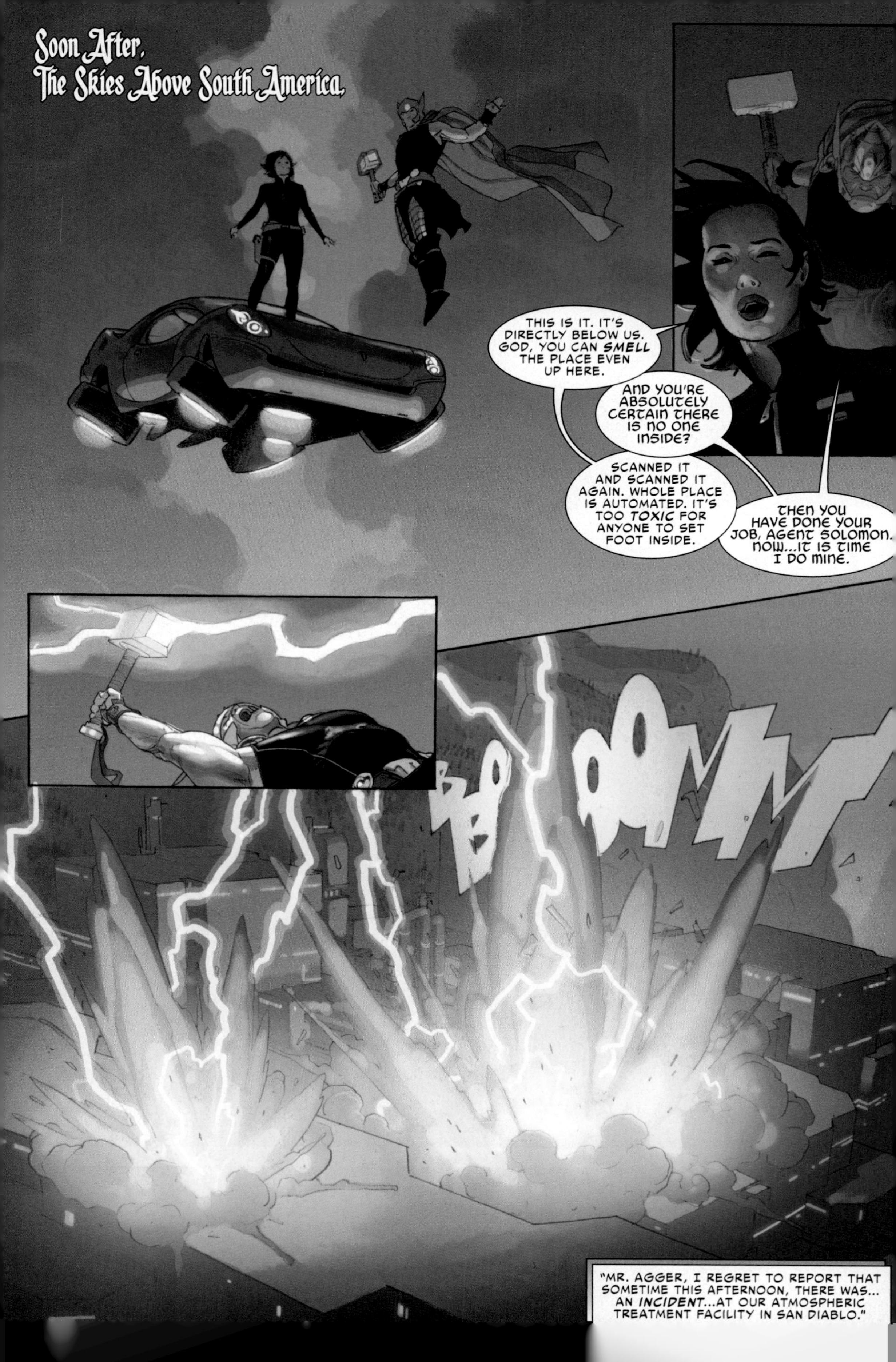
Soon After, The Skies Above South America,
THIS IS IT. IT'S DIRECTLY BELOW US. GOD, YOU CAN SMELL THE PLACE EVEN UP HERE.
AND YOU'RE ABSOLUTELY CERTAIN THERE IS NO ONE INSIDE?
SCANNED IT AND SCANNED IT AGAIN. WHOLE PLACE IS AUTOMATED. IT'S TOO TOXIC FOR ANYONE TO SET FOOT INSIDE.
THEN YOU HAVE DONE YOUR JOB, AGENT SOLOMON. NOW...IT IS TIME I DO MINE.
BOOM
"MR. AGGER, I REGRET TO REPORT THAT SOMETIME THIS AFTERNOON, THERE WAS... AN INCIDENT...AT OUR ATMOSPHERIC TREATMENT FACILITY IN SAN DIABLO."

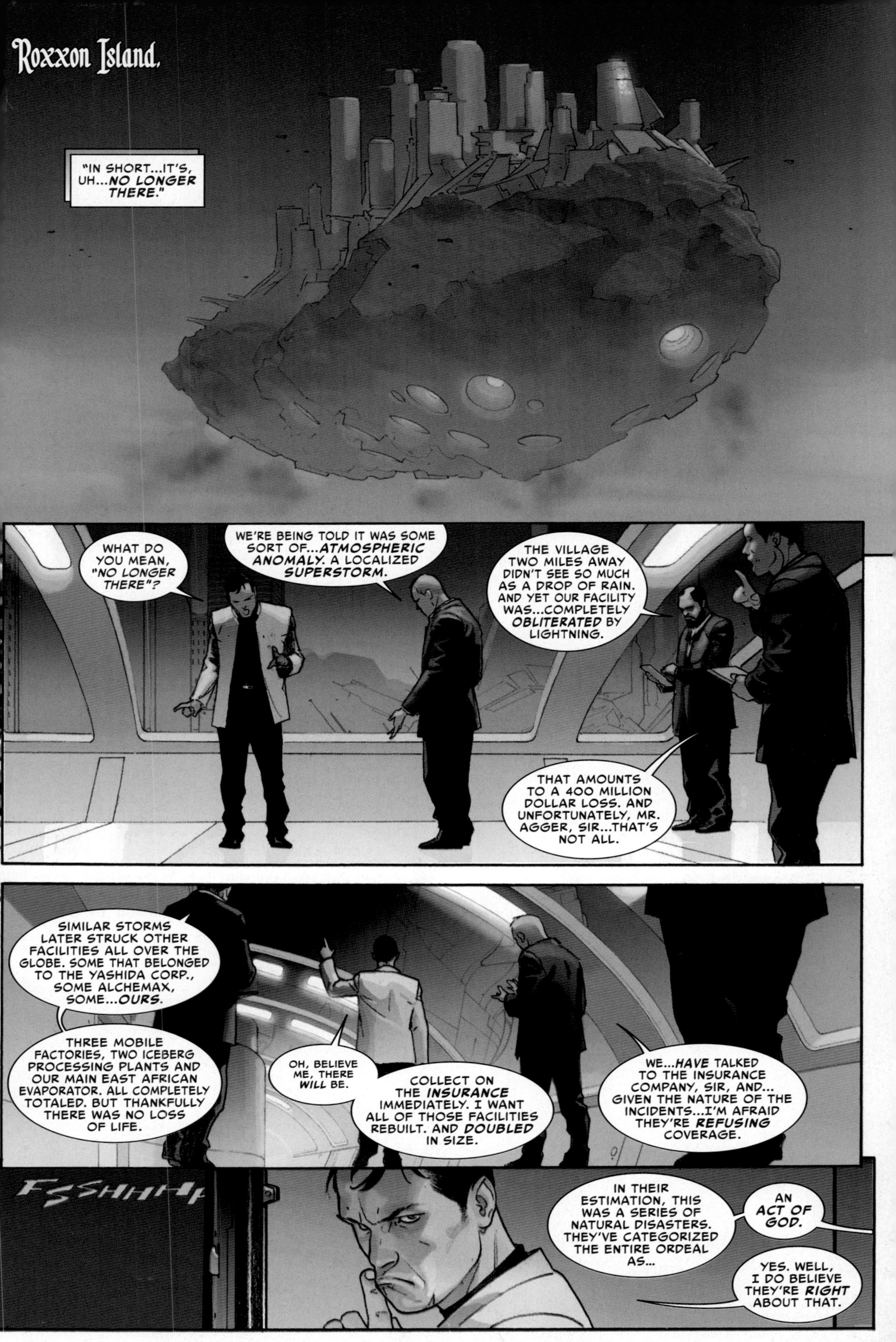
Roxxon Island.
"IN SHORT...IT'S, UH...NO LONGER THERE."
WHAT DO YOU MEAN, "NO LONGER THERE"?
WE'RE BEING TOLD IT WAS SOME SORT OF...ATMOSPHERIC ANOMALY. A LOCALIZED SUPERSTORM.
THE VILLAGE TWO MILES AWAY DIDN'T SEE SO MUCH AS A DROP OF RAIN. AND YET OUR FACILITY WAS...COMPLETELY OBLITERATED BY LIGHTNING.
THAT AMOUNTS TO A 400 MILLION DOLLAR LOSS. AND UNFORTUNATELY, MR. AGGER, SIR...THAT'S NOT ALL.
SIMILAR STORMS LATER STRUCK OTHER FACILITIES ALL OVER THE GLOBE. SOME THAT BELONGED TO THE YASHIDA CORP., SOME ALCHEMAX, SOME...OURS.
THREE MOBILE FACTORIES, TWO ICEBERG PROCESSING PLANTS AND OUR MAIN EAST AFRICAN EVAPORATOR. ALL COMPLETELY TOTALED. BUT THANKFULLY THERE WAS NO LOSS OF LIFE.
OH, BELIEVE ME, THERE WILL BE.
COLLECT ON THE INSURANCE IMMEDIATELY. I WANT ALL OF THOSE FACILITIES REBUILT. AND DOUBLED IN SIZE.
WE...HAVE TALKED TO THE INSURANCE COMPANY, SIR, AND... GIVEN THE NATURE OF THE INCIDENTS...I'M AFRAID THEY'RE REFUSING COVERAGE.
FSSHHHP
IN THEIR ESTIMATION, THIS WAS A SERIES OF NATURAL DISASTERS. THEY'VE CATEGORIZED THE ENTIRE ORDEAL AS...
AN ACT OF GOD.
YES. WELL, I DO BELIEVE THEY'RE RIGHT ABOUT THAT.

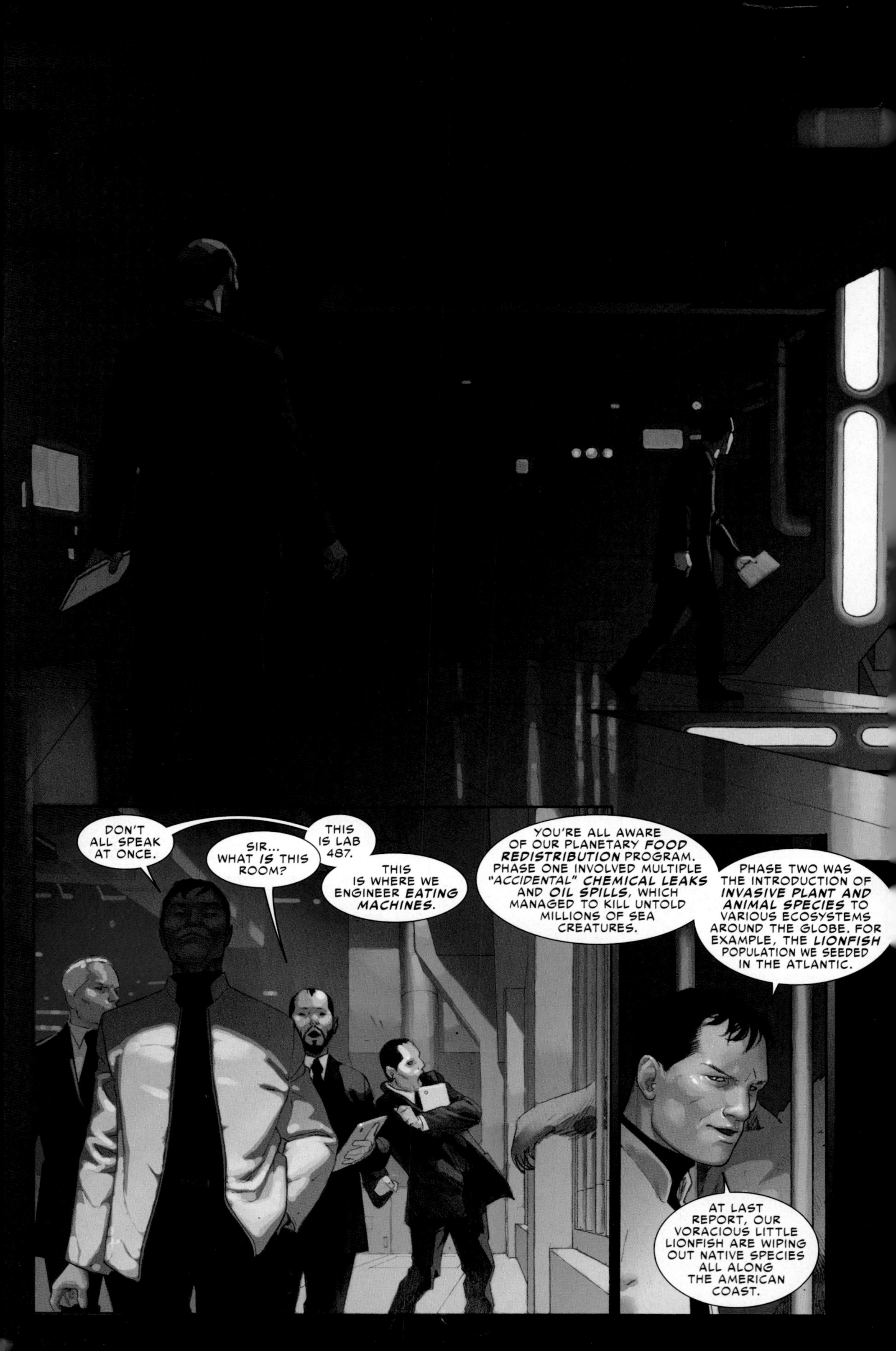
DON'T ALL SPEAK AT ONCE.
SIR... WHAT *IS* THIS ROOM?
THIS IS LAB 487.
THIS IS WHERE WE ENGINEER *EATING MACHINES*.
YOU'RE ALL AWARE OF OUR PLANETARY *FOOD REDISTRIBUTION* PROGRAM. PHASE ONE INVOLVED MULTIPLE *"ACCIDENTAL" CHEMICAL LEAKS* AND *OIL SPILLS*, WHICH MANAGED TO KILL UNTOLD MILLIONS OF SEA CREATURES.
PHASE TWO WAS THE INTRODUCTION OF *INVASIVE PLANT AND ANIMAL SPECIES* TO VARIOUS ECOSYSTEMS AROUND THE GLOBE. FOR EXAMPLE, THE *LIONFISH* POPULATION WE SEEDED IN THE ATLANTIC.
AT LAST REPORT, OUR VORACIOUS LITTLE LIONFISH ARE WIPING OUT NATIVE SPECIES ALL ALONG THE AMERICAN COAST.

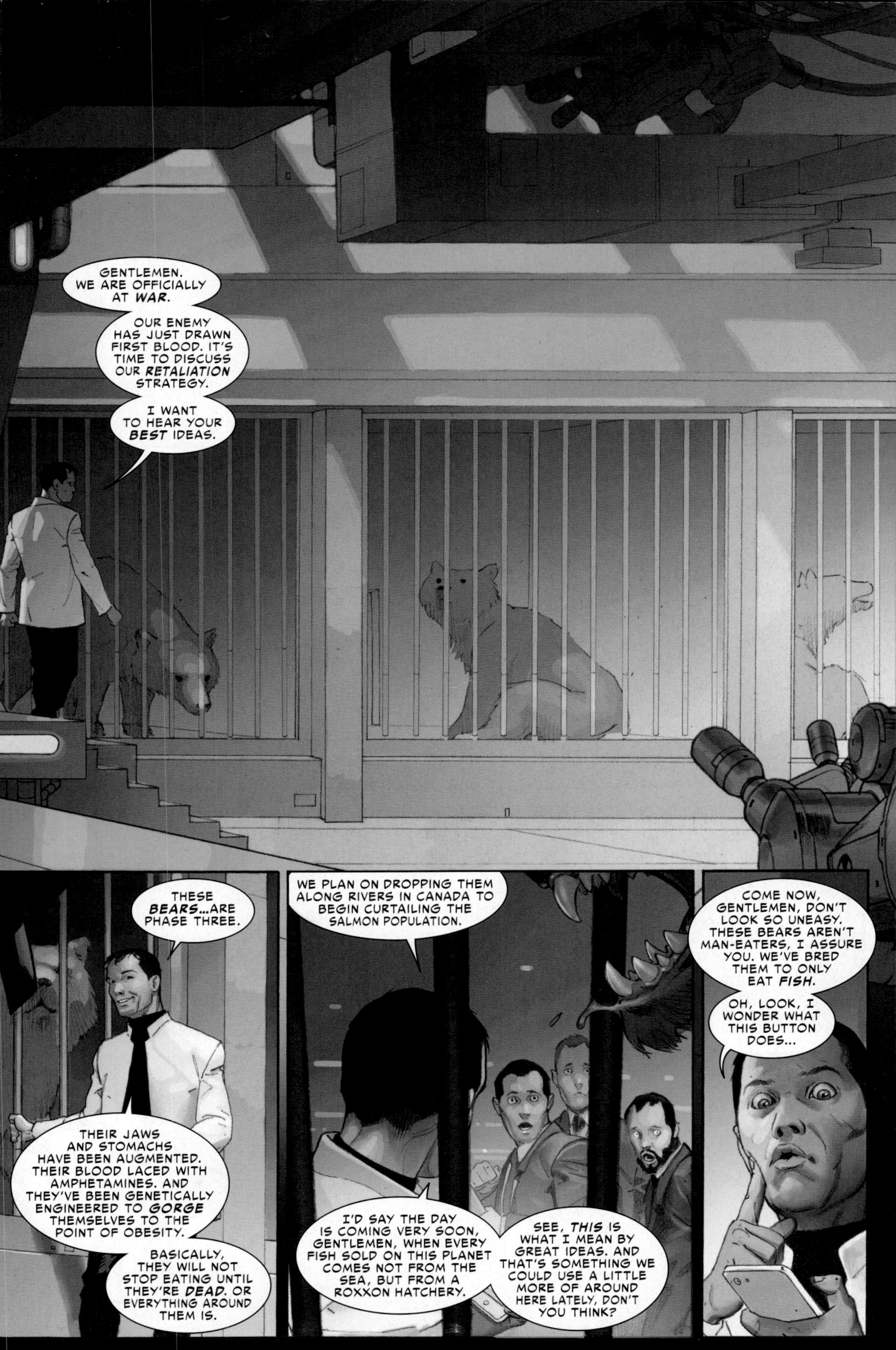
GENTLEMEN. WE ARE OFFICIALLY AT WAR.
OUR ENEMY HAS JUST DRAWN FIRST BLOOD. IT'S TIME TO DISCUSS OUR RETALIATION STRATEGY.
I WANT TO HEAR YOUR BEST IDEAS.
THESE BEARS...ARE PHASE THREE.
THEIR JAWS AND STOMACHS HAVE BEEN AUGMENTED. THEIR BLOOD LACED WITH AMPHETAMINES. AND THEY'VE BEEN GENETICALLY ENGINEERED TO GORGE THEMSELVES TO THE POINT OF OBESITY.
BASICALLY, THEY WILL NOT STOP EATING UNTIL THEY'RE DEAD. OR EVERYTHING AROUND THEM IS.
WE PLAN ON DROPPING THEM ALONG RIVERS IN CANADA TO BEGIN CURTAILING THE SALMON POPULATION.
I'D SAY THE DAY IS COMING VERY SOON, GENTLEMEN, WHEN EVERY FISH SOLD ON THIS PLANET COMES NOT FROM THE SEA, BUT FROM A ROXXON HATCHERY.
SEE, THIS IS WHAT I MEAN BY GREAT IDEAS. AND THAT'S SOMETHING WE COULD USE A LITTLE MORE OF AROUND HERE LATELY, DON'T YOU THINK?
COME NOW, GENTLEMEN, DON'T LOOK SO UNEASY. THESE BEARS AREN'T MAN-EATERS, I ASSURE YOU. WE'VE BRED THEM TO ONLY EAT FISH.
OH, LOOK, I WONDER WHAT THIS BUTTON DOES...

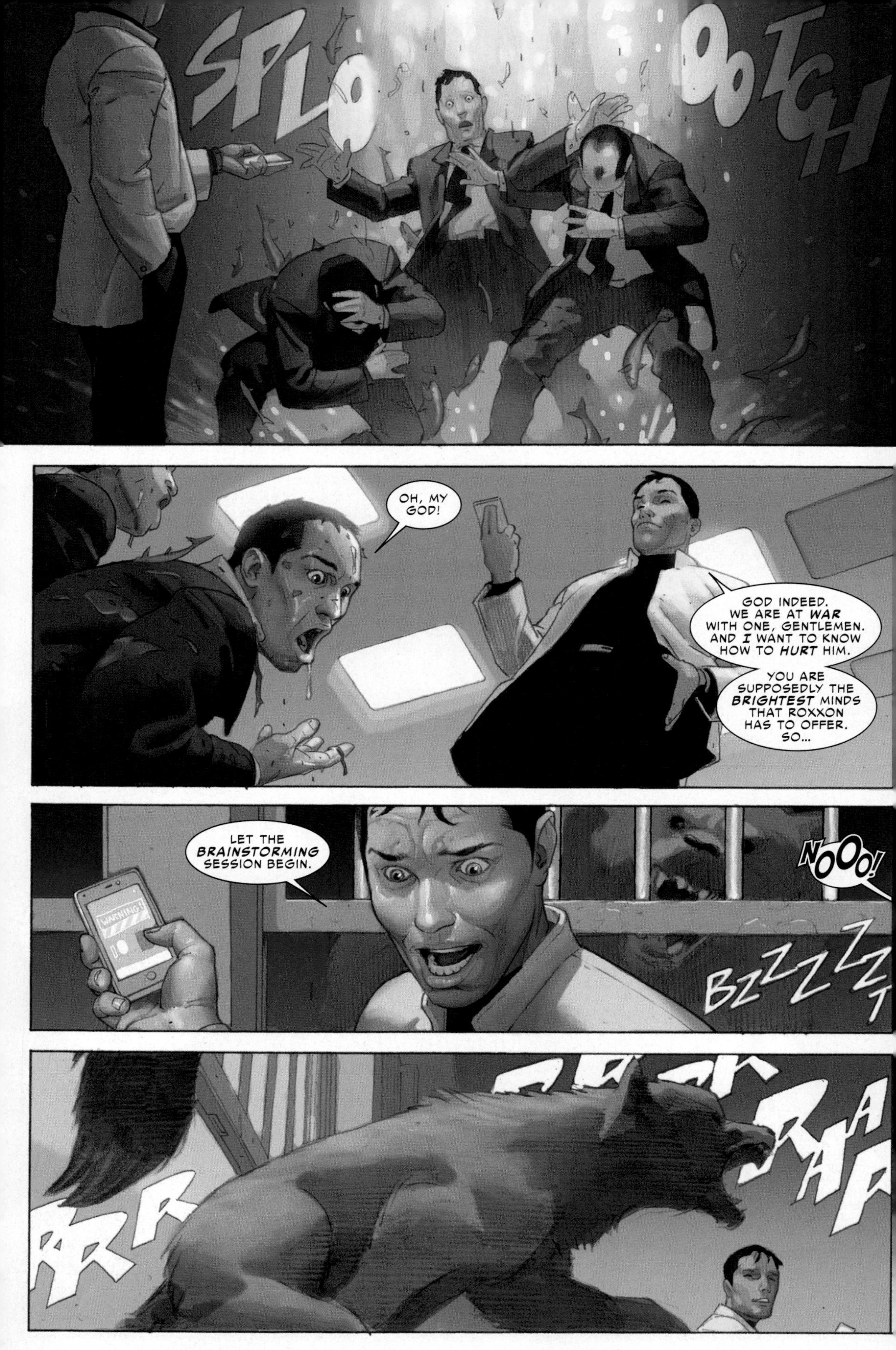
SPLOOOTCH
OH, MY GOD!
GOD INDEED. WE ARE AT WAR WITH ONE, GENTLEMEN. AND I WANT TO KNOW HOW TO HURT HIM.
YOU ARE SUPPOSEDLY THE BRIGHTEST MINDS THAT ROXXON HAS TO OFFER. SO...
LET THE BRAINSTORMING SESSION BEGIN.
WARNING!
NOOO!
BZZZZZT
RRRAAA

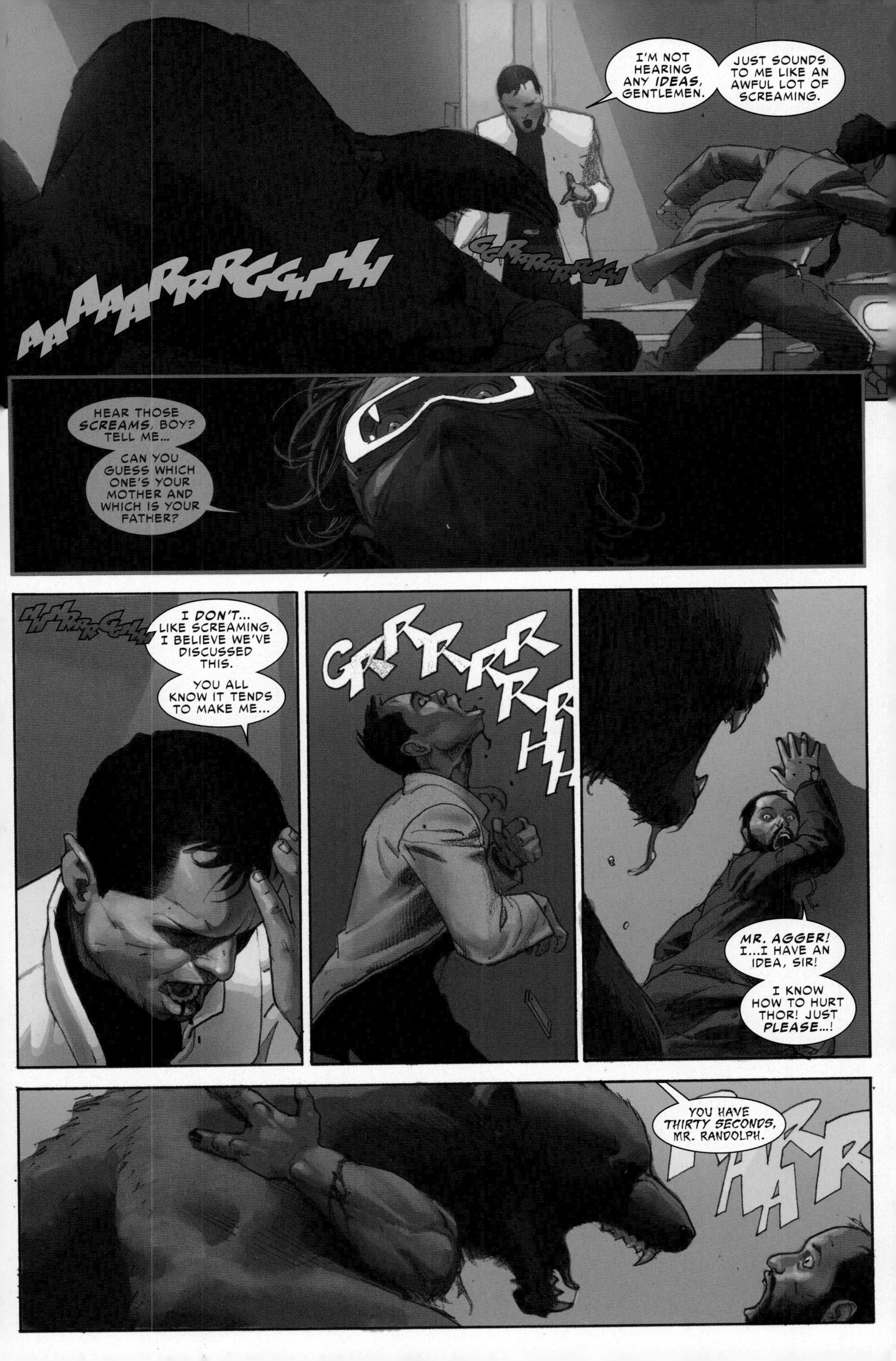
I'M NOT HEARING ANY IDEAS, GENTLEMEN.
JUST SOUNDS TO ME LIKE AN AWFUL LOT OF SCREAMING.
AAAAARRRGGHHH
GGRRRRRRGGH
HEAR THOSE SCREAMS, BOY? TELL ME...
CAN YOU GUESS WHICH ONE'S YOUR MOTHER AND WHICH IS YOUR FATHER?
I DON'T... LIKE SCREAMING. I BELIEVE WE'VE DISCUSSED THIS.
YOU ALL KNOW IT TENDS TO MAKE ME...
GRRRRRRH
MR. AGGER! I...I HAVE AN IDEA, SIR!
I KNOW HOW TO HURT THOR! JUST PLEASE...!
YOU HAVE THIRTY SECONDS, MR. RANDOLPH.

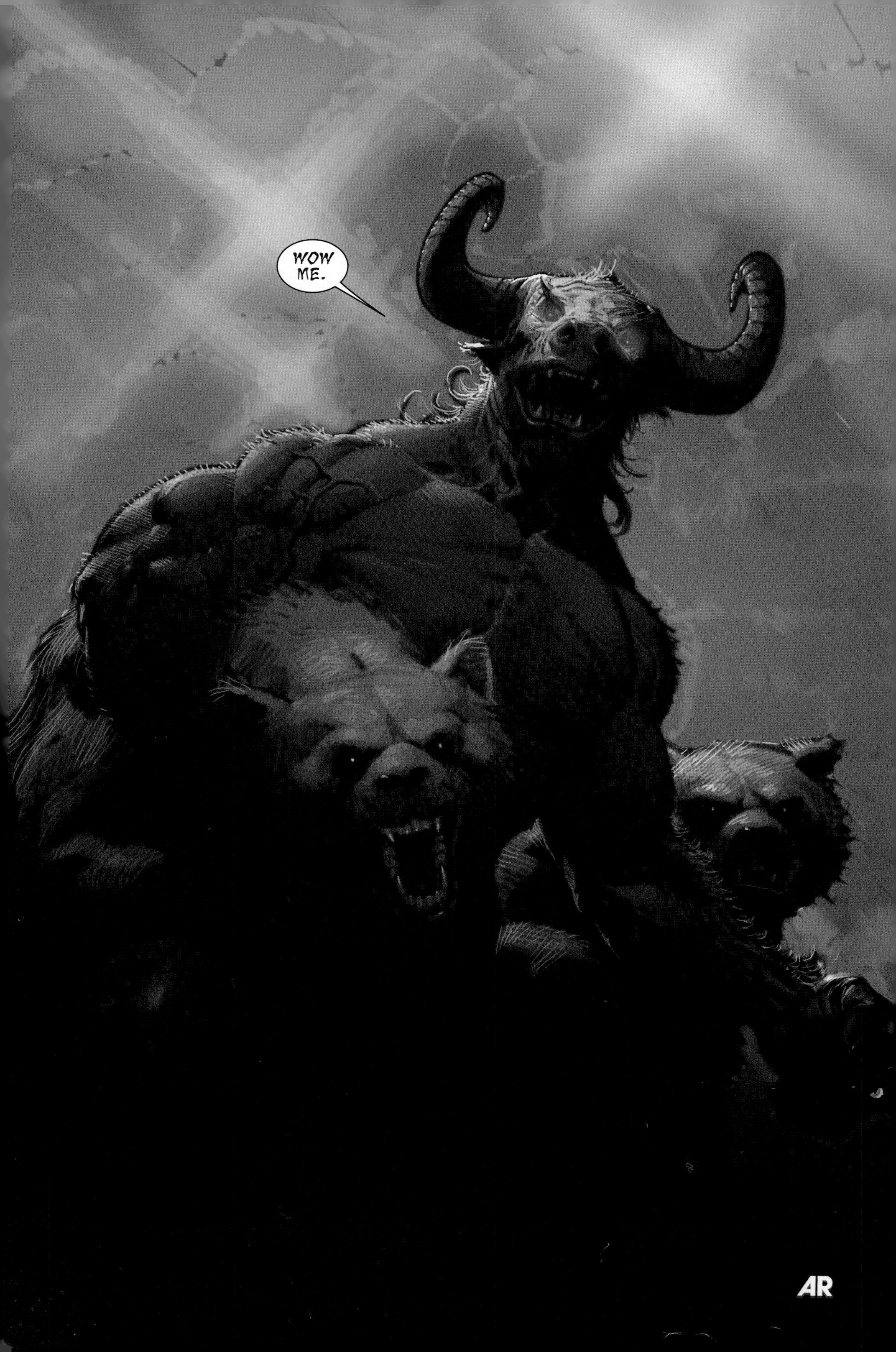
WOW ME.
AR

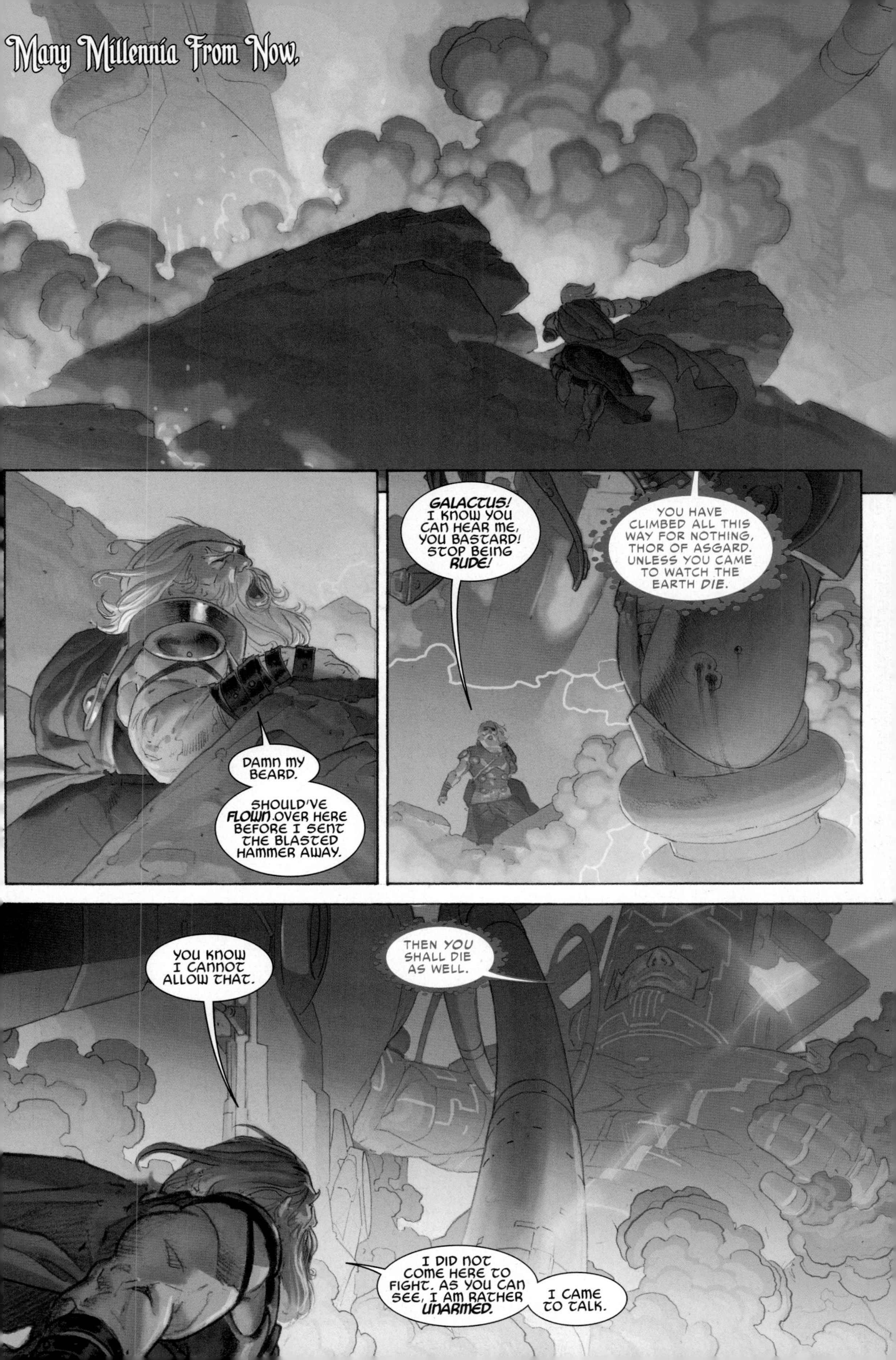
Many Millennia From Now,
DAMN MY BEARD.
SHOULD'VE FLOWN OVER HERE BEFORE I SENT THE BLASTED HAMMER AWAY.
GALACTUS! I KNOW YOU CAN HEAR ME, YOU BASTARD! STOP BEING RUDE!
YOU HAVE CLIMBED ALL THIS WAY FOR NOTHING, THOR OF ASGARD. UNLESS YOU CAME TO WATCH THE EARTH DIE.
YOU KNOW I CANNOT ALLOW THAT.
THEN YOU SHALL DIE AS WELL.
I DID NOT COME HERE TO FIGHT. AS YOU CAN SEE, I AM RATHER UNARMED.
I CAME TO TALK.

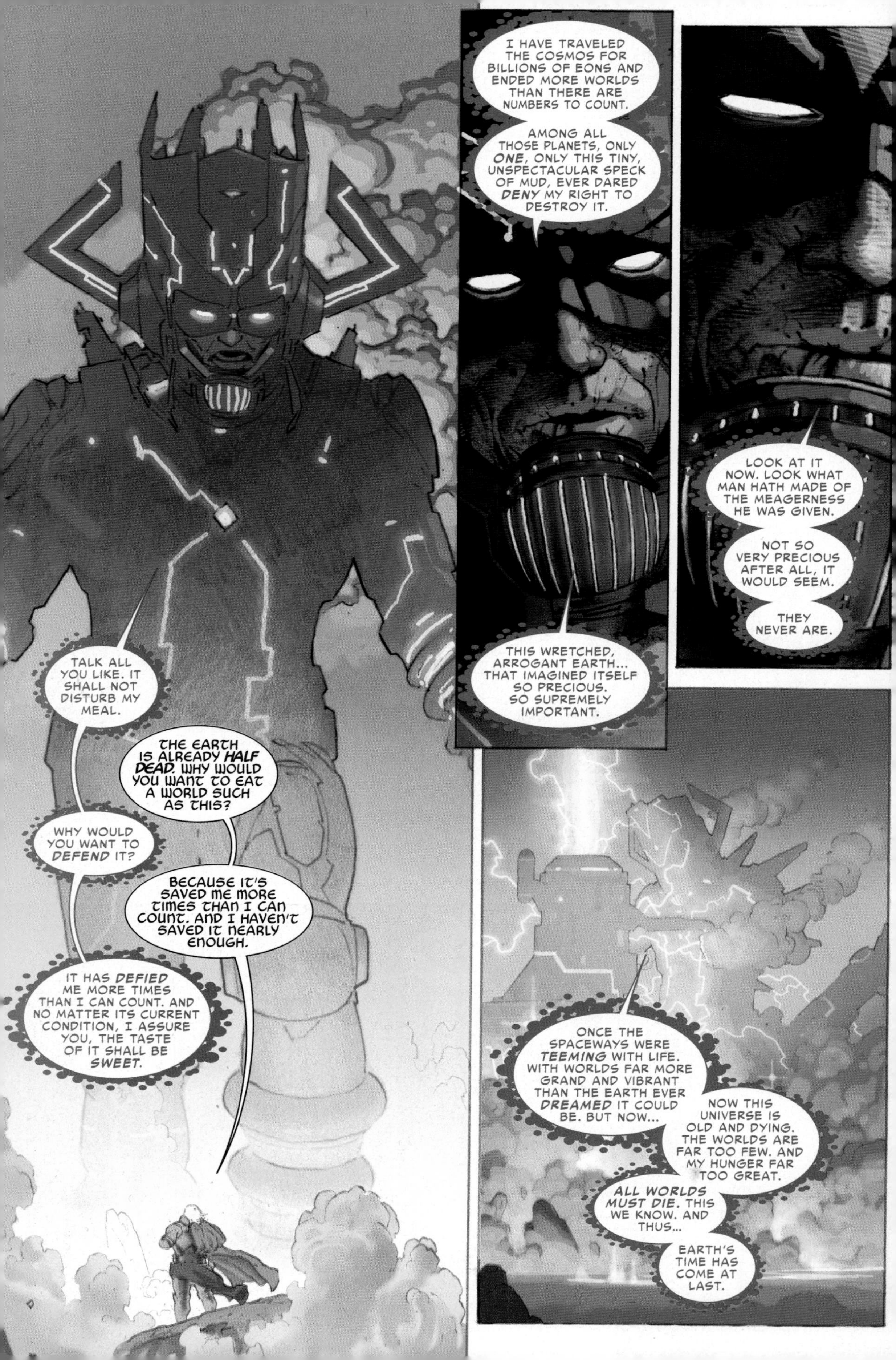

I HAVE TRAVELED THE COSMOS FOR BILLIONS OF EONS AND ENDED MORE WORLDS THAN THERE ARE NUMBERS TO COUNT.
AMONG ALL THOSE PLANETS, ONLY ONE, ONLY THIS TINY, UNSPECTACULAR SPECK OF MUD, EVER DARED DENY MY RIGHT TO DESTROY IT.
THIS WRETCHED, ARROGANT EARTH... THAT IMAGINED ITSELF SO PRECIOUS. SO SUPREMELY IMPORTANT.
LOOK AT IT NOW. LOOK WHAT MAN HATH MADE OF THE MEAGERNESS HE WAS GIVEN.
NOT SO VERY PRECIOUS AFTER ALL, IT WOULD SEEM.
THEY NEVER ARE.
TALK ALL YOU LIKE. IT SHALL NOT DISTURB MY MEAL.
THE EARTH IS ALREADY HALF DEAD. WHY WOULD YOU WANT TO EAT A WORLD SUCH AS THIS?
WHY WOULD YOU WANT TO DEFEND IT?
BECAUSE IT'S SAVED ME MORE TIMES THAN I CAN COUNT. AND I HAVEN'T SAVED IT NEARLY ENOUGH.
IT HAS DEFIED ME MORE TIMES THAN I CAN COUNT. AND NO MATTER ITS CURRENT CONDITION, I ASSURE YOU, THE TASTE OF IT SHALL BE SWEET.
ONCE THE SPACEWAYS WERE TEEMING WITH LIFE. WITH WORLDS FAR MORE GRAND AND VIBRANT THAN THE EARTH EVER DREAMED IT COULD BE. BUT NOW...
NOW THIS UNIVERSE IS OLD AND DYING. THE WORLDS ARE FAR TOO FEW. AND MY HUNGER FAR TOO GREAT.
ALL WORLDS MUST DIE. THIS WE KNOW. AND THUS...
EARTH'S TIME HAS COME AT LAST.

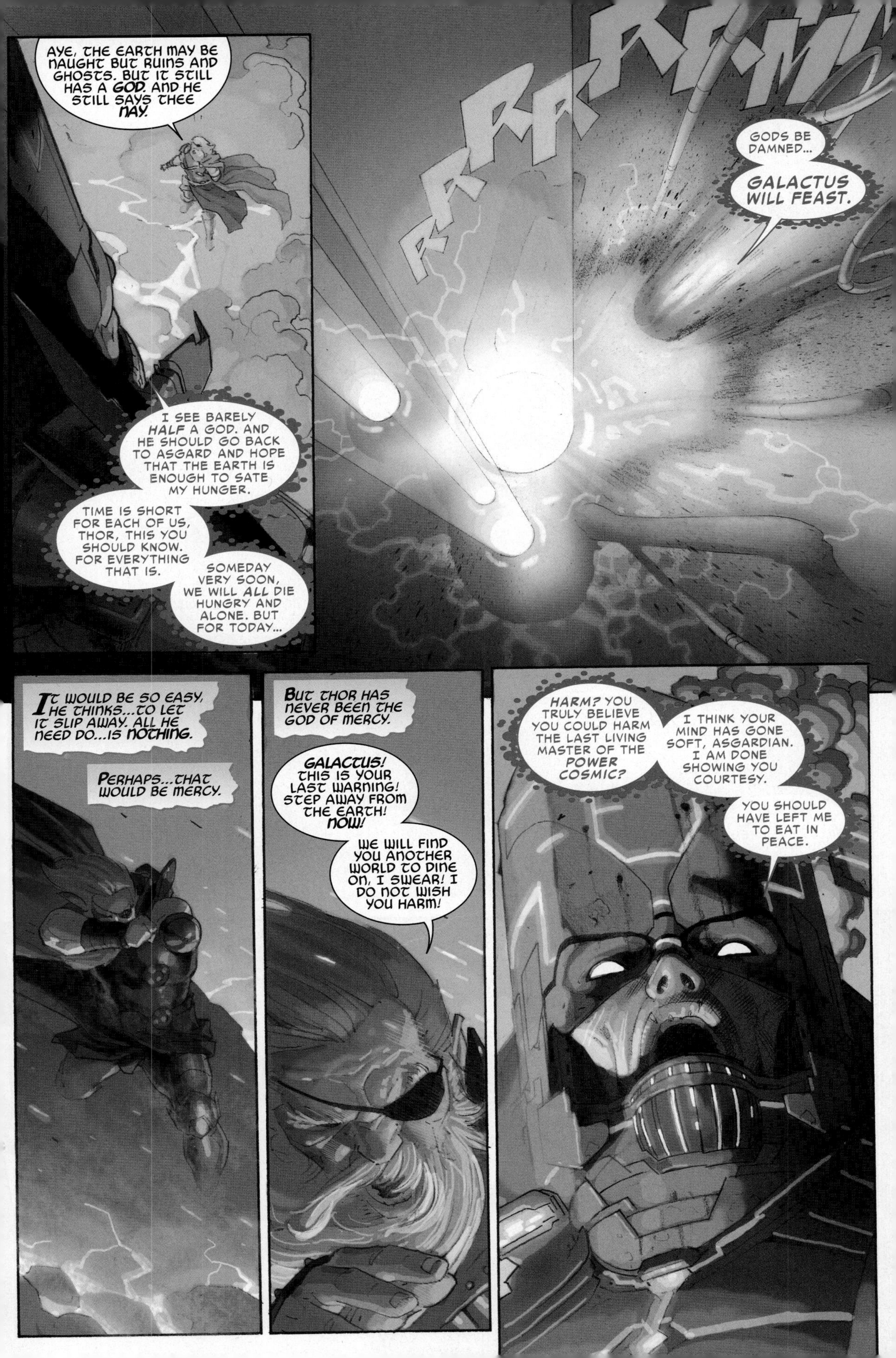
AYE, THE EARTH MAY BE NAUGHT BUT RUINS AND GHOSTS. BUT IT STILL HAS A GOD. AND HE STILL SAYS THEE NAY.
I SEE BARELY HALF A GOD. AND HE SHOULD GO BACK TO ASGARD AND HOPE THAT THE EARTH IS ENOUGH TO SATE MY HUNGER.
TIME IS SHORT FOR EACH OF US, THOR, THIS YOU SHOULD KNOW. FOR EVERYTHING THAT IS.
SOMEDAY VERY SOON, WE WILL ALL DIE HUNGRY AND ALONE. BUT FOR TODAY...
GODS BE DAMNED...
GALACTUS WILL FEAST.
IT WOULD BE SO EASY, HE THINKS...TO LET IT SLIP AWAY. ALL HE NEED DO...IS NOTHING.
PERHAPS...THAT WOULD BE MERCY.
BUT THOR HAS NEVER BEEN THE GOD OF MERCY.
GALACTUS! THIS IS YOUR LAST WARNING! STEP AWAY FROM THE EARTH! NOW!
WE WILL FIND YOU ANOTHER WORLD TO DINE ON, I SWEAR! I DO NOT WISH YOU HARM!
HARM? YOU TRULY BELIEVE YOU COULD HARM THE LAST LIVING MASTER OF THE POWER COSMIC?
I THINK YOUR MIND HAS GONE SOFT, ASGARDIAN. I AM DONE SHOWING YOU COURTESY.
YOU SHOULD HAVE LEFT ME TO EAT IN PEACE.

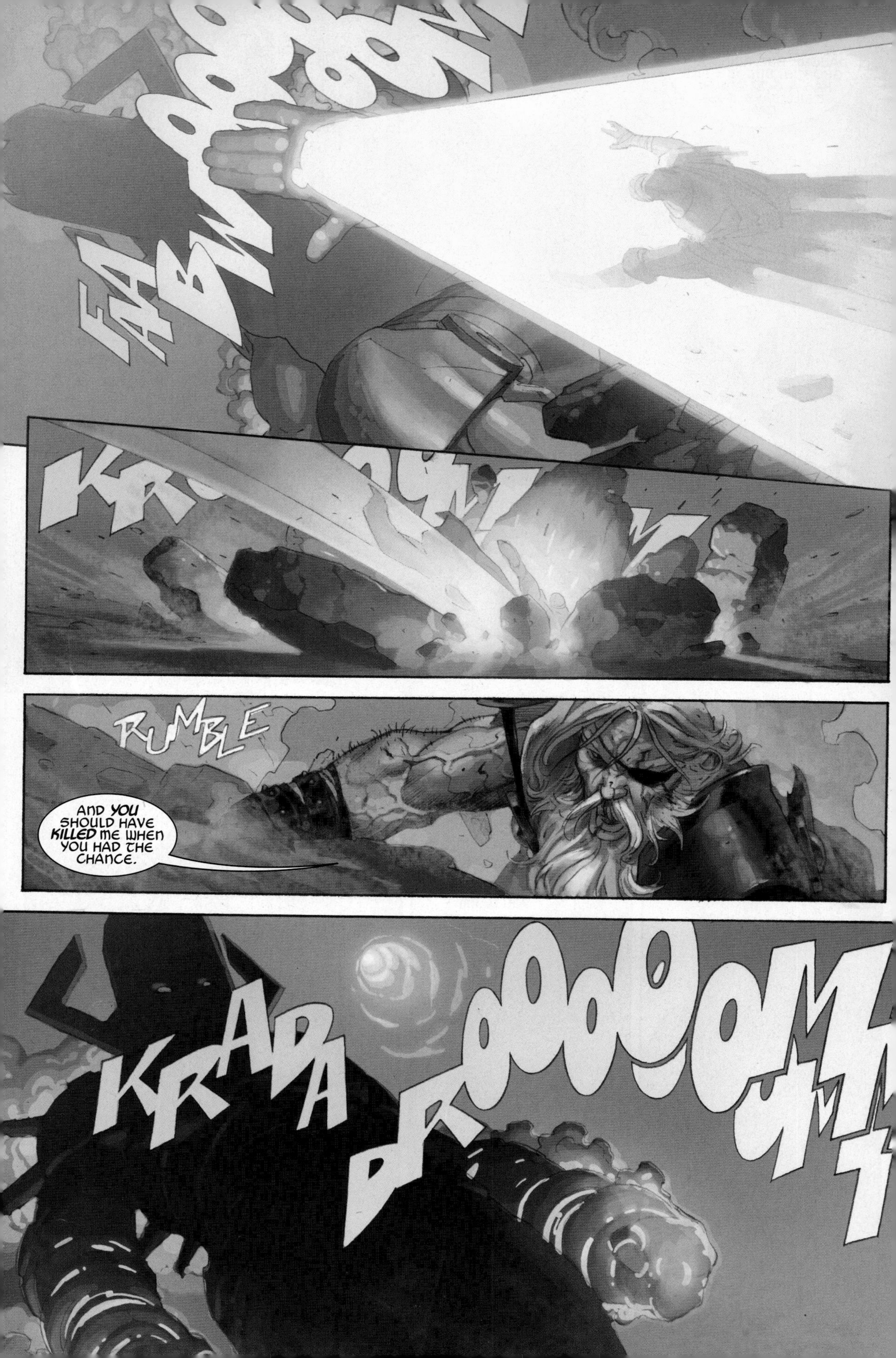
RUMBLE
AND YOU SHOULD HAVE KILLED ME WHEN YOU HAD THE CHANCE.
KRADA

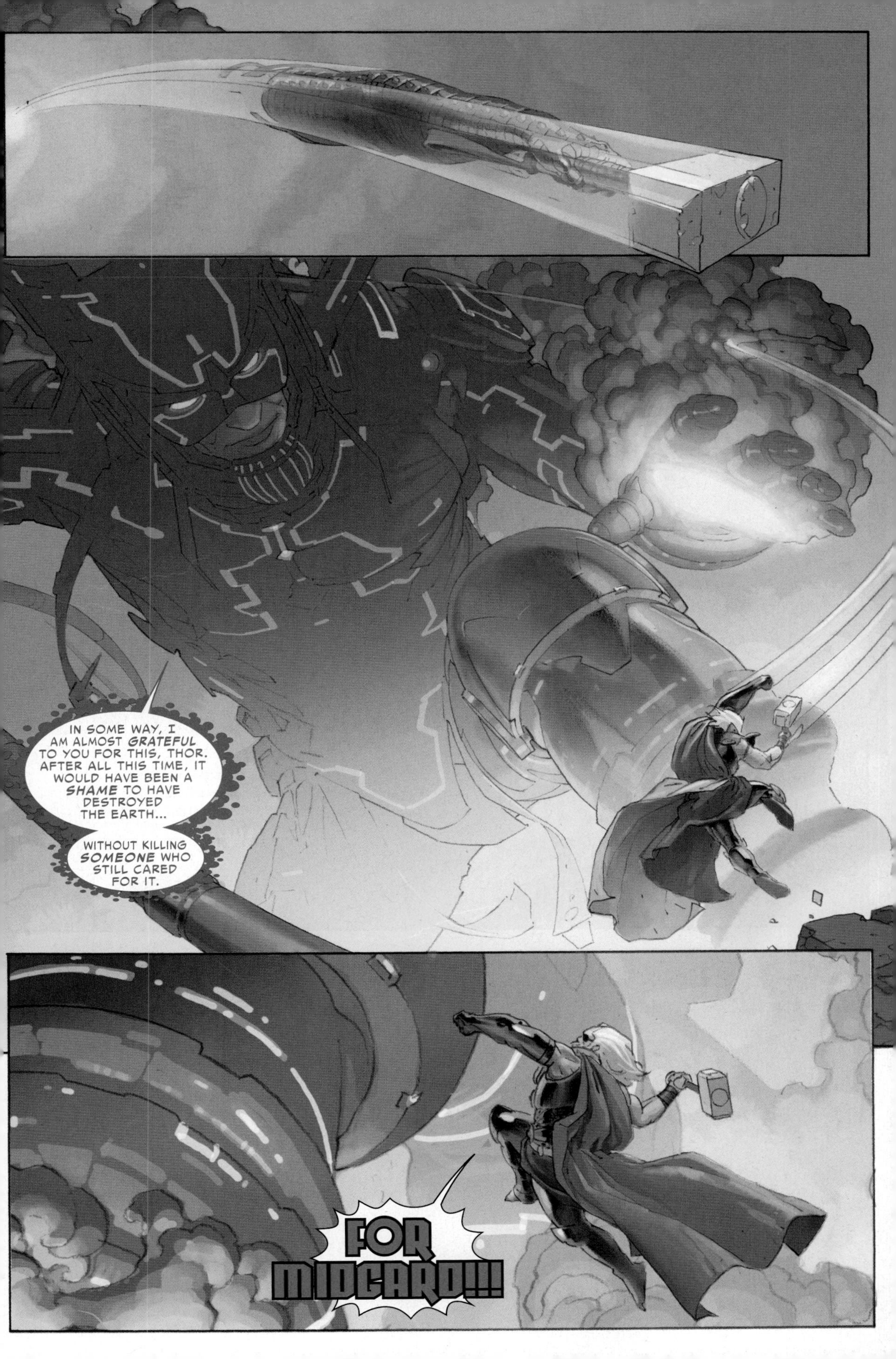
IN SOME WAY, I AM ALMOST GRATEFUL TO YOU FOR THIS, THOR. AFTER ALL THIS TIME, IT WOULD HAVE BEEN A SHAME TO HAVE DESTROYED THE EARTH...
WITHOUT KILLING SOMEONE WHO STILL CARED FOR IT.
FOR MIDGARD!!!

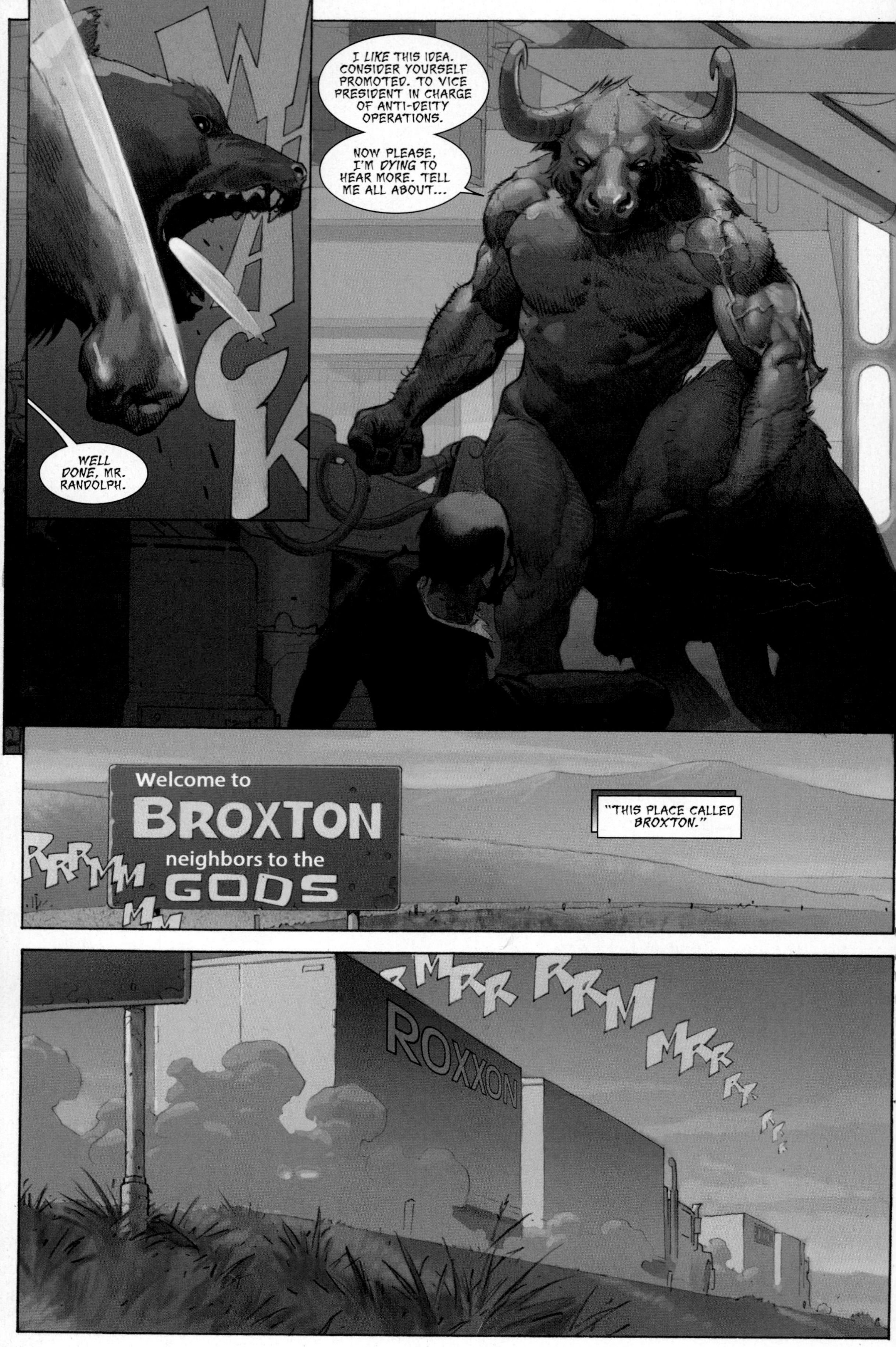
WHACK
I LIKE THIS IDEA. CONSIDER YOURSELF PROMOTED. TO VICE PRESIDENT IN CHARGE OF ANTI-DEITY OPERATIONS.
NOW PLEASE, I'M DYING TO HEAR MORE. TELL ME ALL ABOUT...
WELL DONE, MR. RANDOLPH.
Welcome to BROXTON neighbors to the GODS
RRRMMM
"THIS PLACE CALLED BROXTON."
RRMRR RRRM MRRR
ROXXON

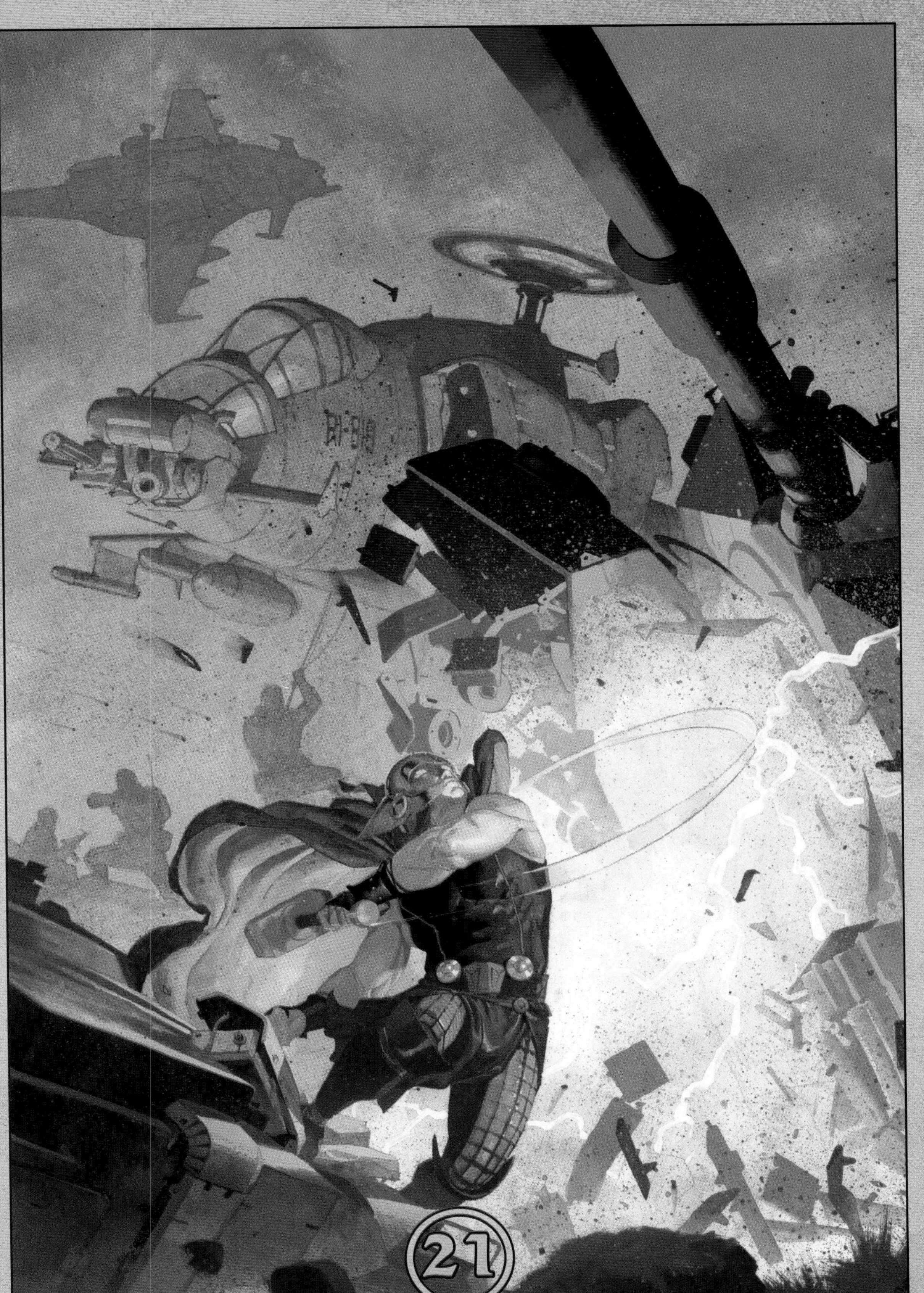
21

The Last Days of Midgard — Part 3:
God, Inc.

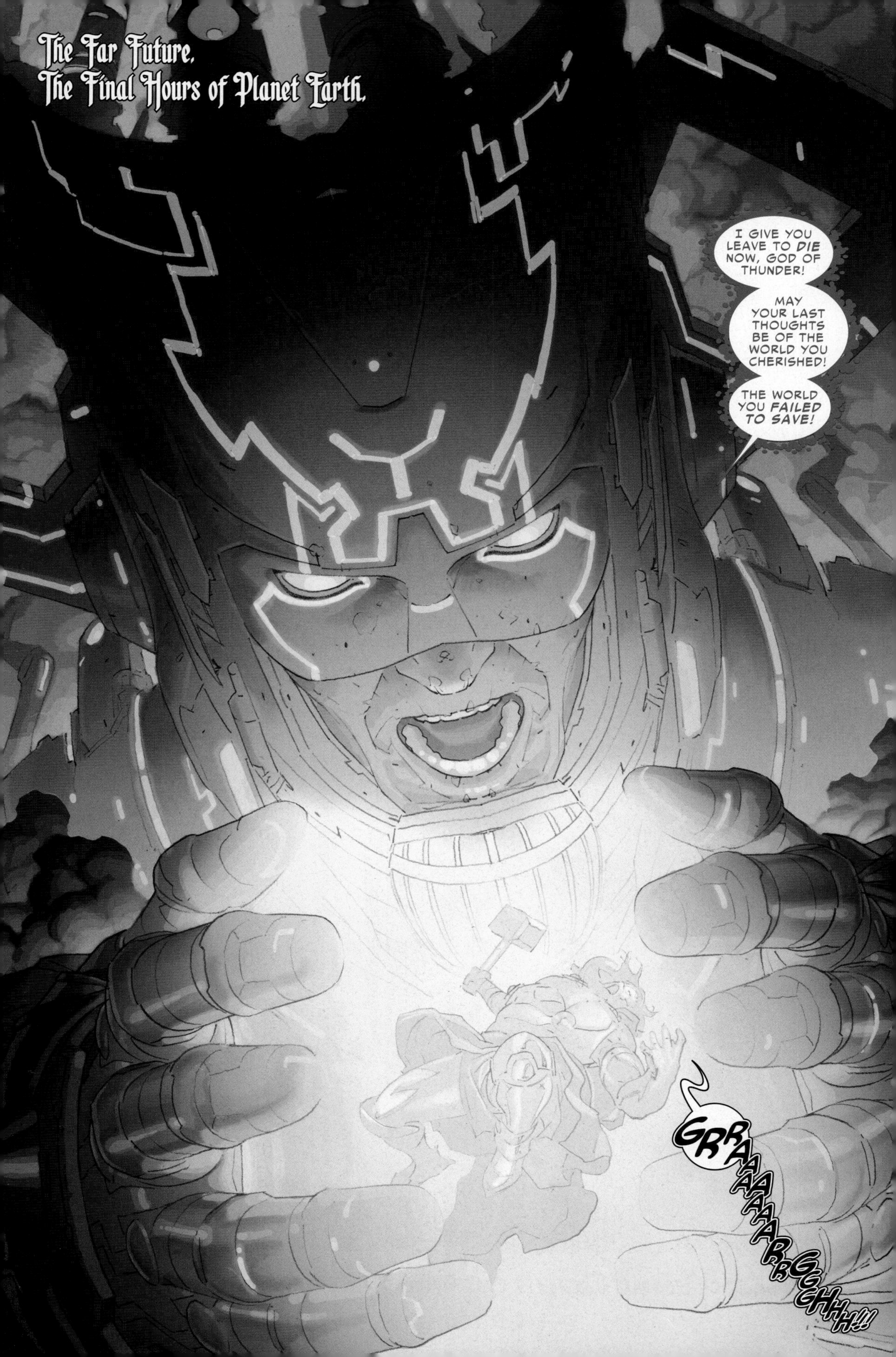
The Far Future.
The Final Hours of Planet Earth.
I GIVE YOU LEAVE TO *DIE* NOW, GOD OF THUNDER!
MAY YOUR LAST THOUGHTS BE OF THE WORLD YOU CHERISHED!
THE WORLD YOU *FAILED* TO *SAVE!*
GRRAAAAARRGGHHH!!

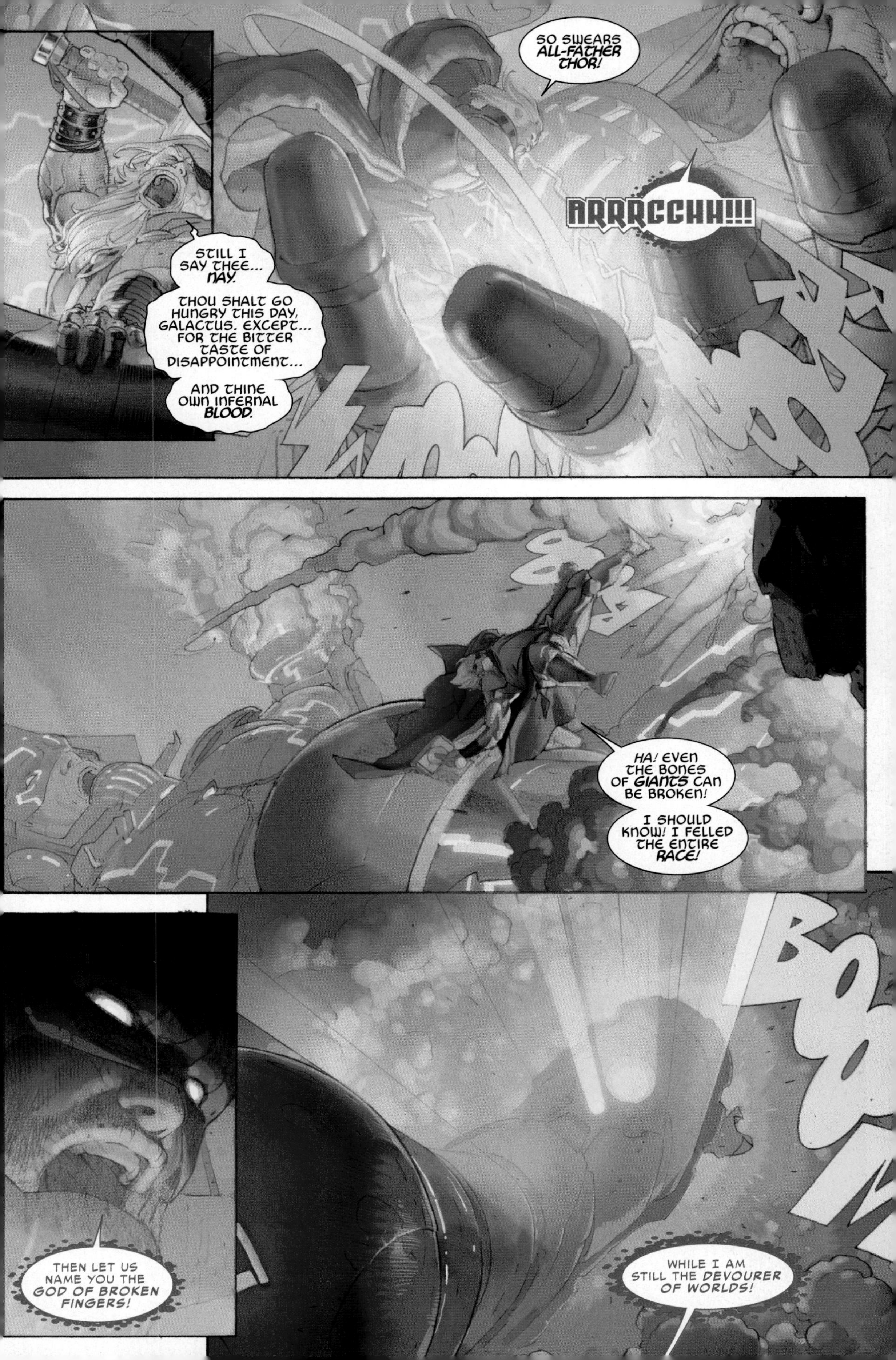

STILL I SAY THEE... NAY.
THOU SHALT GO HUNGRY THIS DAY, GALACTUS. EXCEPT... FOR THE BITTER TASTE OF DISAPPOINTMENT...
AND THINE OWN INFERNAL BLOOD.
SO SWEARS ALL-FATHER THOR!
ARRRGCHH!!!
HA! EVEN THE BONES OF GIANTS CAN BE BROKEN!
I SHOULD KNOW! I FELLED THE ENTIRE RACE!
THEN LET US NAME YOU THE GOD OF BROKEN FINGERS!
WHILE I AM STILL THE DEVOURER OF WORLDS!
BOOM

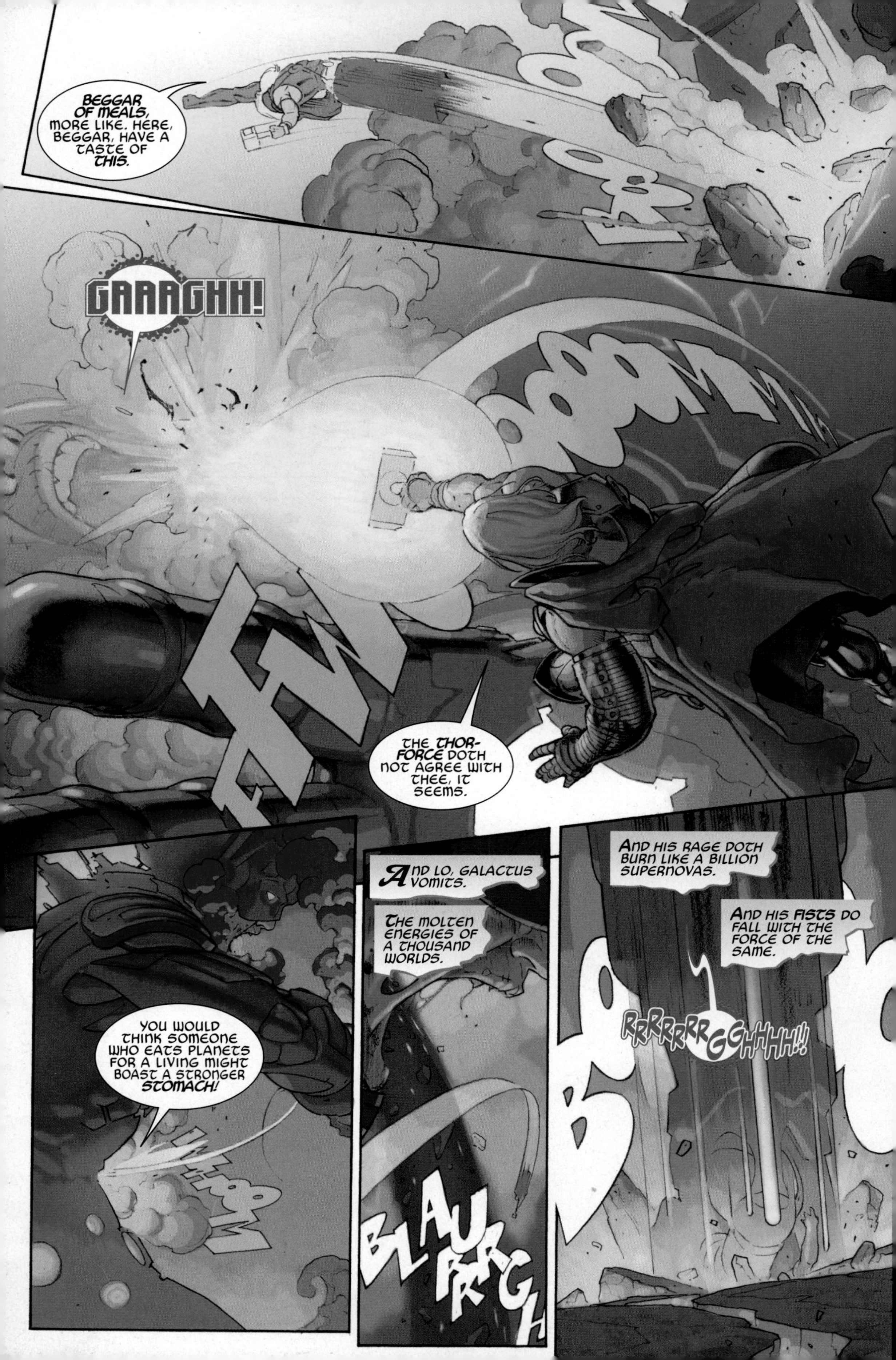
BEGGAR OF MEALS, MORE LIKE. HERE, BEGGAR, HAVE A TASTE OF THIS.
GAAAGHH!
THE THOR-FORCE DOTH NOT AGREE WITH THEE, IT SEEMS.
YOU WOULD THINK SOMEONE WHO EATS PLANETS FOR A LIVING MIGHT BOAST A STRONGER STOMACH!
AND LO, GALACTUS VOMITS.
THE MOLTEN ENERGIES OF A THOUSAND WORLDS.
BLAURRRGH
AND HIS RAGE DOTH BURN LIKE A BILLION SUPERNOVAS.
AND HIS FISTS DO FALL WITH THE FORCE OF THE SAME.
RRRRRRRGGHHHH!!!

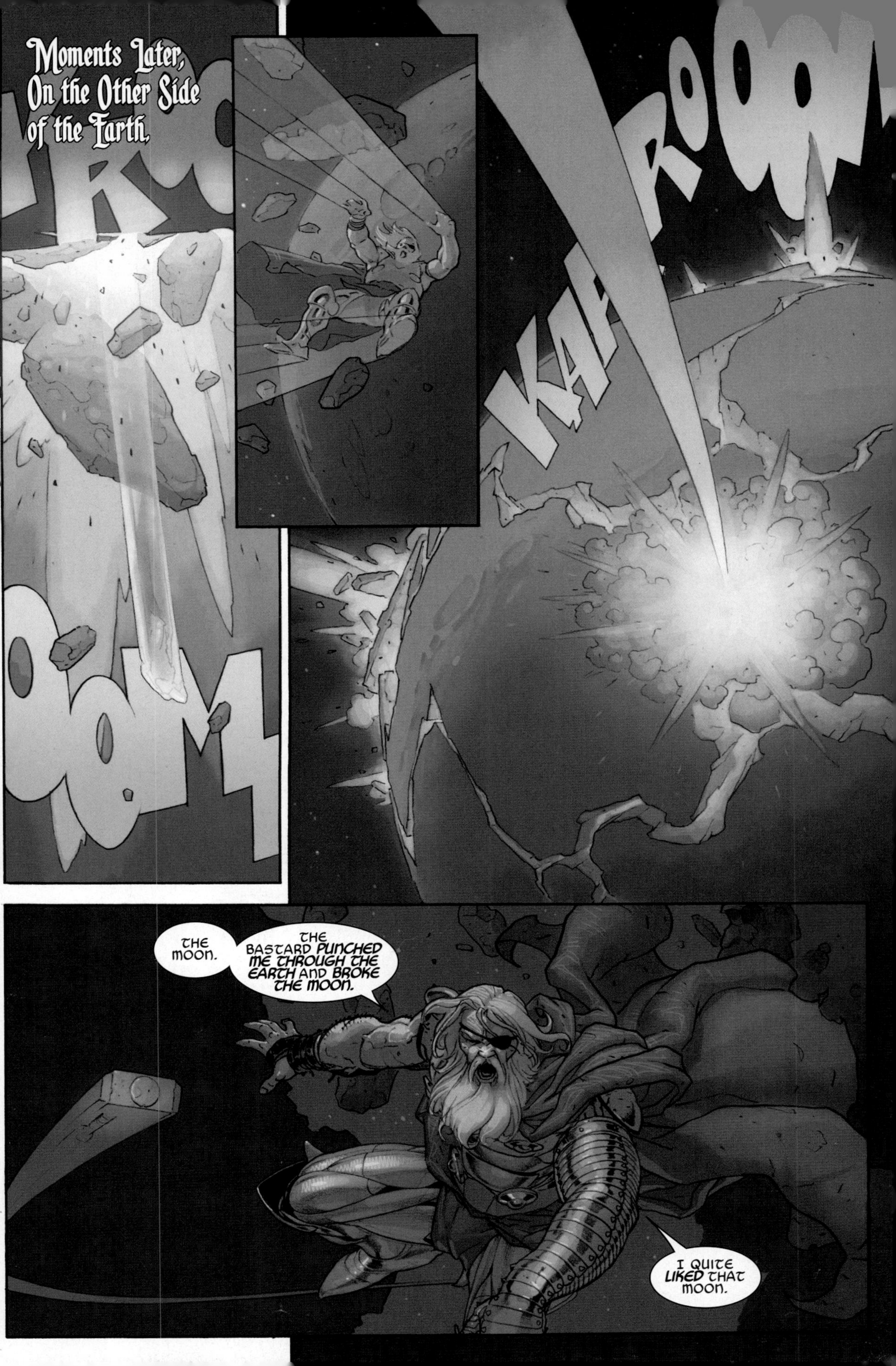
Moments Later, On the Other Side of the Earth,
THE MOON.
THE BASTARD PUNCHED ME THROUGH THE EARTH AND BROKE THE MOON.
I QUITE LIKED THAT MOON.

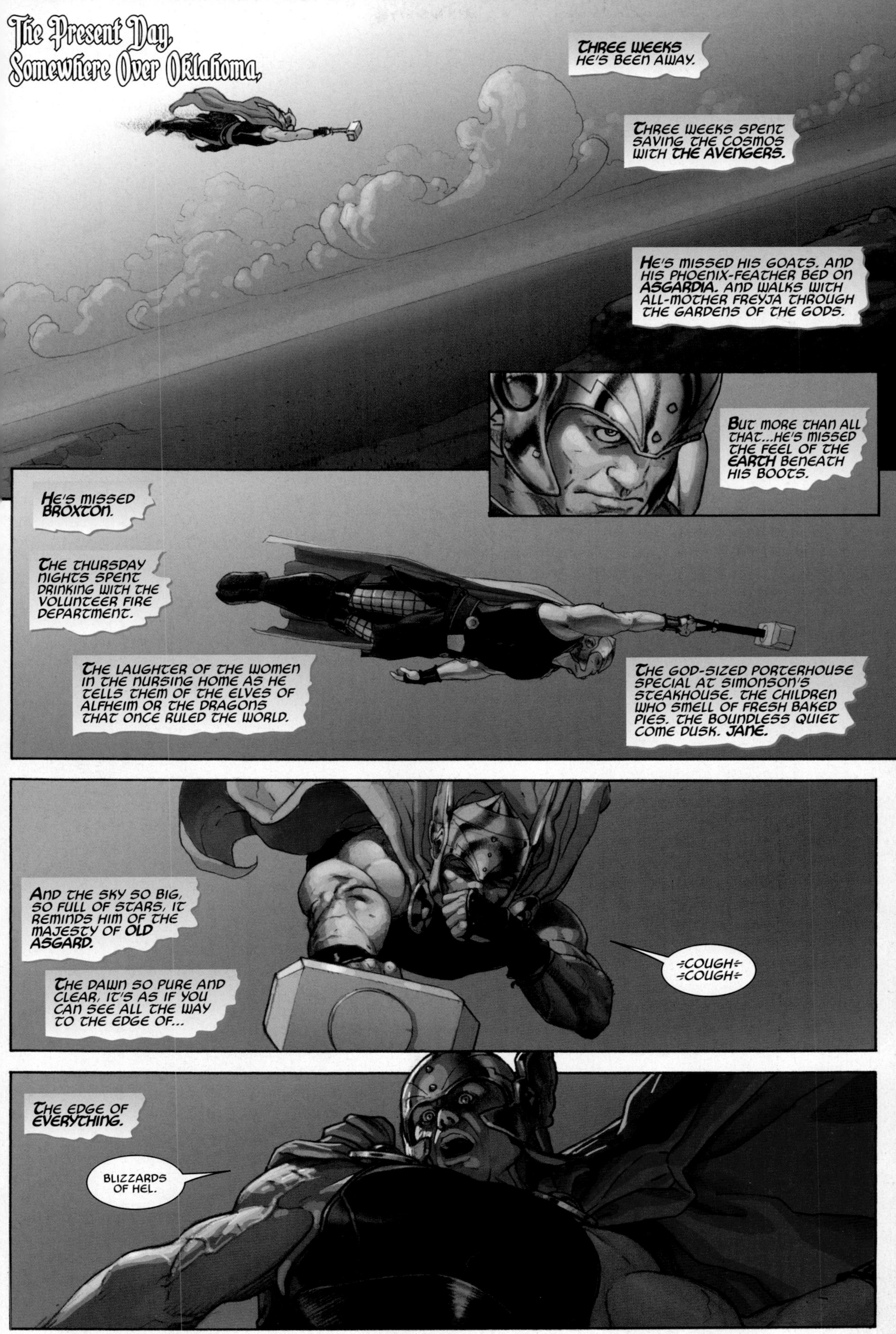
The Present Day, Somewhere Over Oklahoma.
THREE WEEKS HE'S BEEN AWAY.
THREE WEEKS SPENT SAVING THE COSMOS WITH THE AVENGERS.
HE'S MISSED HIS GOATS. AND HIS PHOENIX-FEATHER BED ON ASGARDIA. AND WALKS WITH ALL-MOTHER FREYJA THROUGH THE GARDENS OF THE GODS.
BUT MORE THAN ALL THAT...HE'S MISSED THE FEEL OF THE EARTH BENEATH HIS BOOTS.
HE'S MISSED BROXTON.
THE THURSDAY NIGHTS SPENT DRINKING WITH THE VOLUNTEER FIRE DEPARTMENT.
THE LAUGHTER OF THE WOMEN IN THE NURSING HOME AS HE TELLS THEM OF THE ELVES OF ALFHEIM OR THE DRAGONS THAT ONCE RULED THE WORLD.
THE GOD-SIZED PORTERHOUSE SPECIAL AT SIMONSON'S STEAKHOUSE. THE CHILDREN WHO SMELL OF FRESH BAKED PIES. THE BOUNDLESS QUIET COME DUSK. JANE.
AND THE SKY SO BIG, SO FULL OF STARS, IT REMINDS HIM OF THE MAJESTY OF OLD ASGARD.
THE DAWN SO PURE AND CLEAR, IT'S AS IF YOU CAN SEE ALL THE WAY TO THE EDGE OF...
COUGH COUGH
THE EDGE OF EVERYTHING.
BLIZZARDS OF HEL.

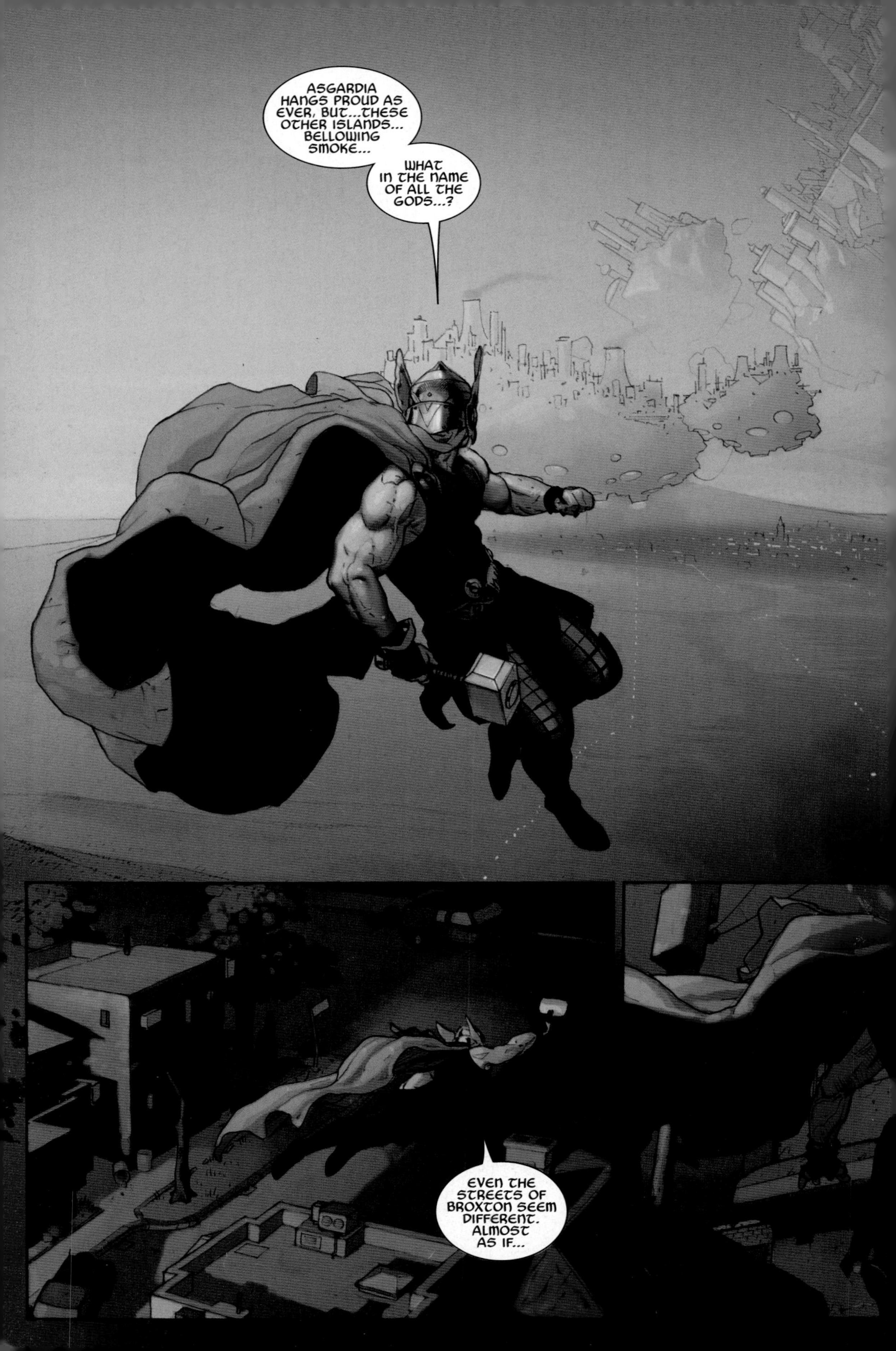

ASGARDIA HANGS PROUD AS EVER, BUT...THESE OTHER ISLANDS... BELLOWING SMOKE...
WHAT IN THE NAME OF ALL THE GODS...?
EVEN THE STREETS OF BROXTON SEEM DIFFERENT. ALMOST AS IF...

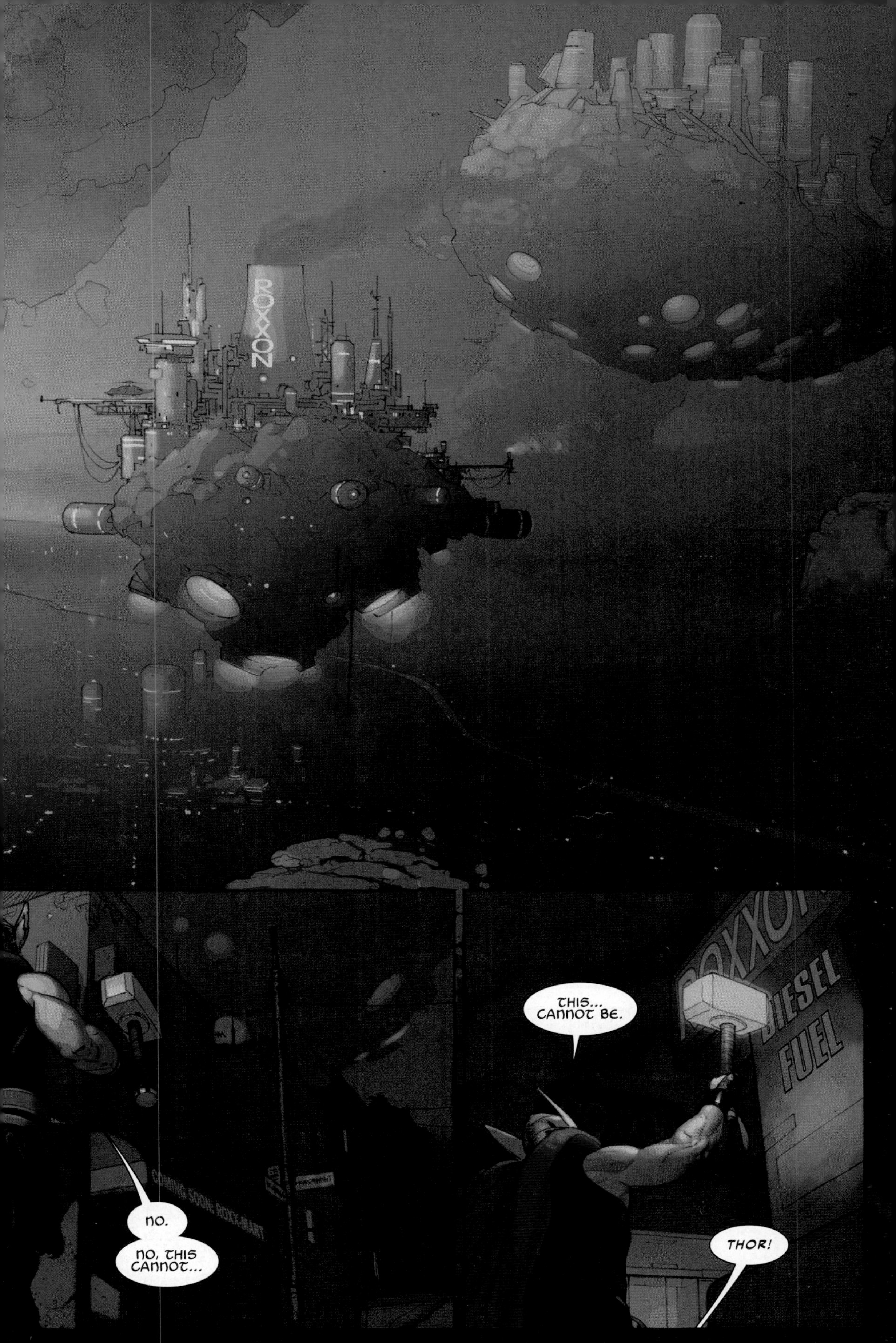
ROXXON
COMING SOON: ROXX-MART
NO.
NO, THIS CANNOT...
THIS... CANNOT BE.
DIESEL FUEL
THOR!

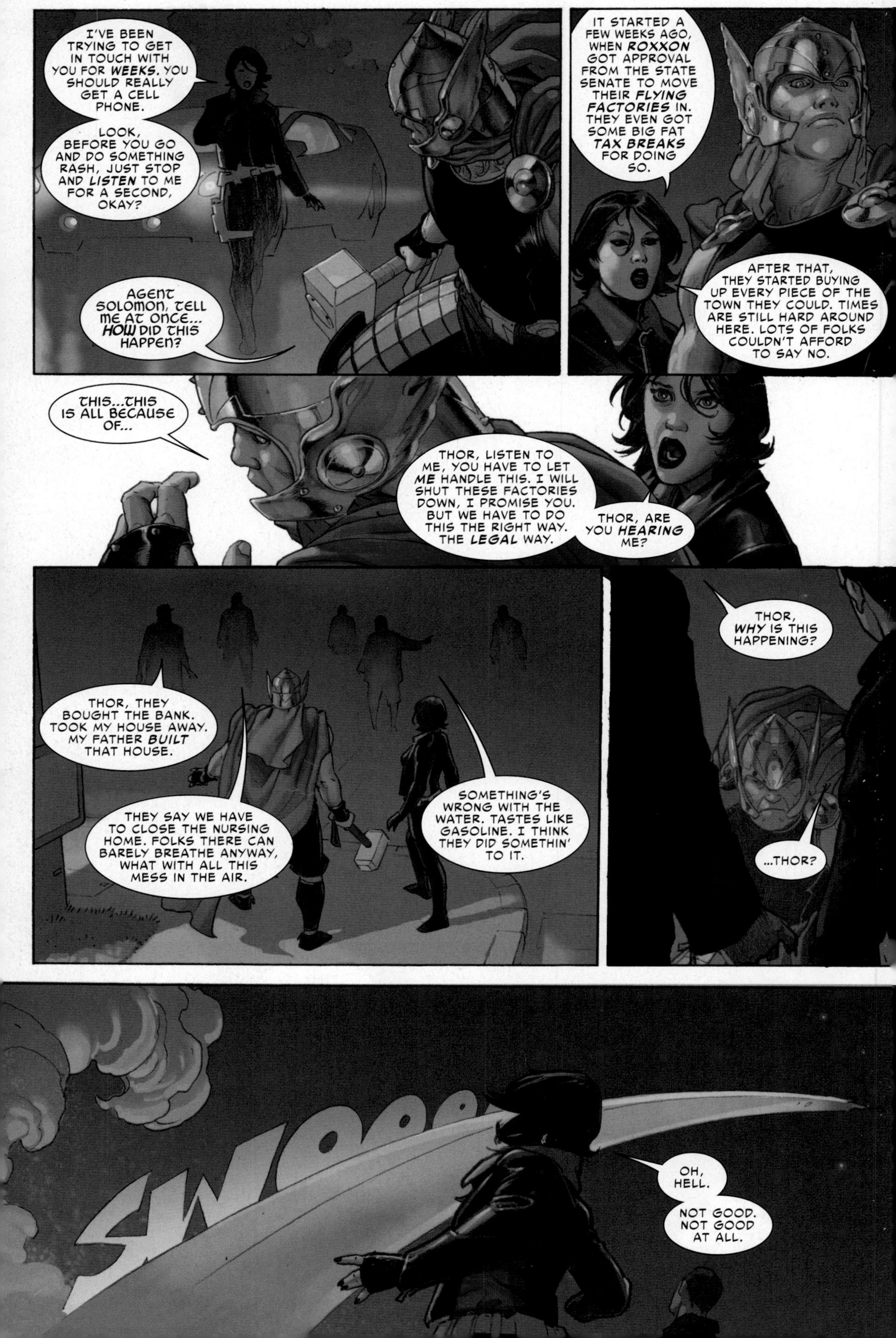
I'VE BEEN TRYING TO GET IN TOUCH WITH YOU FOR WEEKS. YOU SHOULD REALLY GET A CELL PHONE.
LOOK, BEFORE YOU GO AND DO SOMETHING RASH, JUST STOP AND LISTEN TO ME FOR A SECOND, OKAY?
AGENT SOLOMON, TELL ME AT ONCE... HOW DID THIS HAPPEN?
IT STARTED A FEW WEEKS AGO, WHEN ROXXON GOT APPROVAL FROM THE STATE SENATE TO MOVE THEIR FLYING FACTORIES IN. THEY EVEN GOT SOME BIG FAT TAX BREAKS FOR DOING SO.
AFTER THAT, THEY STARTED BUYING UP EVERY PIECE OF THE TOWN THEY COULD. TIMES ARE STILL HARD AROUND HERE. LOTS OF FOLKS COULDN'T AFFORD TO SAY NO.
THIS...THIS IS ALL BECAUSE OF...
THOR, LISTEN TO ME, YOU HAVE TO LET ME HANDLE THIS. I WILL SHUT THESE FACTORIES DOWN, I PROMISE YOU. BUT WE HAVE TO DO THIS THE RIGHT WAY. THE LEGAL WAY.
THOR, ARE YOU HEARING ME?
THOR, THEY BOUGHT THE BANK. TOOK MY HOUSE AWAY. MY FATHER BUILT THAT HOUSE.
THEY SAY WE HAVE TO CLOSE THE NURSING HOME. FOLKS THERE CAN BARELY BREATHE ANYWAY, WHAT WITH ALL THIS MESS IN THE AIR.
SOMETHING'S WRONG WITH THE WATER. TASTES LIKE GASOLINE. I THINK THEY DID SOMETHIN' TO IT.
THOR, WHY IS THIS HAPPENING?
...THOR?
SWOOO
OH, HELL.
NOT GOOD. NOT GOOD AT ALL.

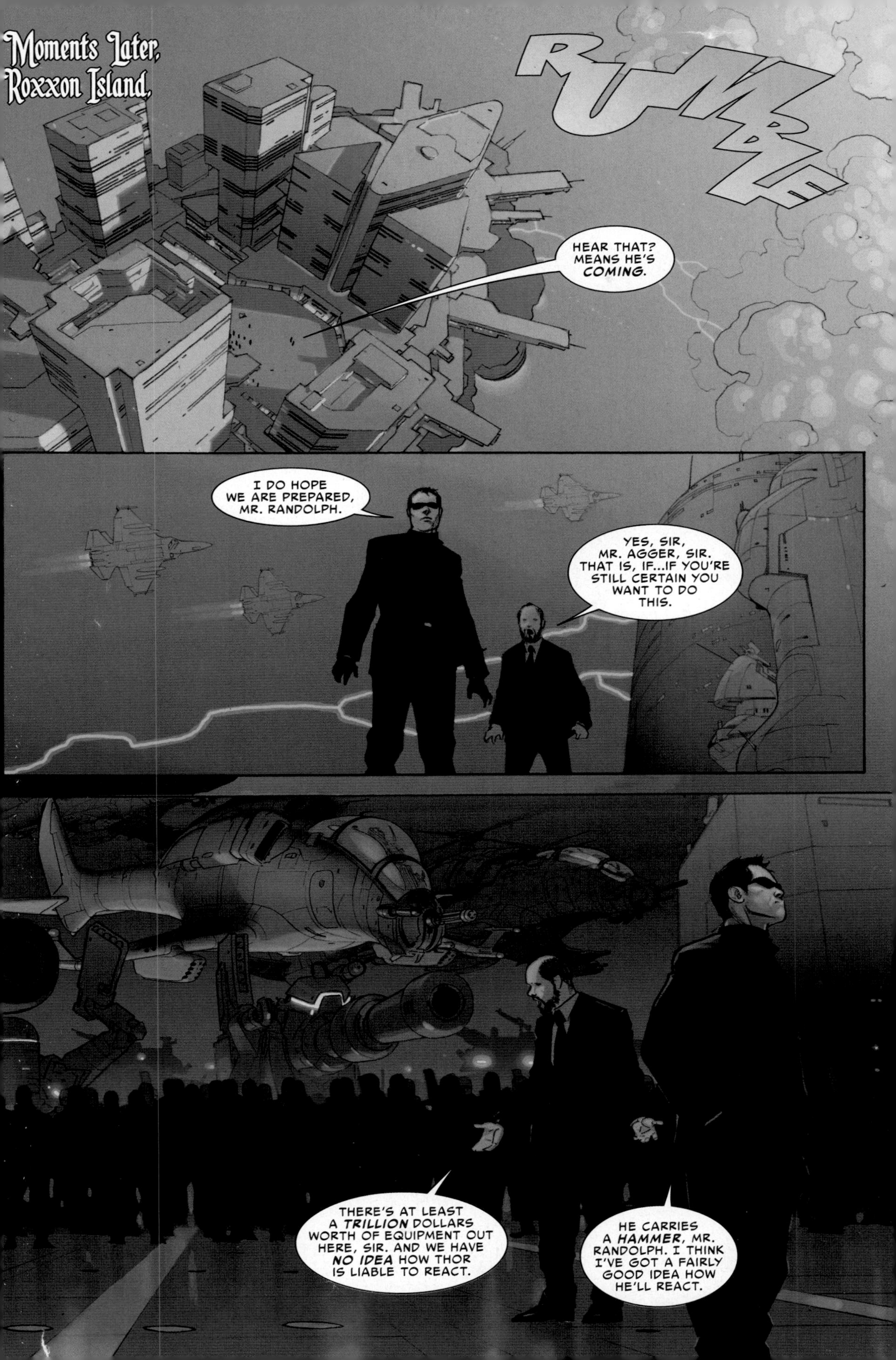
Moments Later, Roxxon Island.
RUMBLE
HEAR THAT? MEANS HE'S *COMING*.
I DO HOPE WE ARE PREPARED, MR. RANDOLPH.
YES, SIR, MR. AGGER, SIR. THAT IS, IF...IF YOU'RE STILL CERTAIN YOU WANT TO DO THIS.
THERE'S AT LEAST A *TRILLION* DOLLARS WORTH OF EQUIPMENT OUT HERE, SIR. AND WE HAVE *NO IDEA* HOW THOR IS LIABLE TO REACT.
HE CARRIES A *HAMMER*, MR. RANDOLPH. I THINK I'VE GOT A FAIRLY GOOD IDEA HOW HE'LL REACT.

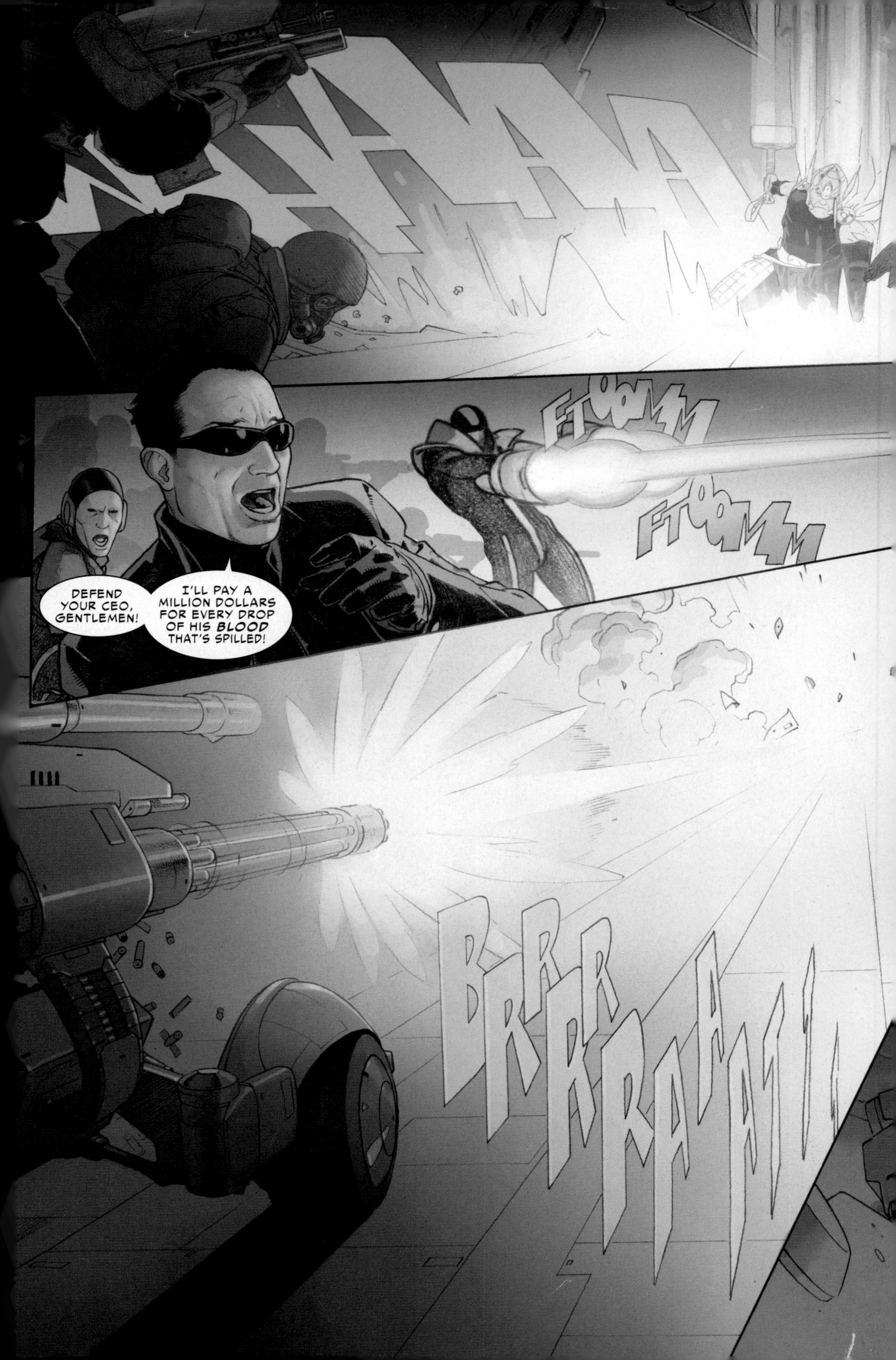
FTOOMM
FTOOMM
DEFEND YOUR CEO, GENTLEMEN!
I'LL PAY A MILLION DOLLARS FOR EVERY DROP OF HIS BLOOD THAT'S SPILLED!

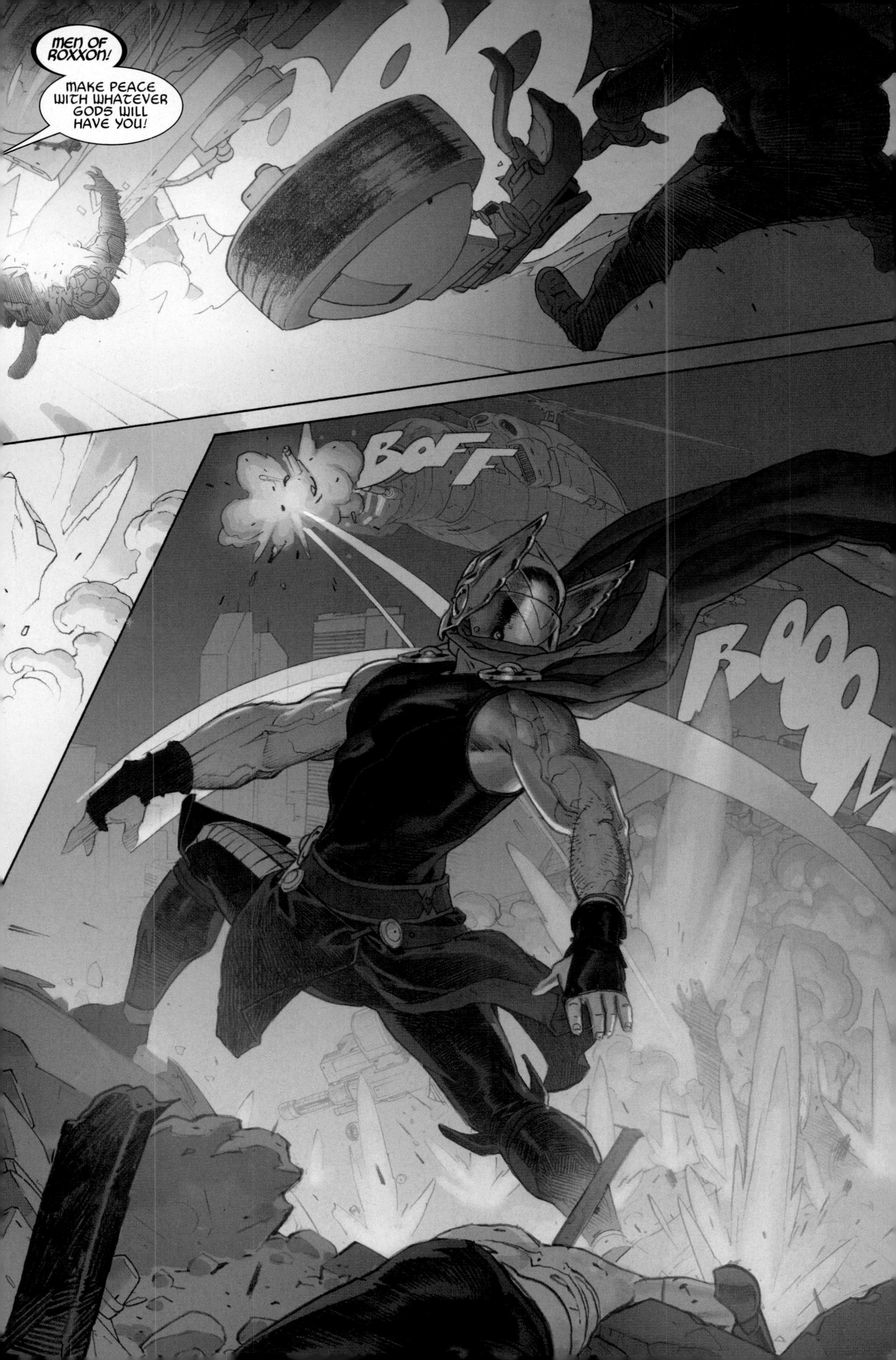
MEN OF ROXXON!
MAKE PEACE WITH WHATEVER GODS WILL HAVE YOU!
BOFF
BOOO

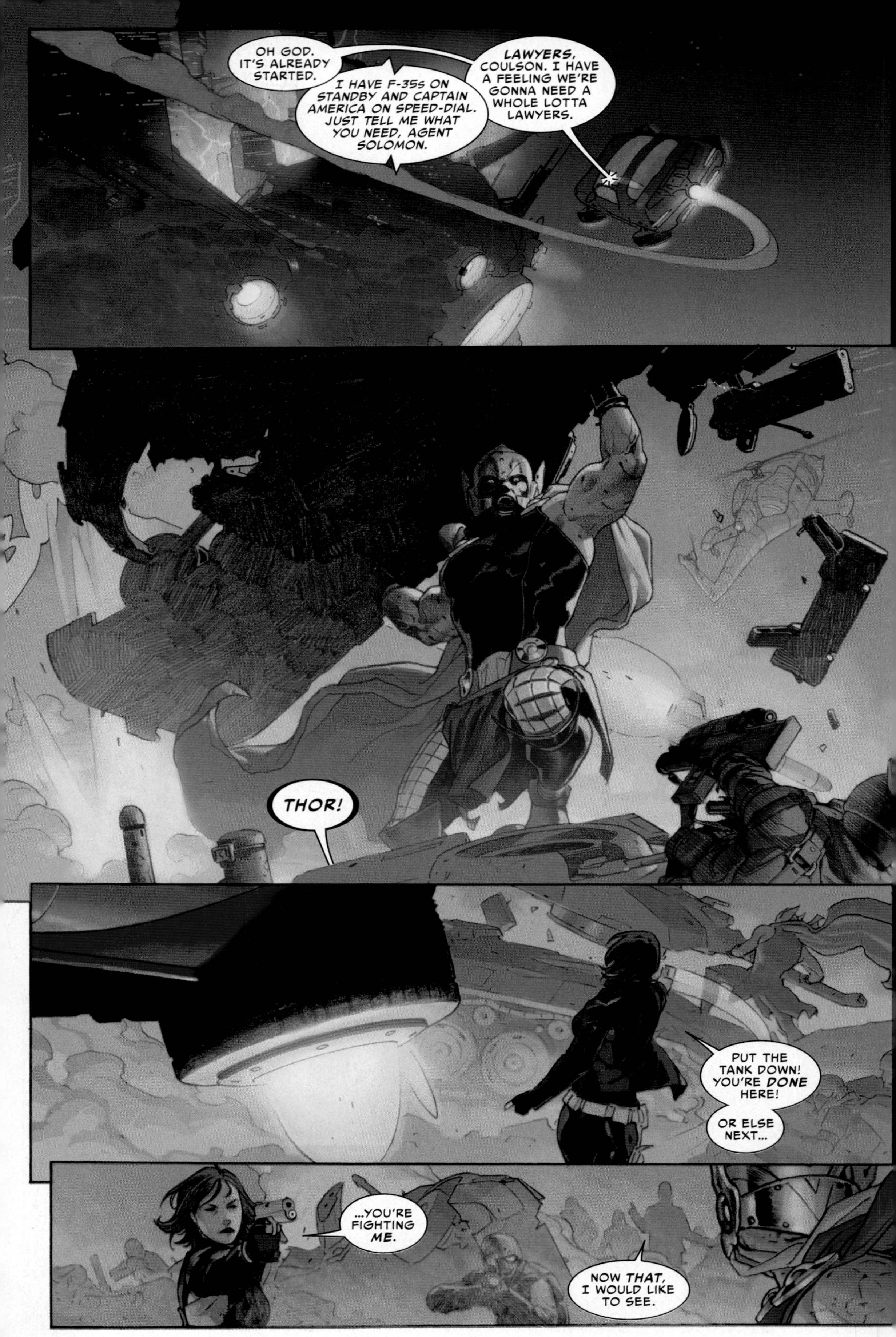
OH GOD. IT'S ALREADY STARTED.
I HAVE F-35s ON STANDBY AND CAPTAIN AMERICA ON SPEED-DIAL. JUST TELL ME WHAT YOU NEED, AGENT SOLOMON.
LAWYERS, COULSON. I HAVE A FEELING WE'RE GONNA NEED A WHOLE LOTTA LAWYERS.
THOR!
PUT THE TANK DOWN! YOU'RE DONE HERE!
OR ELSE NEXT...
...YOU'RE FIGHTING ME.
NOW THAT, I WOULD LIKE TO SEE.

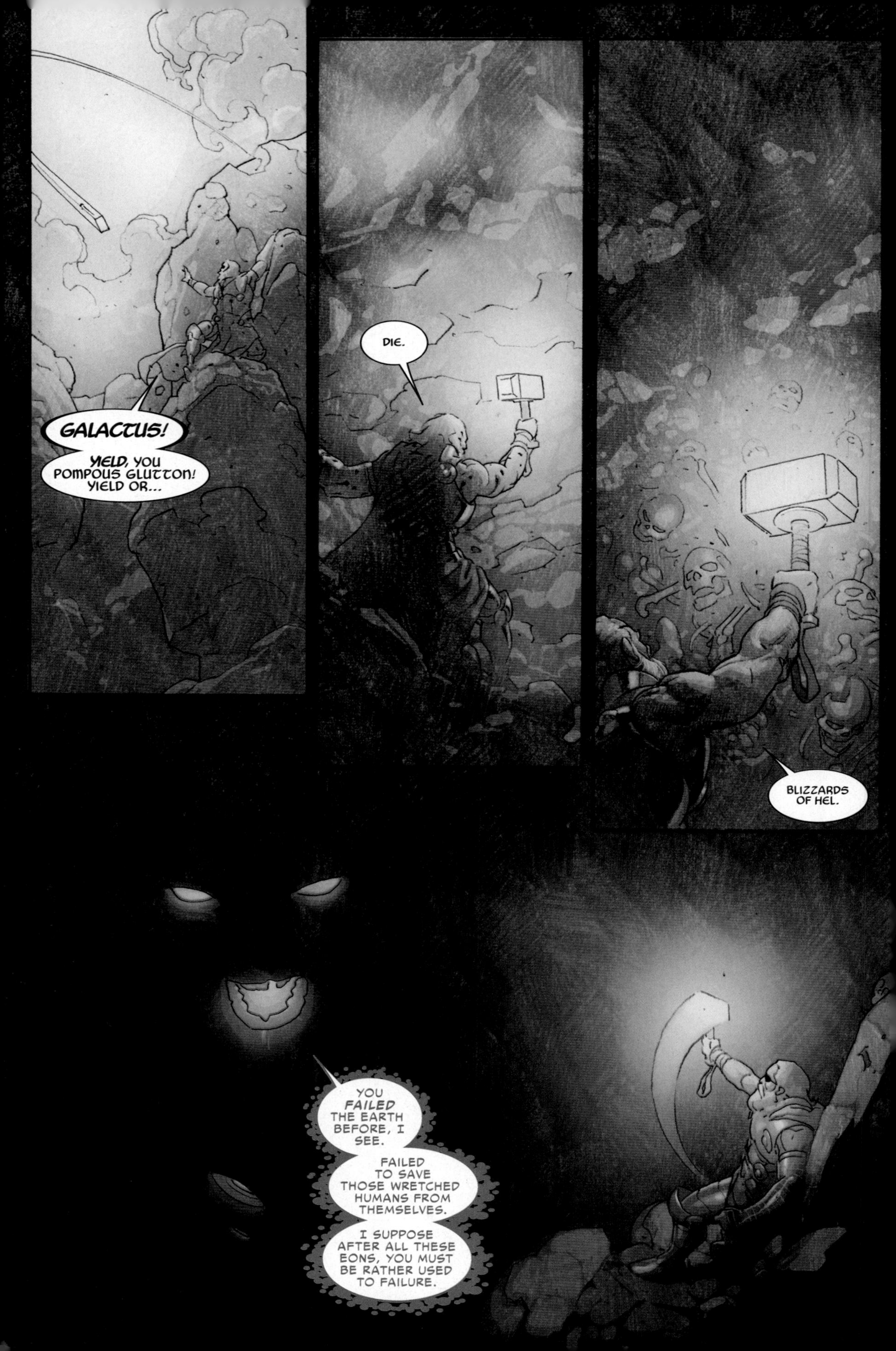
GALACTUS!
YIELD, YOU POMPOUS GLUTTON! YIELD OR...
DIE.
BLIZZARDS OF HEL.
YOU FAILED THE EARTH BEFORE, I SEE.
FAILED TO SAVE THOSE WRETCHED HUMANS FROM THEMSELVES.
I SUPPOSE AFTER ALL THESE EONS, YOU MUST BE RATHER USED TO FAILURE.

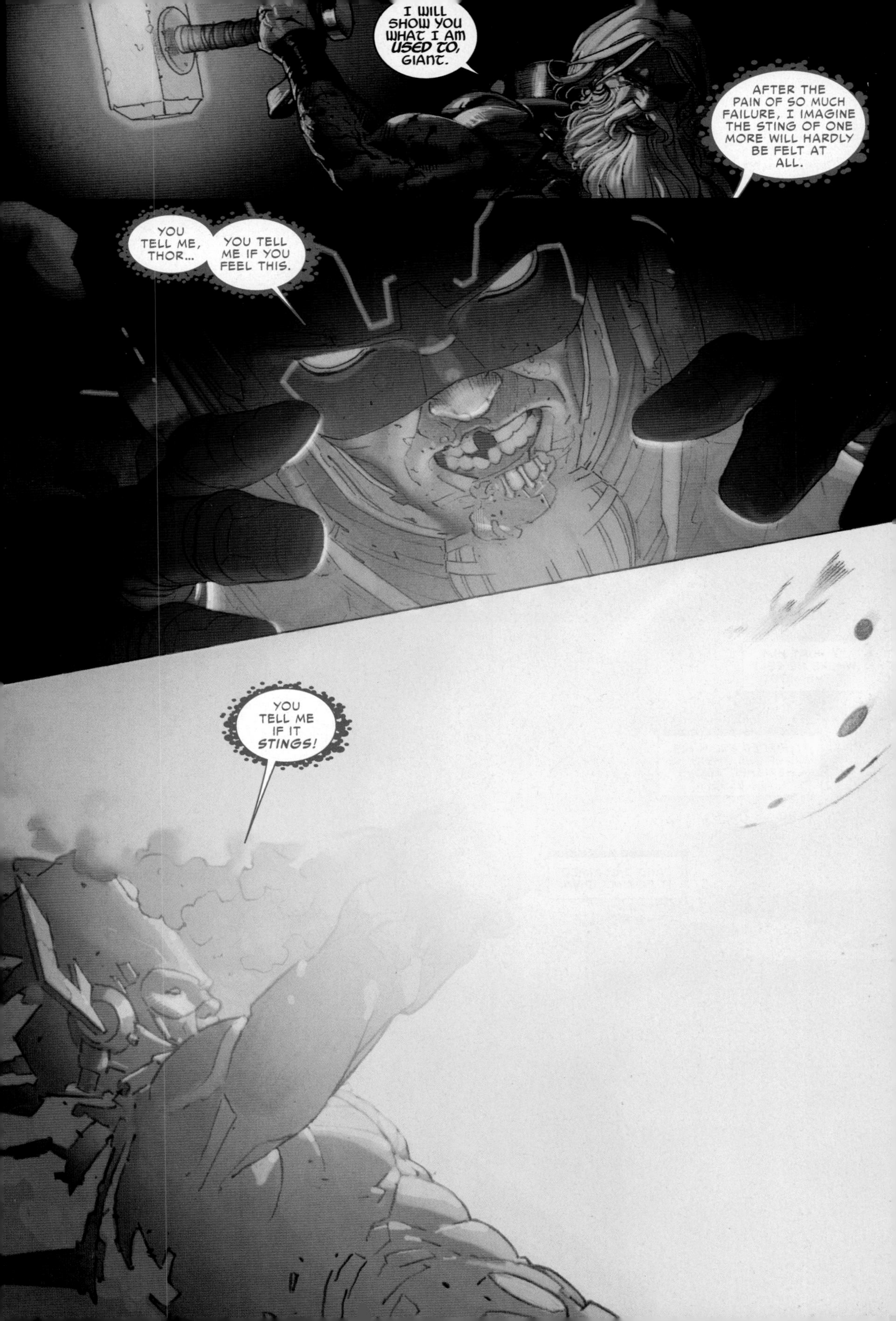
I WILL SHOW YOU WHAT I AM *USED TO,* GIANT.
AFTER THE PAIN OF SO MUCH FAILURE, I IMAGINE THE STING OF ONE MORE WILL HARDLY BE FELT AT ALL.
YOU TELL ME, THOR...
YOU TELL ME IF YOU FEEL THIS.
YOU TELL ME IF IT *STINGS!*

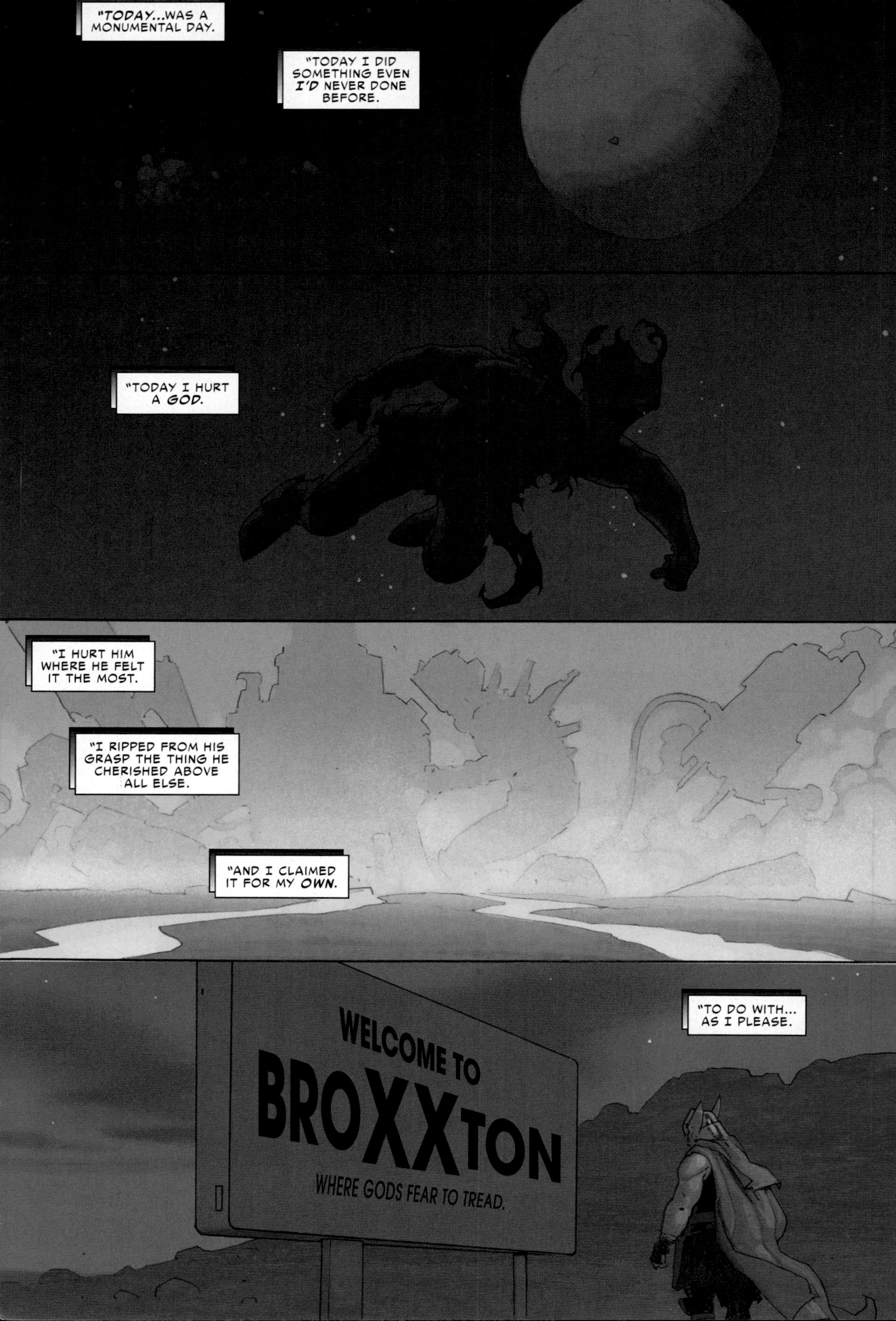
"*TODAY*...WAS A MONUMENTAL DAY.
"TODAY I DID SOMETHING EVEN *I'D* NEVER DONE BEFORE.
"TODAY I HURT A *GOD*.
"I HURT HIM WHERE HE FELT IT THE MOST.
"I RIPPED FROM HIS GRASP THE THING HE CHERISHED ABOVE ALL ELSE.
"AND I CLAIMED IT FOR MY *OWN*.
WELCOME TO
BROXXTON
WHERE GODS FEAR TO TREAD.
"TO DO WITH... AS I PLEASE.

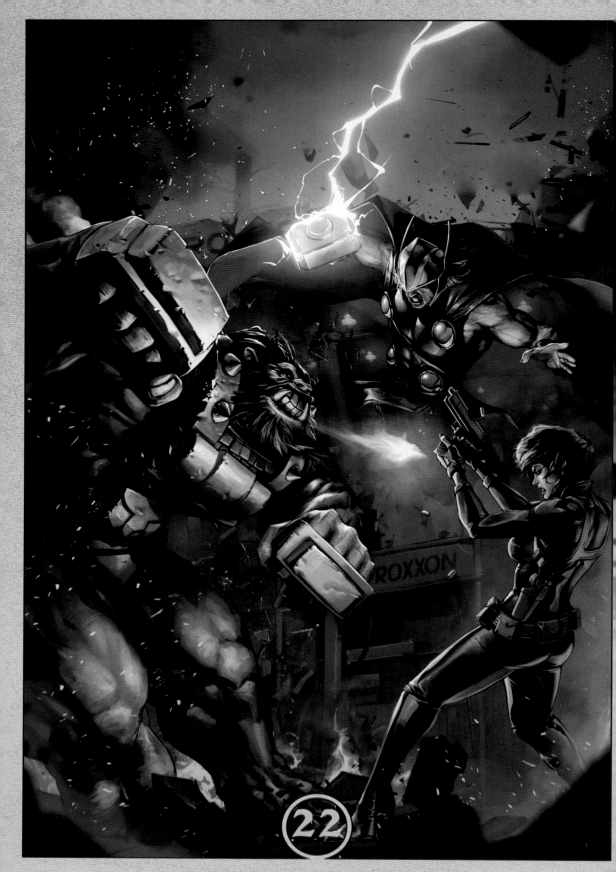

The Last Days of Midgard — Part 4:
For Thor So Loved the World

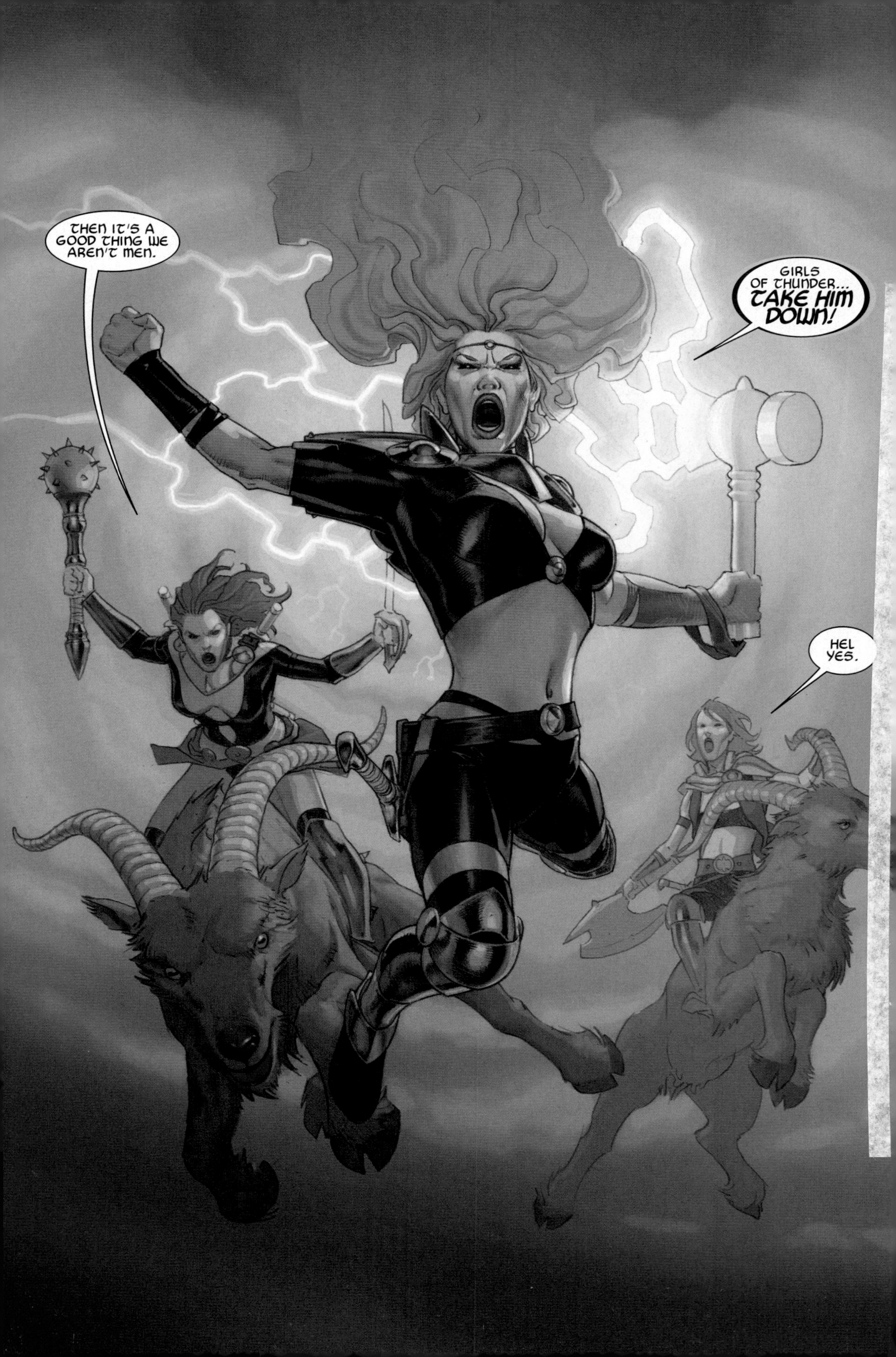
THEN IT'S A GOOD THING WE AREN'T MEN.
GIRLS OF THUNDER... TAKE HIM DOWN!
HEL YES.

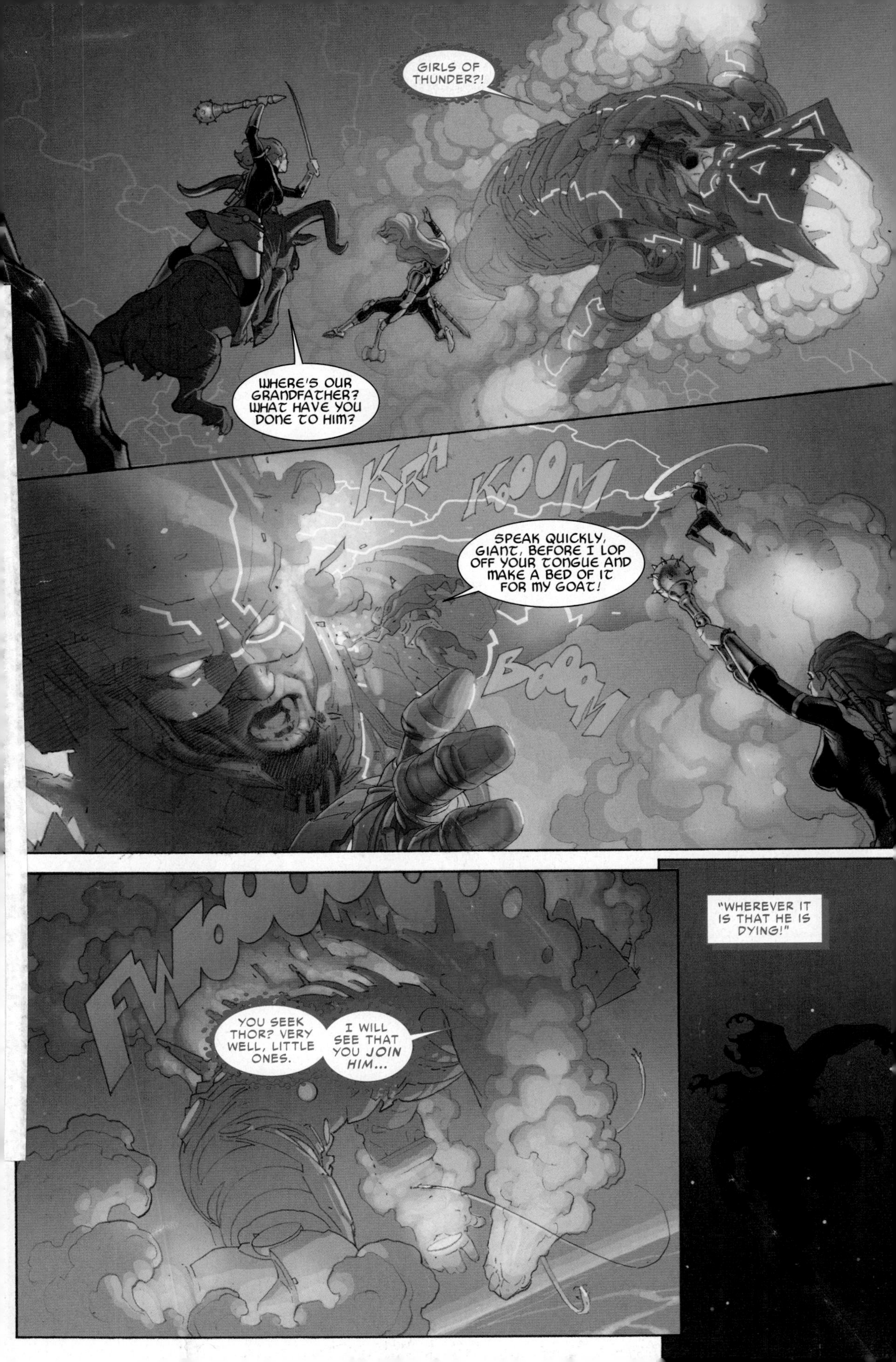
GIRLS OF THUNDER?!
WHERE'S OUR GRANDFATHER? WHAT HAVE YOU DONE TO HIM?
KRA
KOOOM
SPEAK QUICKLY, GIANT, BEFORE I LOP OFF YOUR TONGUE AND MAKE A BED OF IT FOR MY GOAT!
BOOOM
YOU SEEK THOR? VERY WELL, LITTLE ONES.
I WILL SEE THAT YOU JOIN HIM...
"WHEREVER IT IS THAT HE IS DYING!"

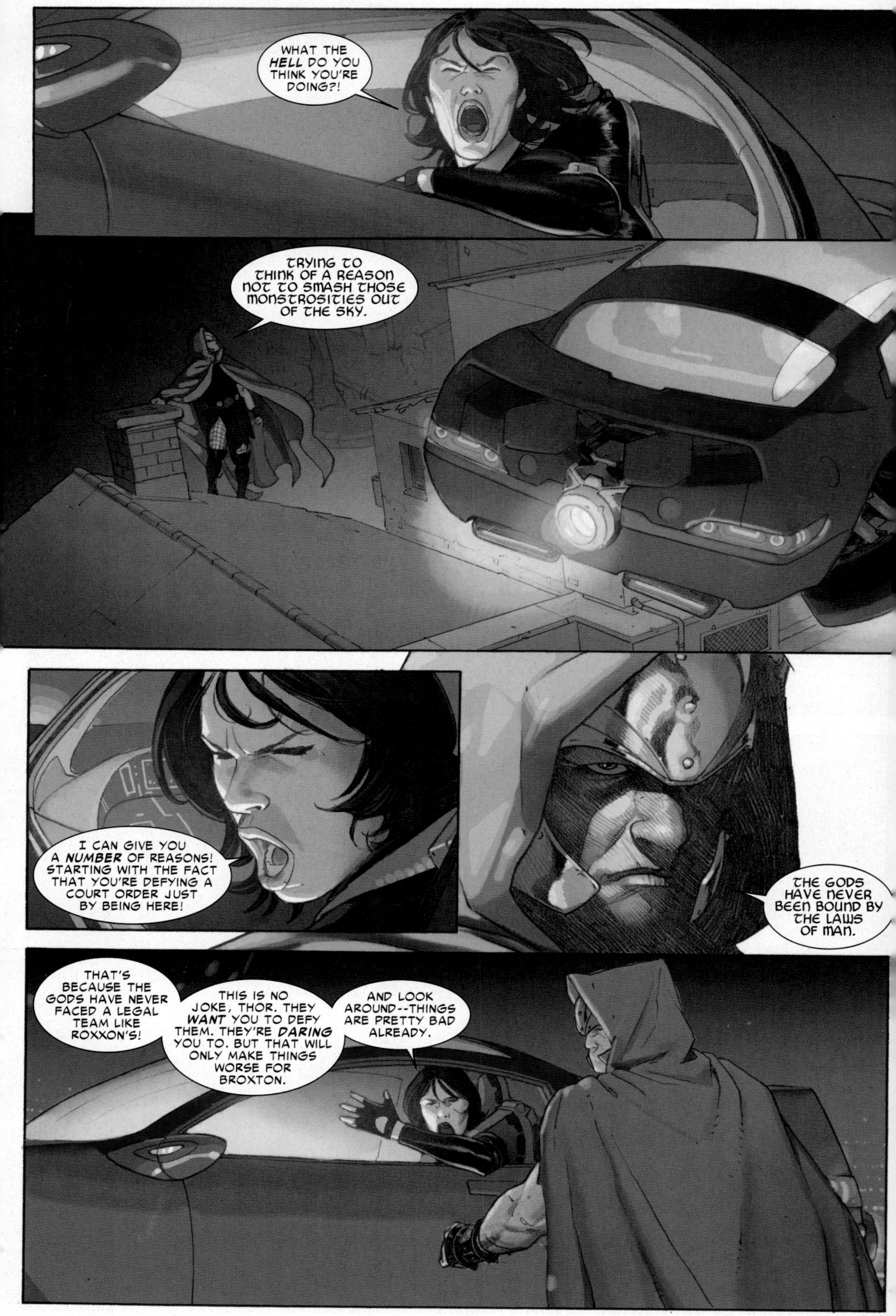
WHAT THE *HELL* DO YOU THINK YOU'RE DOING?!
TRYING TO THINK OF A REASON NOT TO SMASH THOSE MONSTROSITIES OUT OF THE SKY.
I CAN GIVE YOU A *NUMBER* OF REASONS! STARTING WITH THE FACT THAT YOU'RE DEFYING A COURT ORDER JUST BY BEING HERE!
THE GODS HAVE NEVER BEEN BOUND BY THE LAWS OF MAN.
THAT'S BECAUSE THE GODS HAVE NEVER FACED A LEGAL TEAM LIKE ROXXON'S!
THIS IS NO JOKE, THOR. THEY *WANT* YOU TO DEFY THEM. THEY'RE *DARING* YOU TO. BUT THAT WILL ONLY MAKE THINGS WORSE FOR BROXTON.
AND LOOK AROUND--THINGS ARE PRETTY BAD ALREADY.

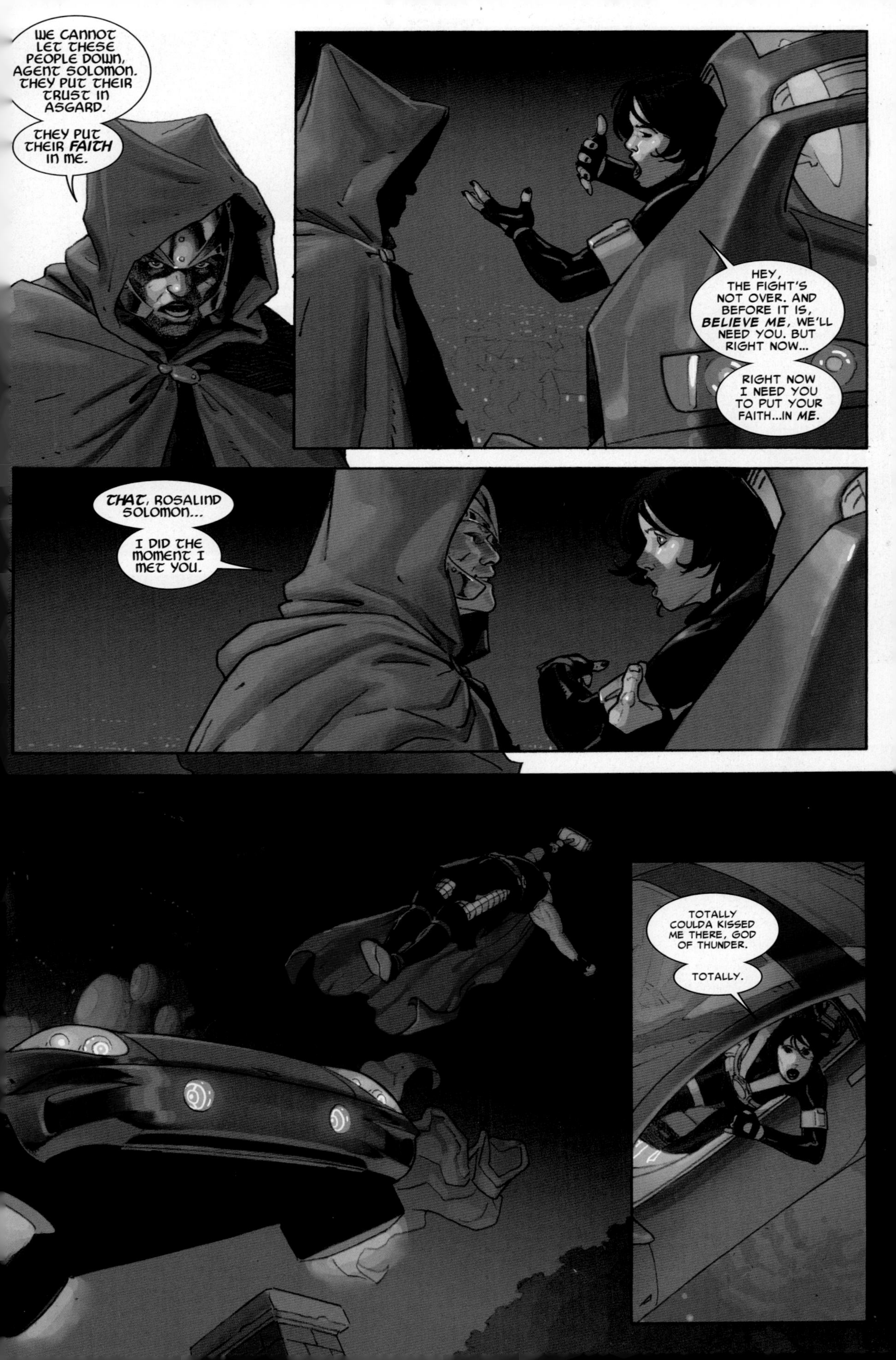

WE CANNOT LET THESE PEOPLE DOWN, AGENT SOLOMON. THEY PUT THEIR TRUST IN ASGARD.
THEY PUT THEIR **FAITH** IN ME.
HEY, THE FIGHT'S NOT OVER. AND BEFORE IT IS, **BELIEVE ME**, WE'LL NEED YOU. BUT RIGHT NOW...
RIGHT NOW I NEED YOU TO PUT YOUR FAITH...IN **ME**.
THAT, ROSALIND SOLOMON...
I DID THE MOMENT I MET YOU.
TOTALLY COULDA KISSED ME THERE, GOD OF THUNDER.
TOTALLY.

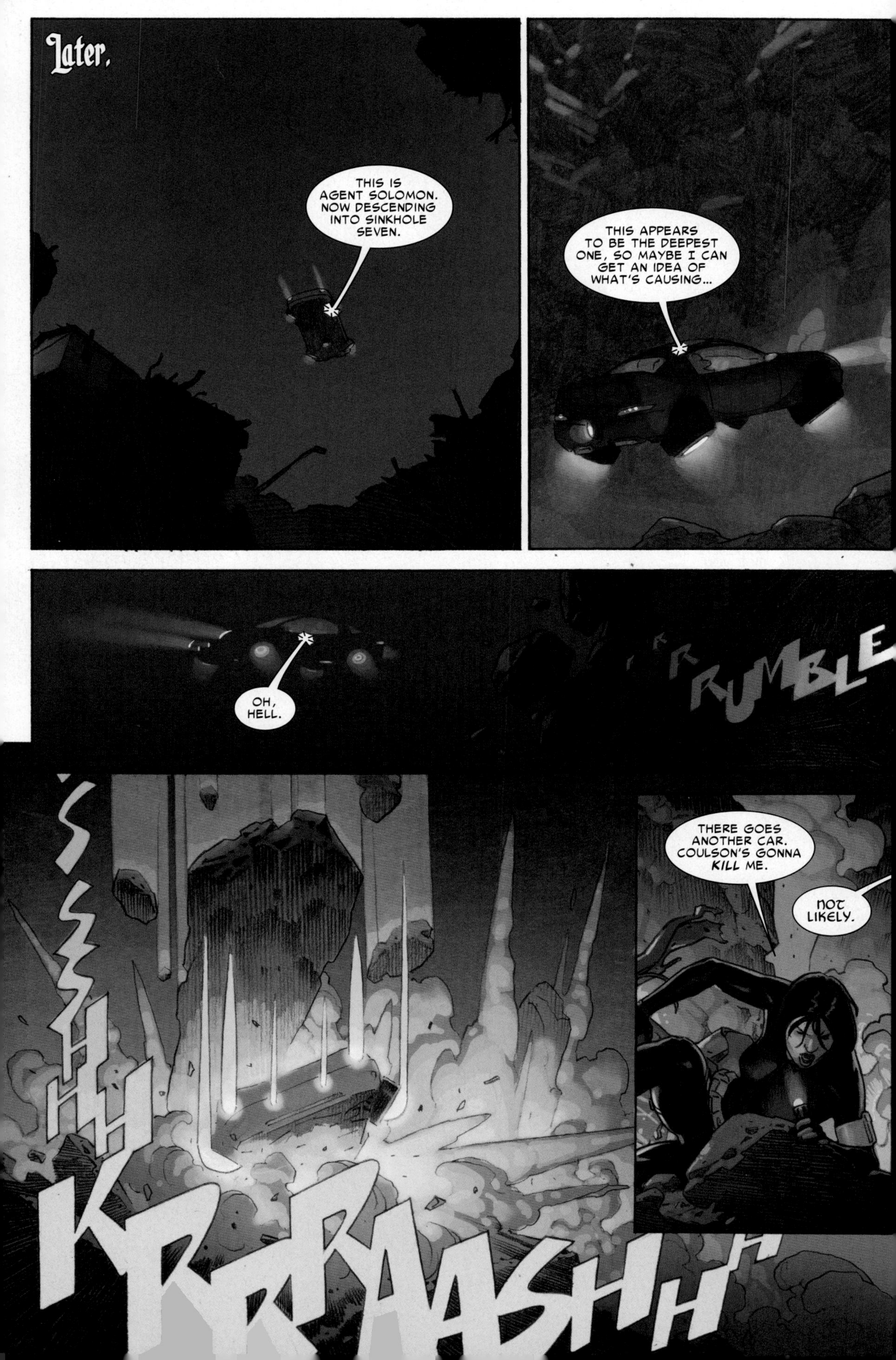
Later,
THIS IS AGENT SOLOMON. NOW DESCENDING INTO SINKHOLE SEVEN.
THIS APPEARS TO BE THE DEEPEST ONE, SO MAYBE I CAN GET AN IDEA OF WHAT'S CAUSING...
OH, HELL.
RUMBLE
KRRAASHH
THERE GOES ANOTHER CAR. COULSON'S GONNA KILL ME.
NOT LIKELY.

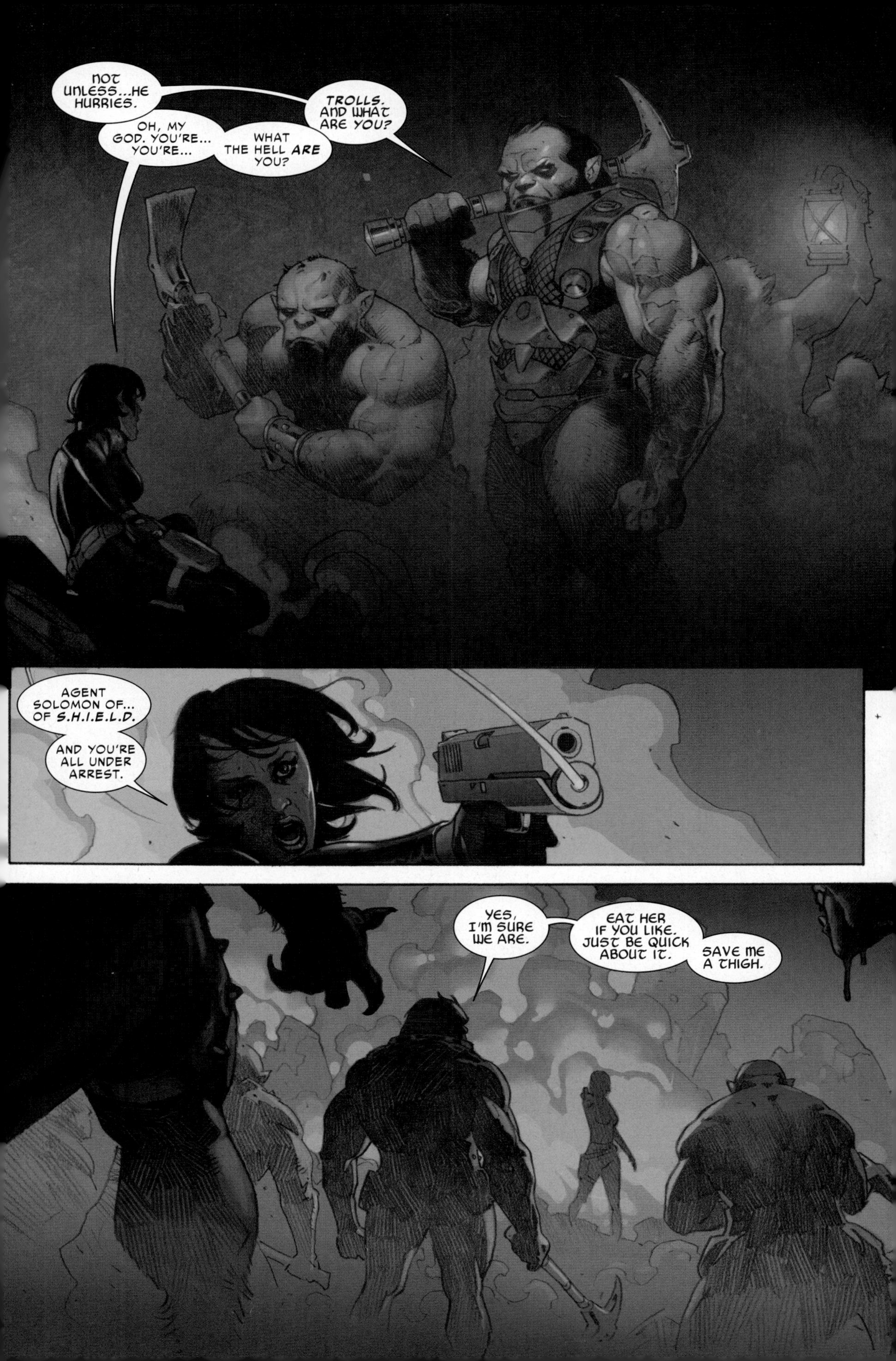
NOT UNLESS...HE HURRIES.
OH, MY GOD. YOU'RE... YOU'RE...
WHAT THE HELL *ARE* YOU?
TROLLS. AND WHAT ARE *YOU?*
AGENT SOLOMON OF... OF *S.H.I.E.L.D.*
AND YOU'RE ALL UNDER ARREST.
YES, I'M SURE WE ARE.
EAT HER IF YOU LIKE. JUST BE QUICK ABOUT IT.
SAVE ME A THIGH.

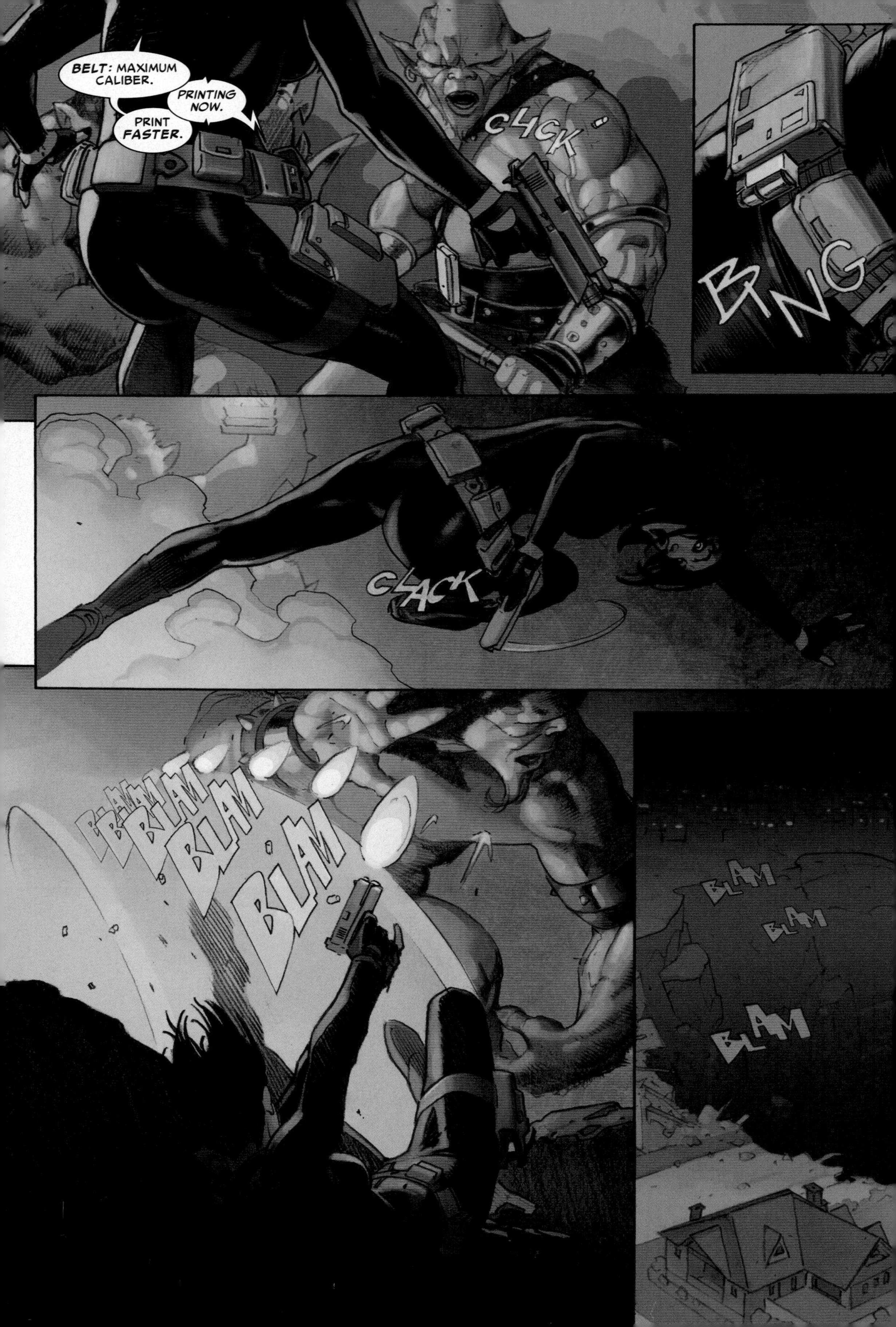

BELT: MAXIMUM CALIBER.
PRINTING NOW.
PRINT FASTER.
CLICK
BING
CLACK
BLAM
BLAM
BLAM
BLAM
BLAM
BLAM
BLAM

ZWOOOOOSSO

The Far Future.

ELLISIV WODENDOTTIR WIELDS THE WEAPONS OF HER GREAT UNCLES FANDRAL AND HOGUN LIKE A WARRIOR BORN.

KROOMM

FWA

BOOOM

BOOM

GRRRRGH!!!

FRIGG FEELS THE LIGHTNING COURSING THROUGH HER, AND WONDERS HOW SHE LIVED THIS LONG WITHOUT A HAMMER LIKE STORMBREAKER BY HER SIDE.

ATLI AND THE GREAT AXE JARNBJORN ARE A MATCH MADE IN VALHALLA. OR HEL.

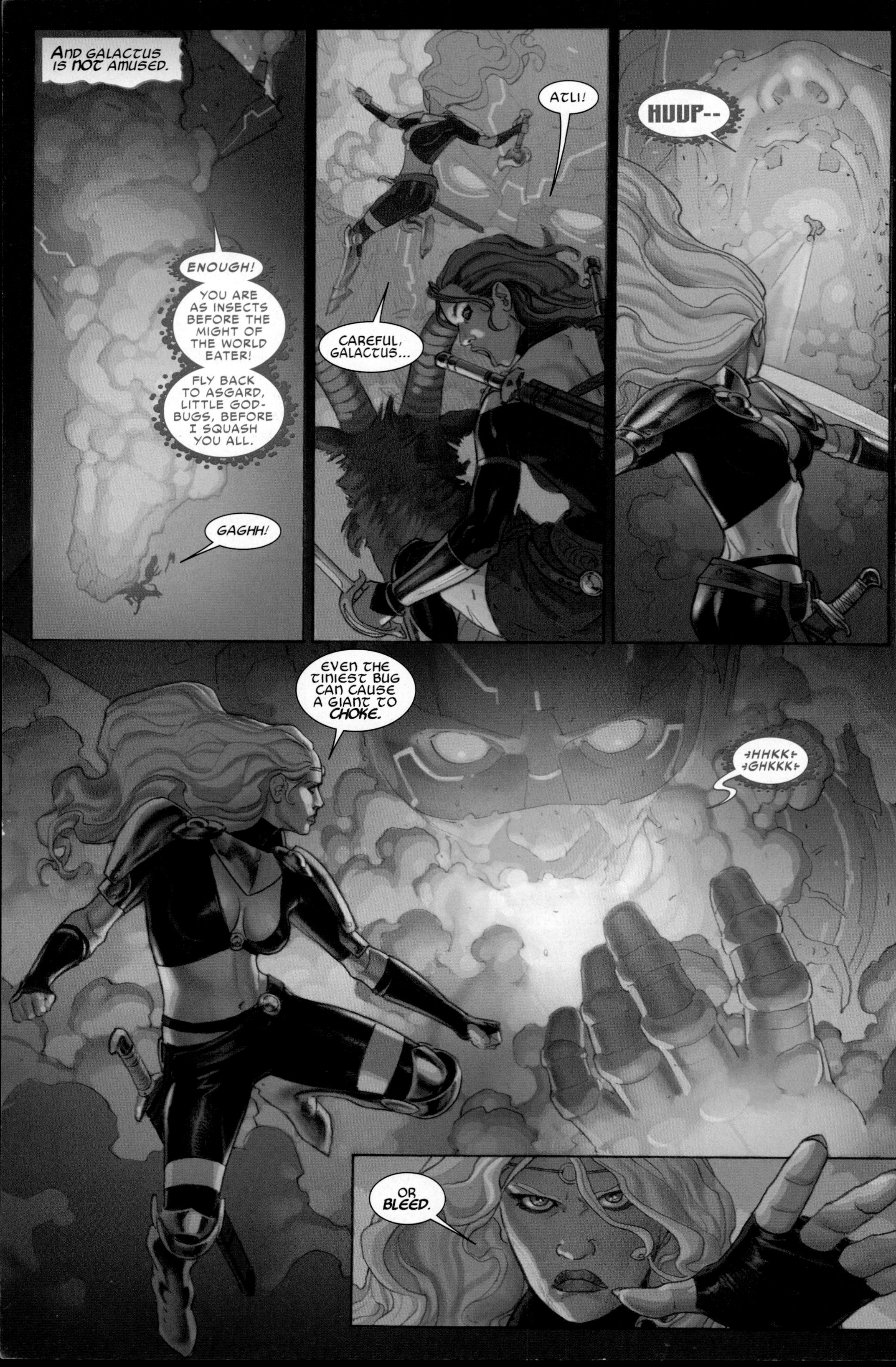
AND GALACTUS IS NOT AMUSED.
ENOUGH!
YOU ARE AS INSECTS BEFORE THE MIGHT OF THE WORLD EATER!
FLY BACK TO ASGARD, LITTLE GOD-BUGS, BEFORE I SQUASH YOU ALL.
GAGHH!
ATLI!
CAREFUL, GALACTUS...
HUUP--
EVEN THE TINIEST BUG CAN CAUSE A GIANT TO CHOKE.
HHKK
GHKKK
OR BLEED.

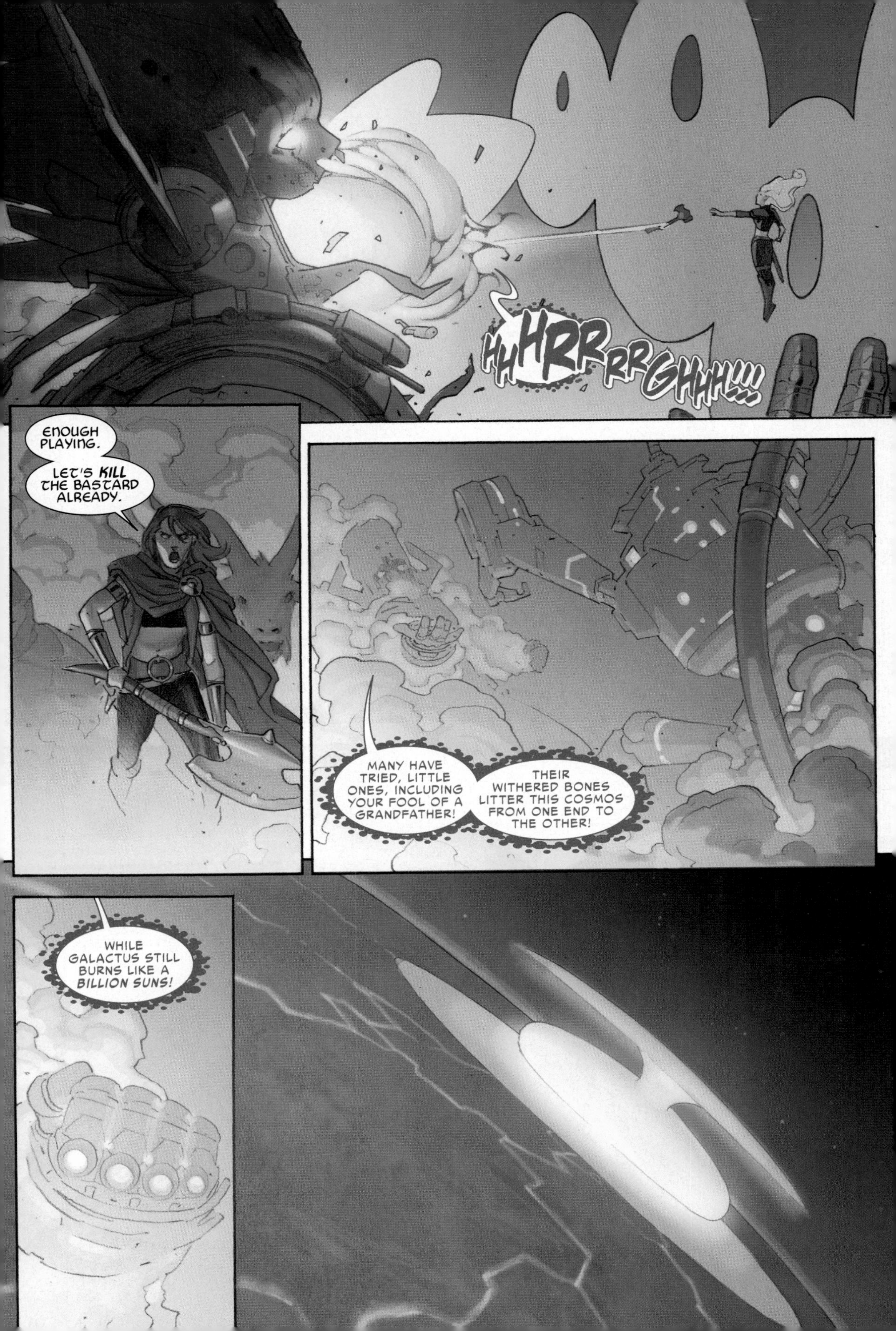

HHHRRRRRGHHH!!!
ENOUGH PLAYING.
LET'S KILL THE BASTARD ALREADY.
MANY HAVE TRIED, LITTLE ONES, INCLUDING YOUR FOOL OF A GRANDFATHER!
THEIR WITHERED BONES LITTER THIS COSMOS FROM ONE END TO THE OTHER!
WHILE GALACTUS STILL BURNS LIKE A BILLION SUNS!

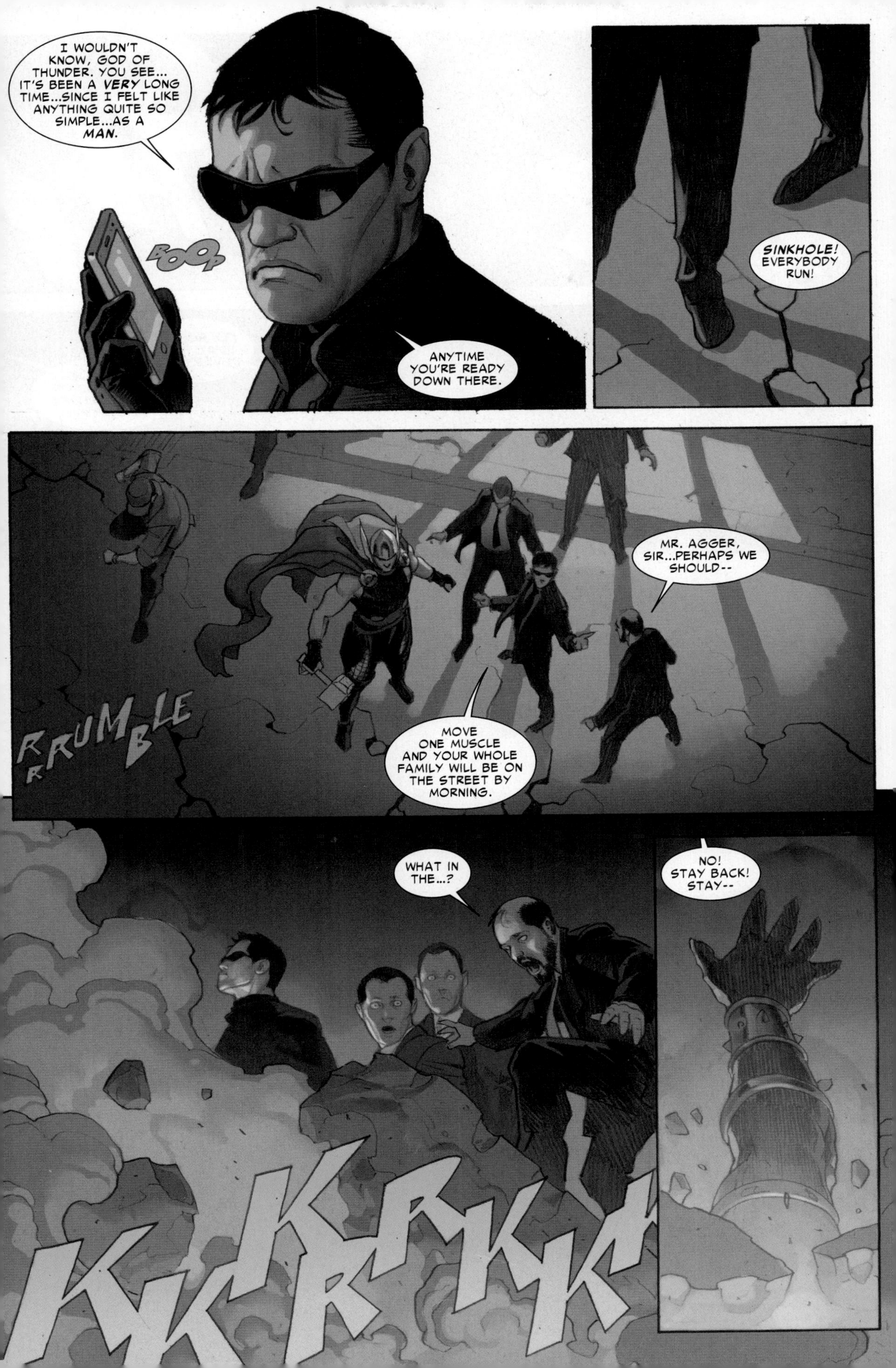
I WOULDN'T KNOW, GOD OF THUNDER. YOU SEE... IT'S BEEN A VERY LONG TIME...SINCE I FELT LIKE ANYTHING QUITE SO SIMPLE...AS A MAN.
BOOP
ANYTIME YOU'RE READY DOWN THERE.
SINKHOLE! EVERYBODY RUN!
MR. AGGER, SIR...PERHAPS WE SHOULD--
RRRUMBLE
MOVE ONE MUSCLE AND YOUR WHOLE FAMILY WILL BE ON THE STREET BY MORNING.
WHAT IN THE...?
NO! STAY BACK! STAY--
KKRKRKK

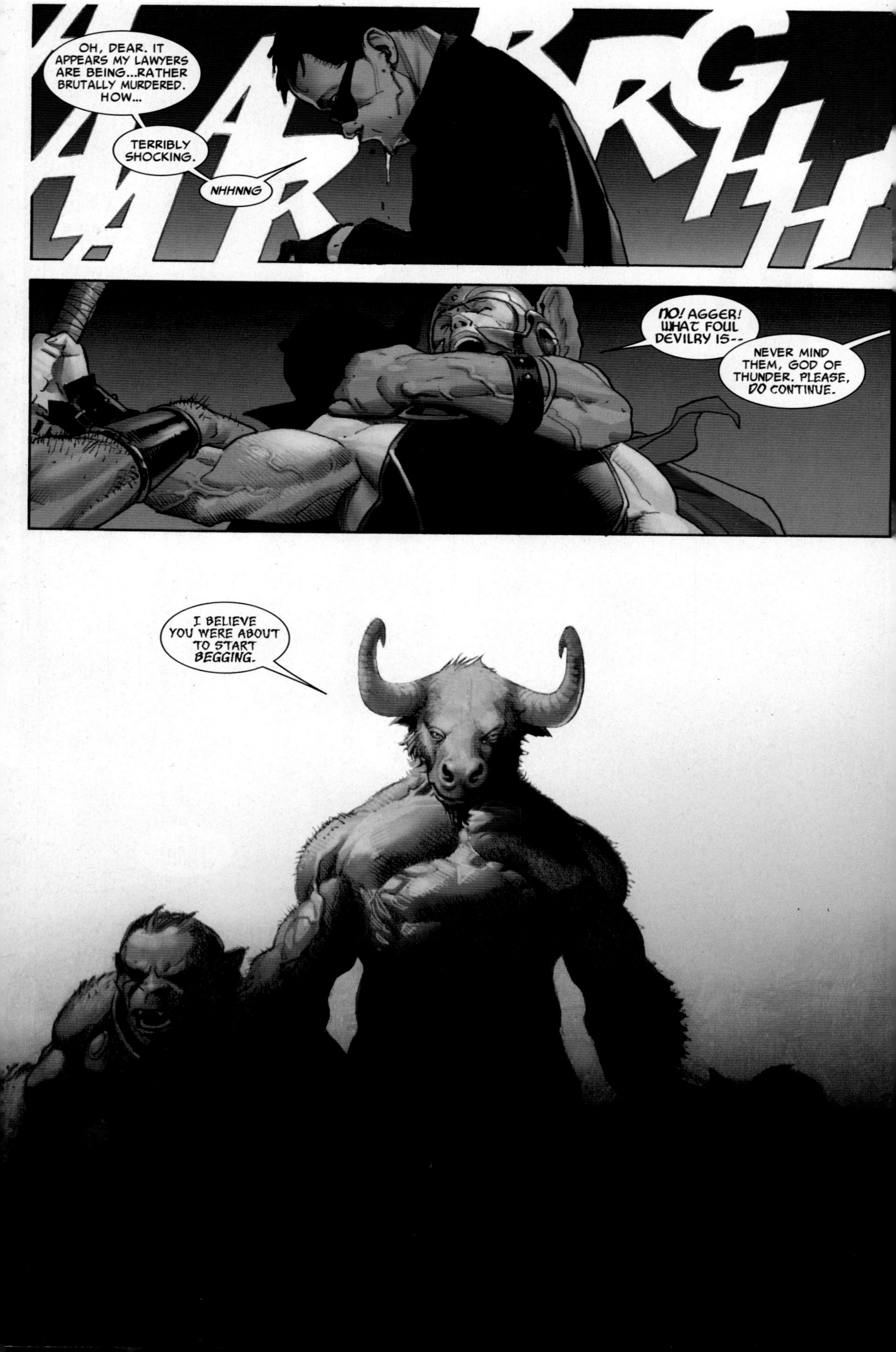

OH, DEAR. IT APPEARS MY LAWYERS ARE BEING...RATHER BRUTALLY MURDERED. HOW...
TERRIBLY SHOCKING.
NHHNNG
NO! AGGER! WHAT FOUL DEVILRY IS--
NEVER MIND THEM, GOD OF THUNDER. PLEASE, DO CONTINUE.
I BELIEVE YOU WERE ABOUT TO START BEGGING.

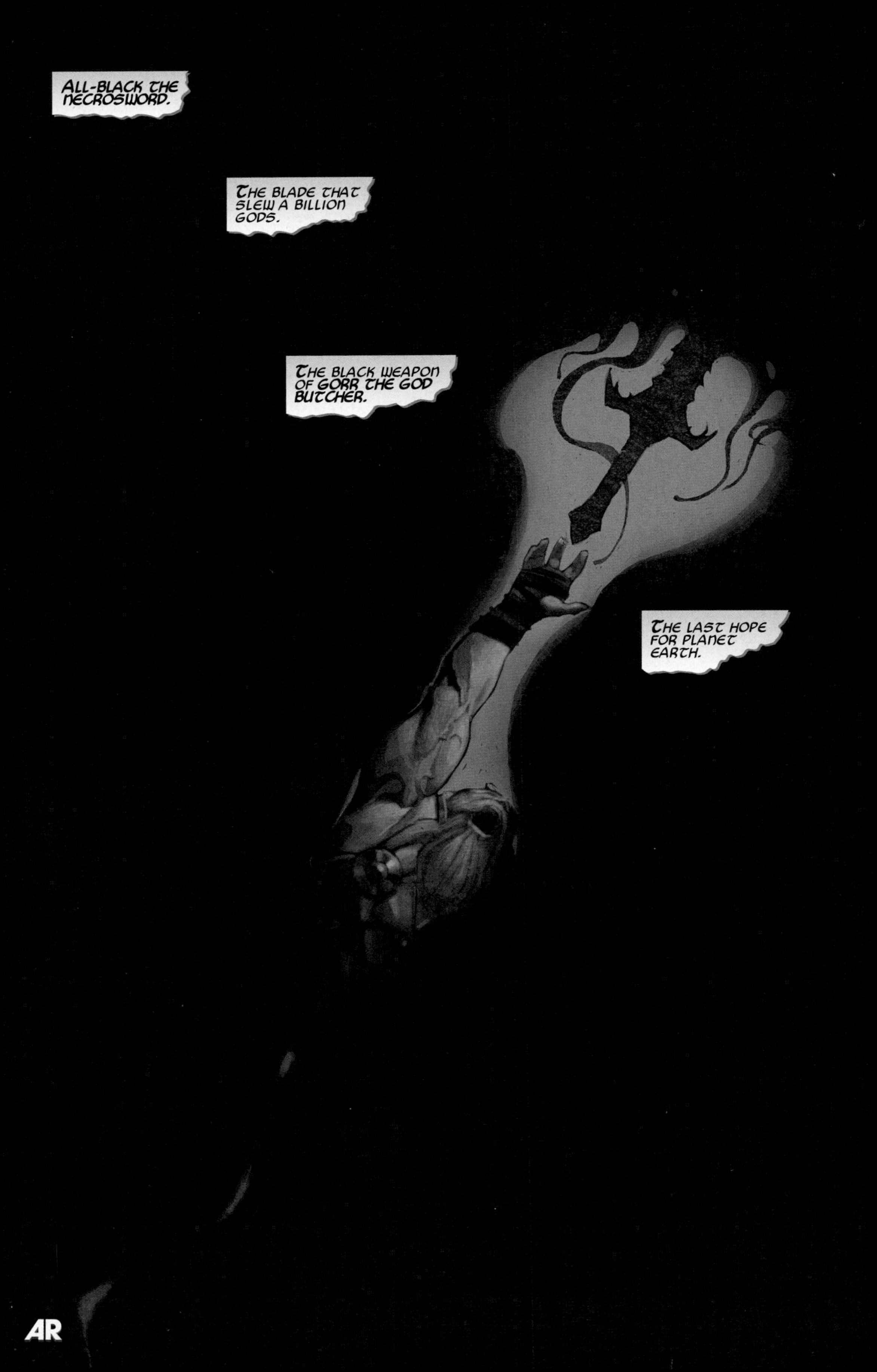
ALL-BLACK THE NECROSWORD.
THE BLADE THAT SLEW A BILLION GODS.
THE BLACK WEAPON OF GORR THE GOD BUTCHER.
THE LAST HOPE FOR PLANET EARTH.
AR

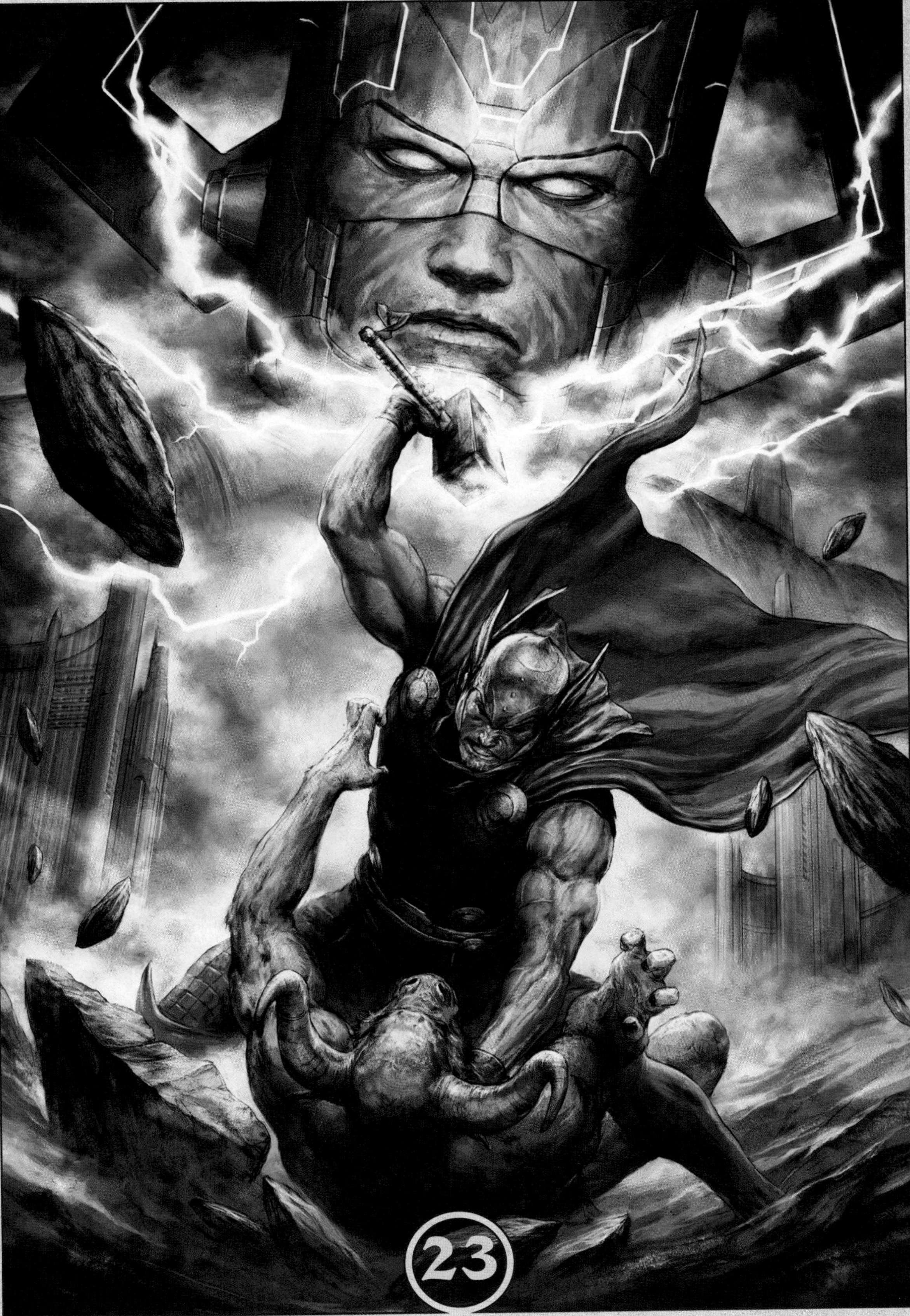
23

The Last Days of Midgard — Part 5:
Blood of the Earth

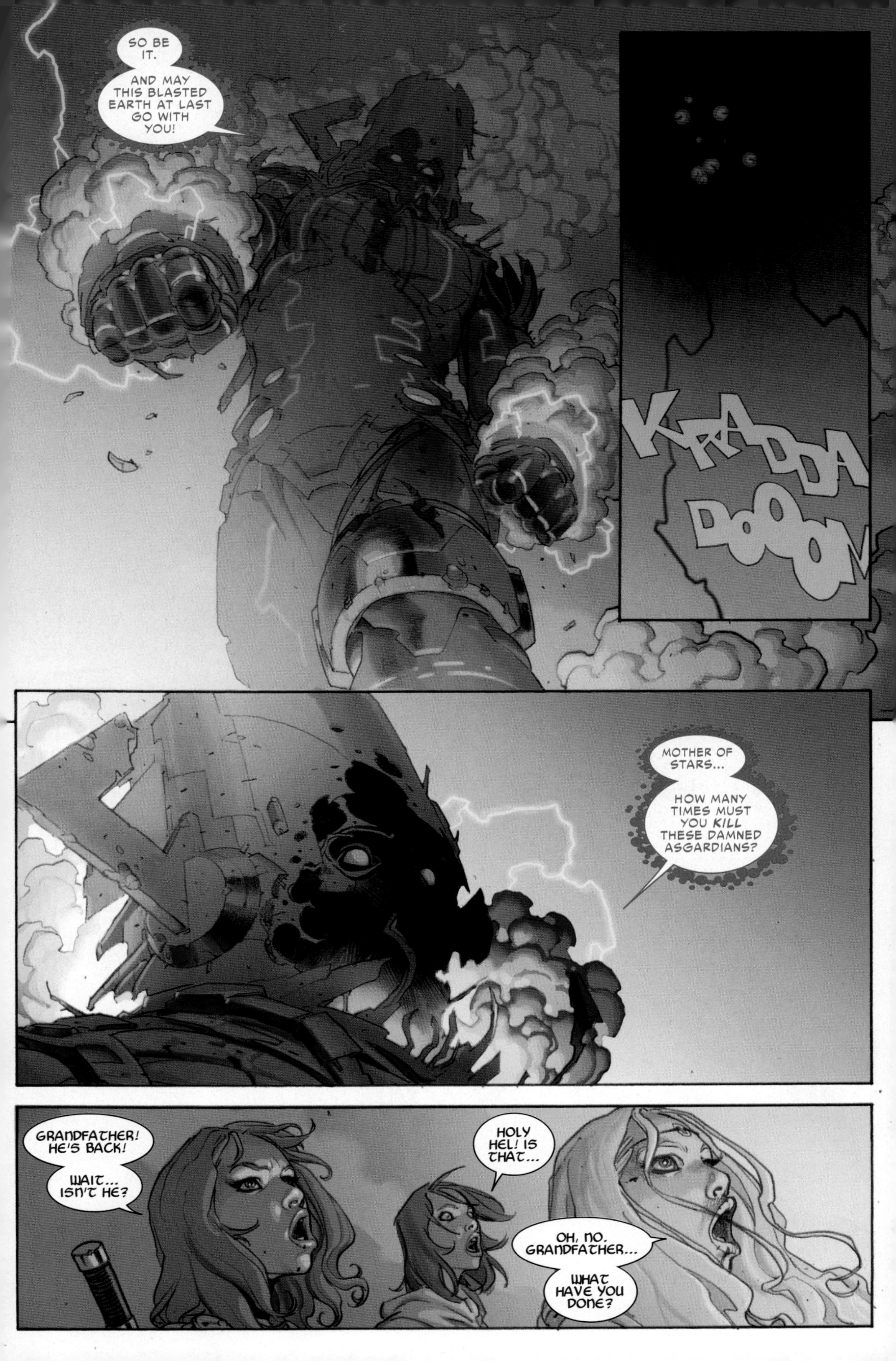
SO BE IT.
AND MAY THIS BLASTED EARTH AT LAST GO WITH YOU!
KRADDA DOOOOM
MOTHER OF STARS...
HOW MANY TIMES MUST YOU *KILL* THESE DAMNED ASGARDIANS?
GRANDFATHER! HE'S BACK!
WAIT... ISN'T HE?
HOLY HEL! IS THAT...
OH, NO. GRANDFATHER...
WHAT HAVE YOU DONE?

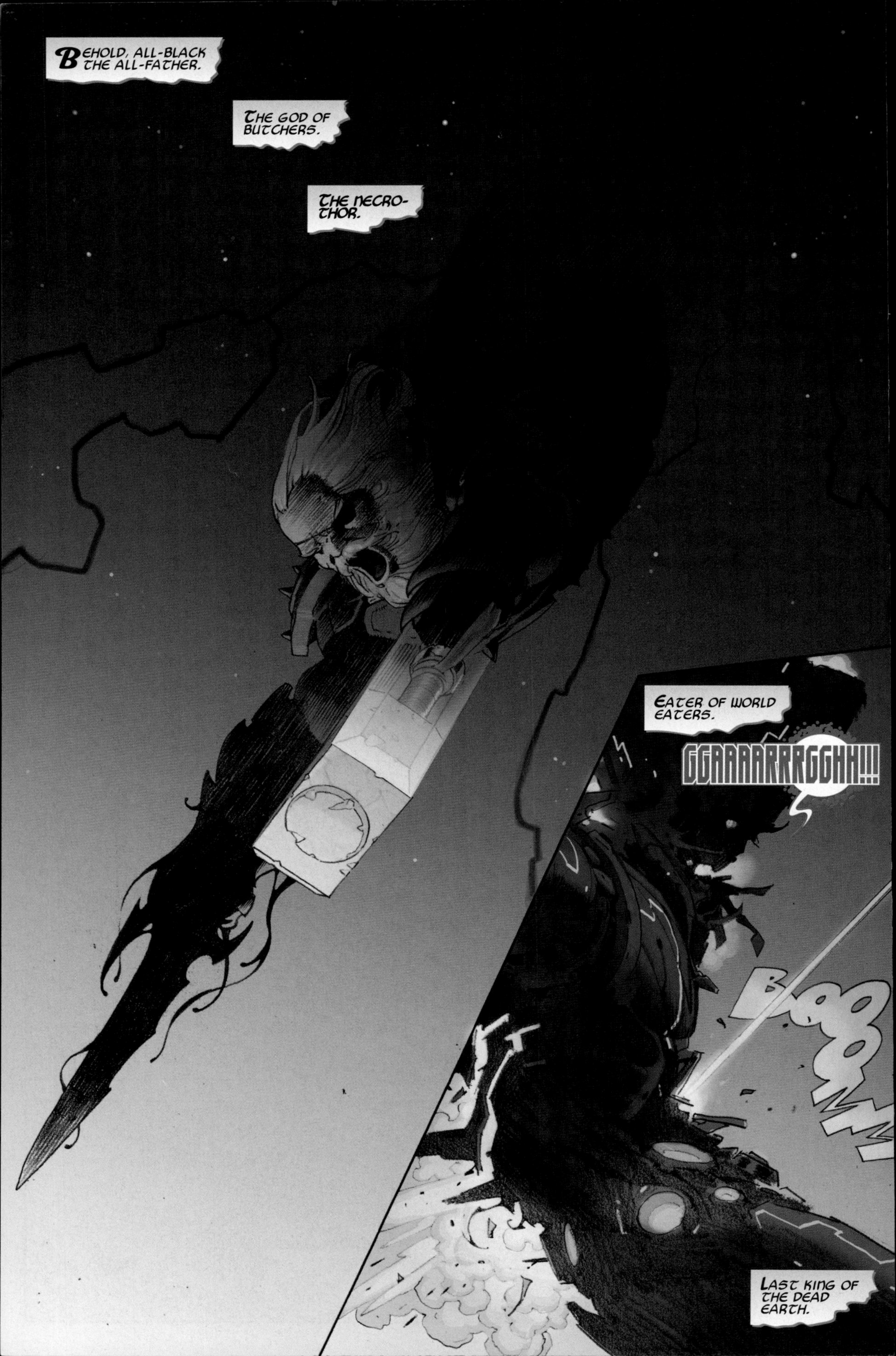
BEHOLD, ALL-BLACK THE ALL-FATHER.
THE GOD OF BUTCHERS.
THE NECRO-THOR.
EATER OF WORLD EATERS.
GGAAAARRRGGHH!!!
LAST KING OF THE DEAD EARTH.

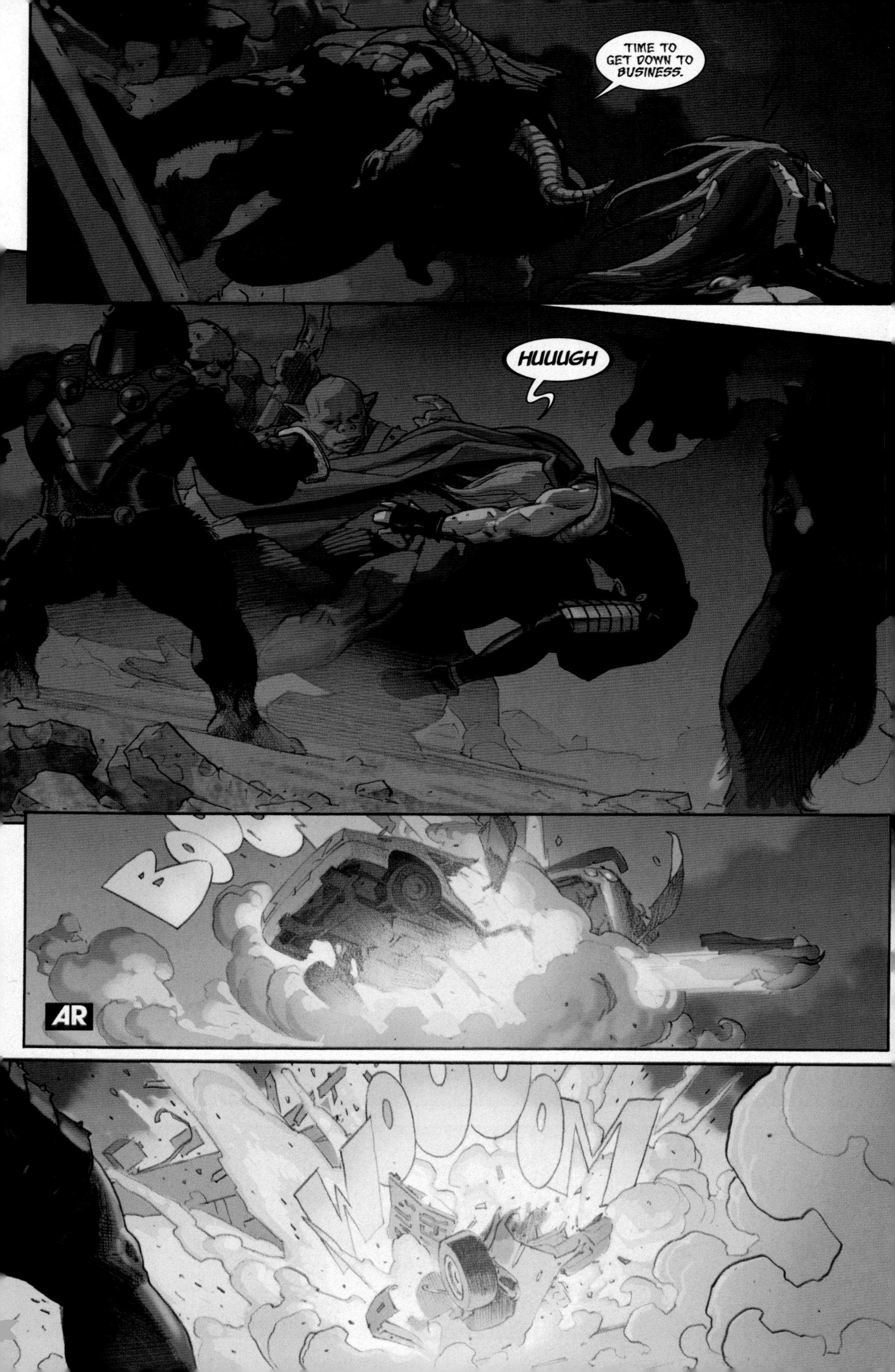
TIME TO GET DOWN TO BUSINESS.
HUUUGH
BOOO
WOOOOM

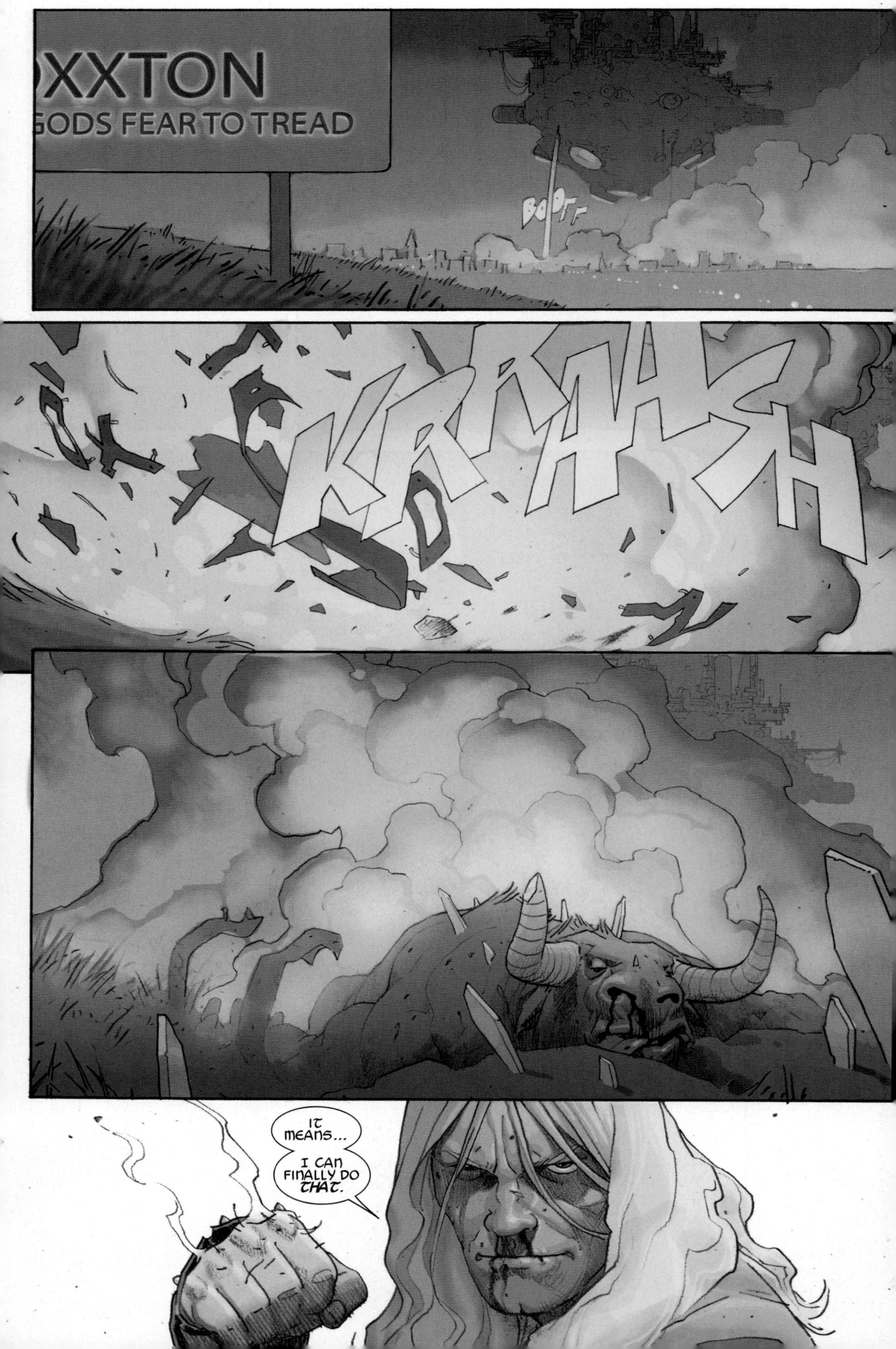

OXXTON
GODS FEAR TO TREAD
BOOFF
KRAAASH
IT MEANS...
I CAN FINALLY DO THAT.

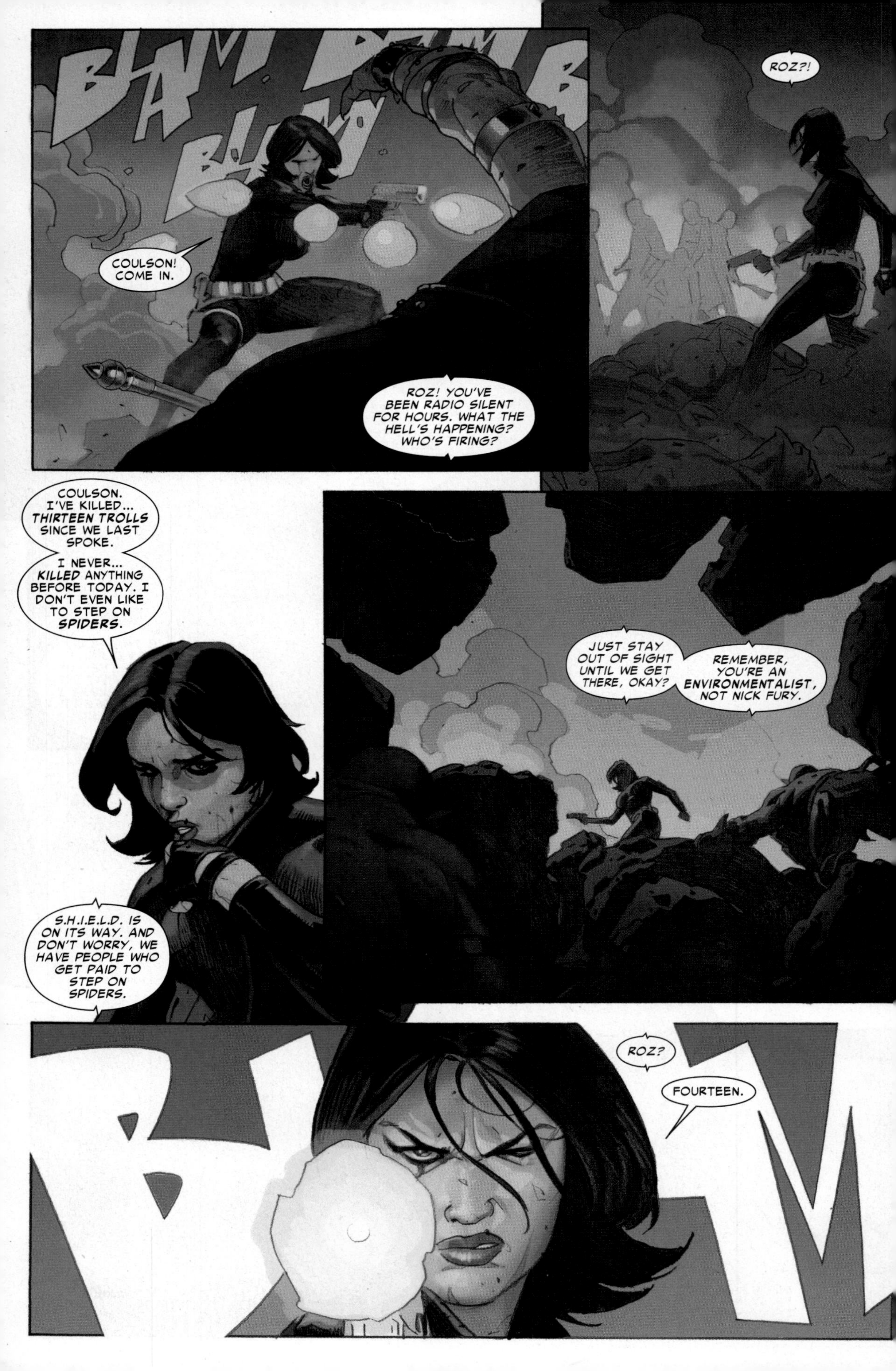
COULSON! COME IN.
ROZ! YOU'VE BEEN RADIO SILENT FOR HOURS. WHAT THE HELL'S HAPPENING? WHO'S FIRING?
ROZ?!
COULSON. I'VE KILLED... THIRTEEN TROLLS SINCE WE LAST SPOKE.
I NEVER... KILLED ANYTHING BEFORE TODAY. I DON'T EVEN LIKE TO STEP ON SPIDERS.
S.H.I.E.L.D. IS ON ITS WAY. AND DON'T WORRY, WE HAVE PEOPLE WHO GET PAID TO STEP ON SPIDERS.
JUST STAY OUT OF SIGHT UNTIL WE GET THERE, OKAY?
REMEMBER, YOU'RE AN ENVIRONMENTALIST, NOT NICK FURY.
ROZ?
FOURTEEN.

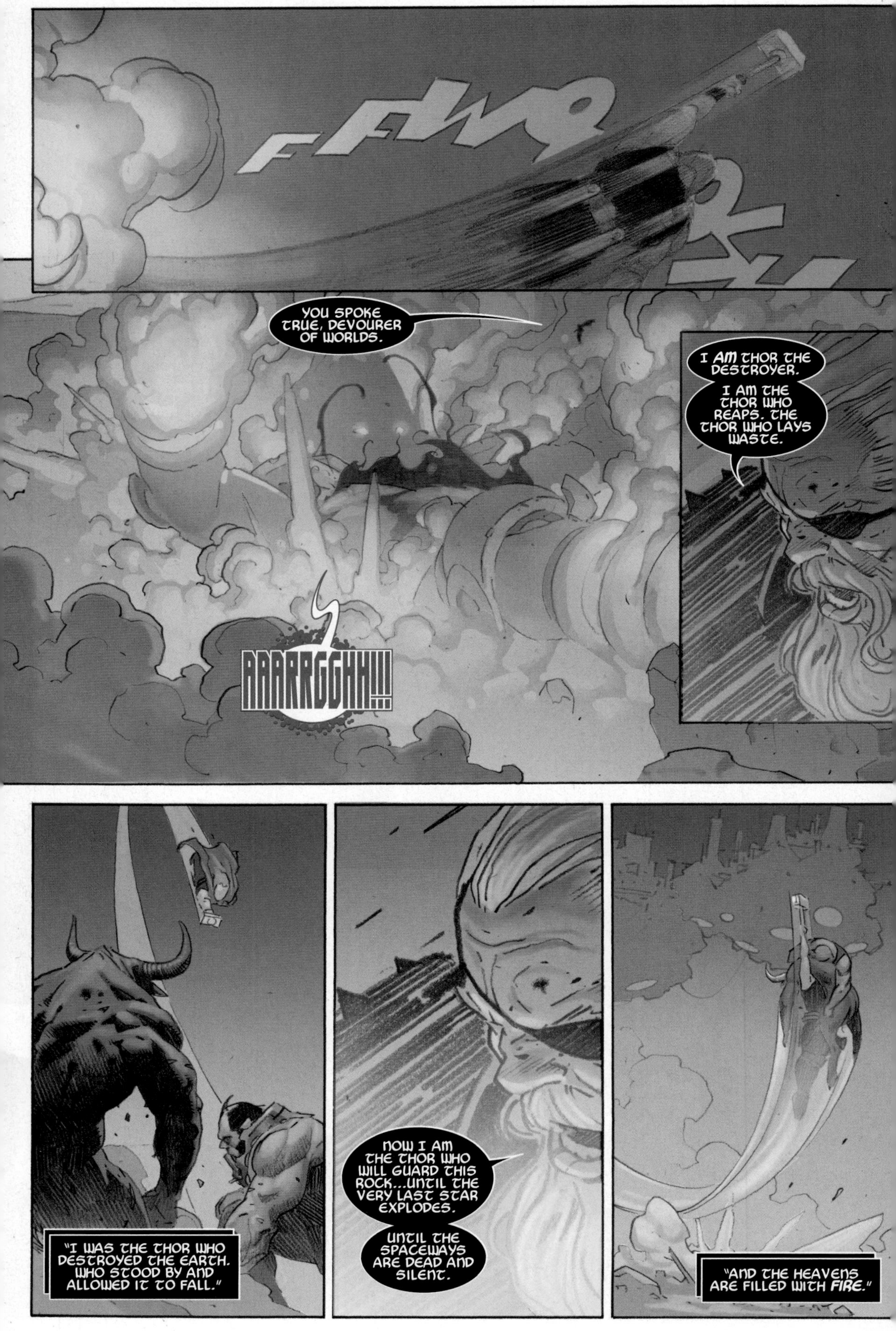
YOU SPOKE TRUE, DEVOURER OF WORLDS.
AAARRGGHH!!!
I *AM* THOR THE DESTROYER.
I AM THE THOR WHO REAPS. THE THOR WHO LAYS WASTE.
"I WAS THE THOR WHO DESTROYED THE EARTH. WHO STOOD BY AND ALLOWED IT TO FALL."
NOW I AM THE THOR WHO WILL GUARD THIS ROCK...UNTIL THE VERY LAST STAR EXPLODES.
UNTIL THE SPACEWAYS ARE DEAD AND SILENT.
"AND THE HEAVENS ARE FILLED WITH *FIRE*."

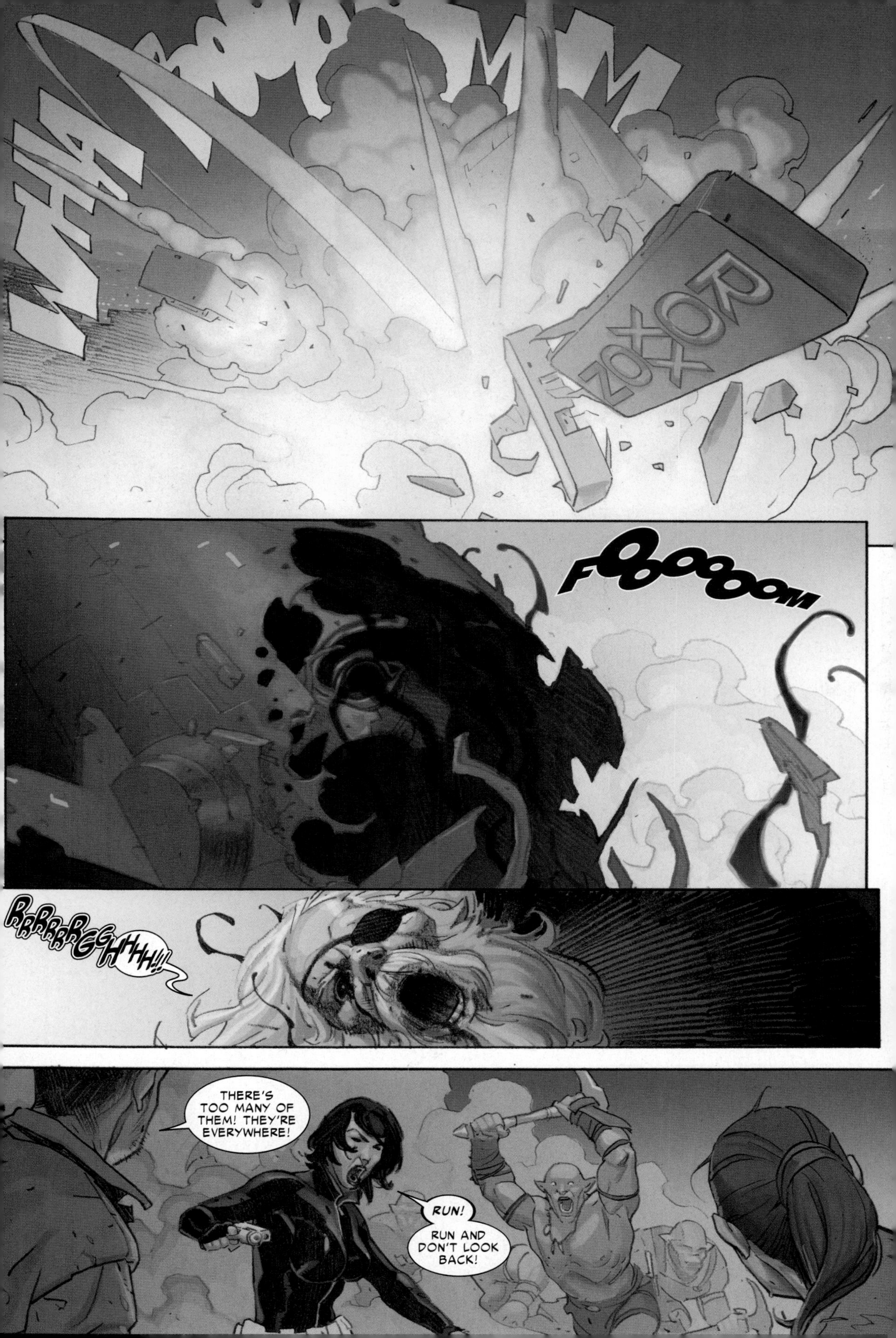
FOOOOOOM
RRRRRRGGHHHH!!
THERE'S TOO MANY OF THEM! THEY'RE EVERYWHERE!
RUN!
RUN AND DON'T LOOK BACK!

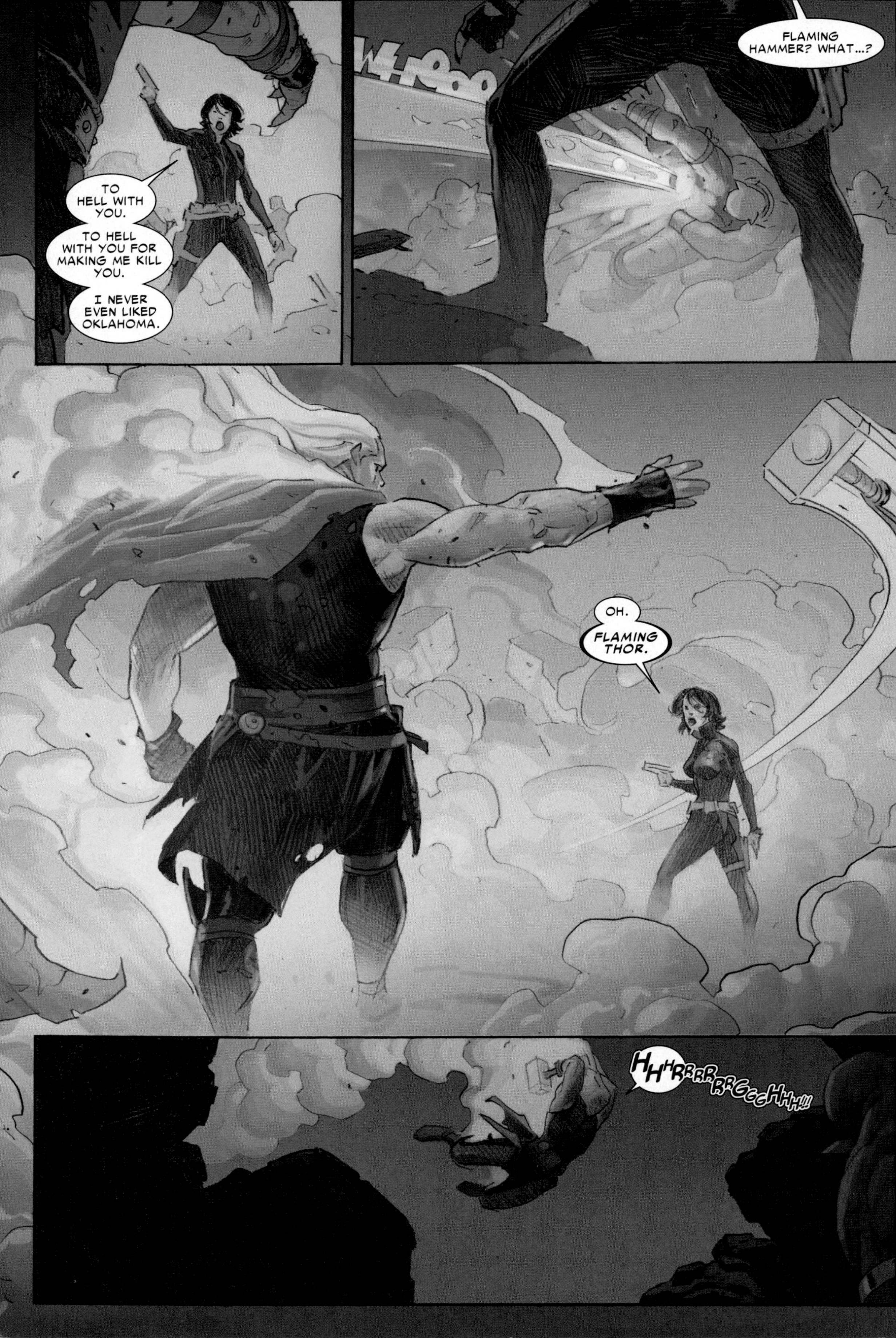

TO HELL WITH YOU.
TO HELL WITH YOU FOR MAKING ME KILL YOU.
I NEVER EVEN LIKED OKLAHOMA.
FLAMING HAMMER? WHAT...?
OH.
FLAMING THOR.
HHHRRRRRRRGGGHHHH!!!

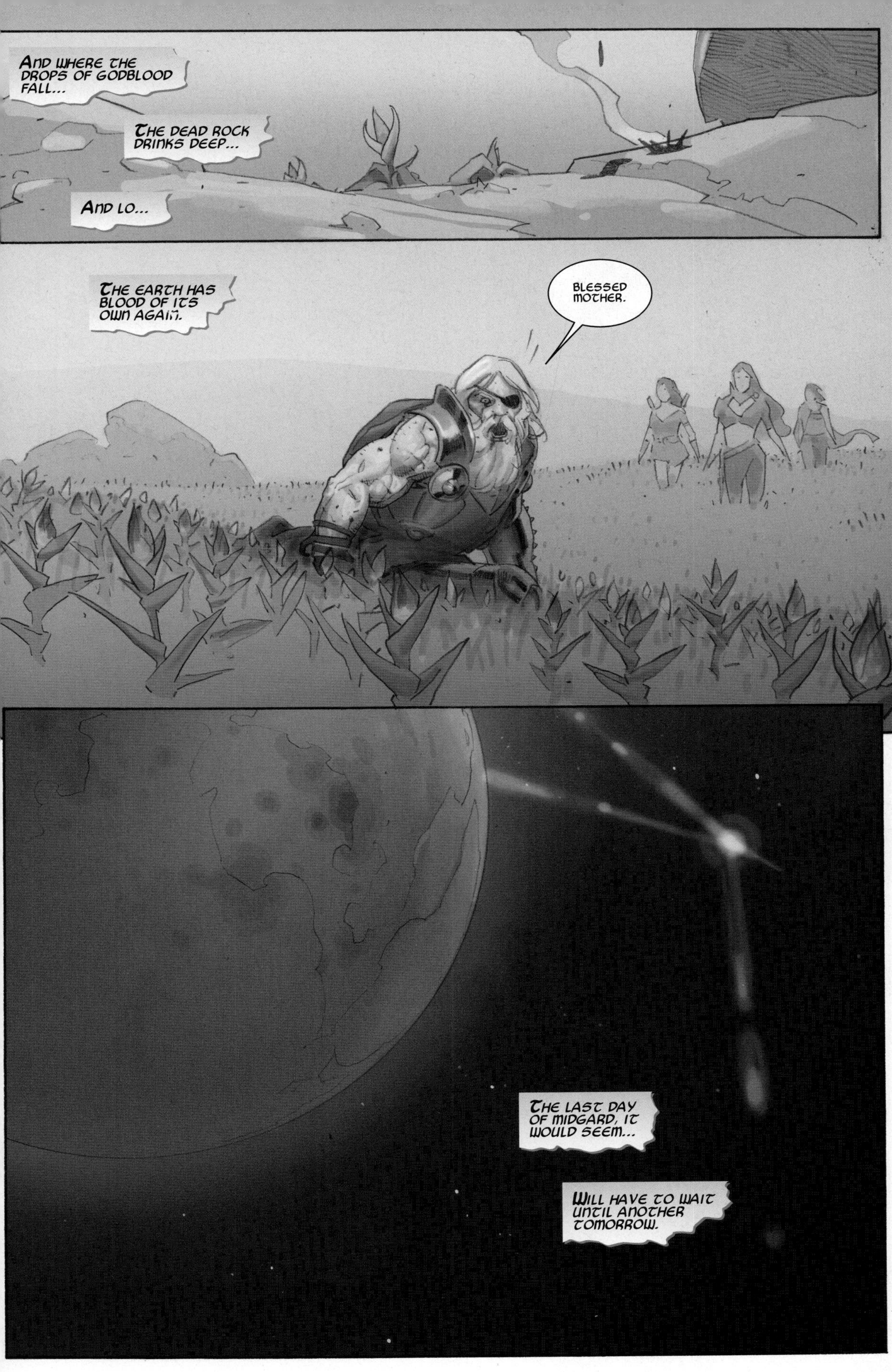
AND WHERE THE DROPS OF GODBLOOD FALL...
THE DEAD ROCK DRINKS DEEP...
AND LO...
THE EARTH HAS BLOOD OF ITS OWN AGAIN.
BLESSED MOTHER.
THE LAST DAY OF MIDGARD, IT WOULD SEEM...
WILL HAVE TO WAIT UNTIL ANOTHER TOMORROW.

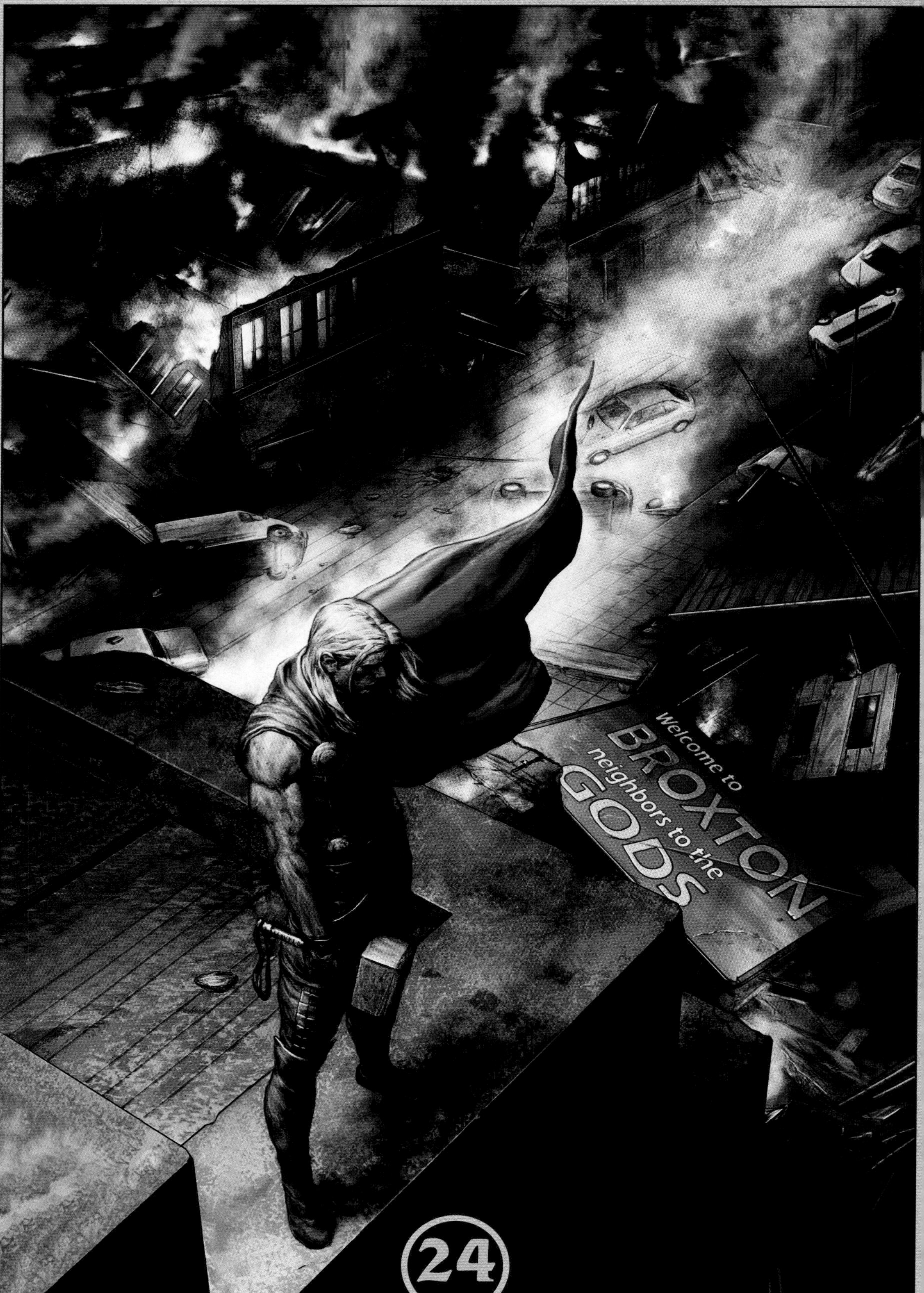
Welcome to
BROXTON
neighbors to the
GODS
24

The Last Days of Midgard — Epilogue: Adieu, Midgard, Adieu

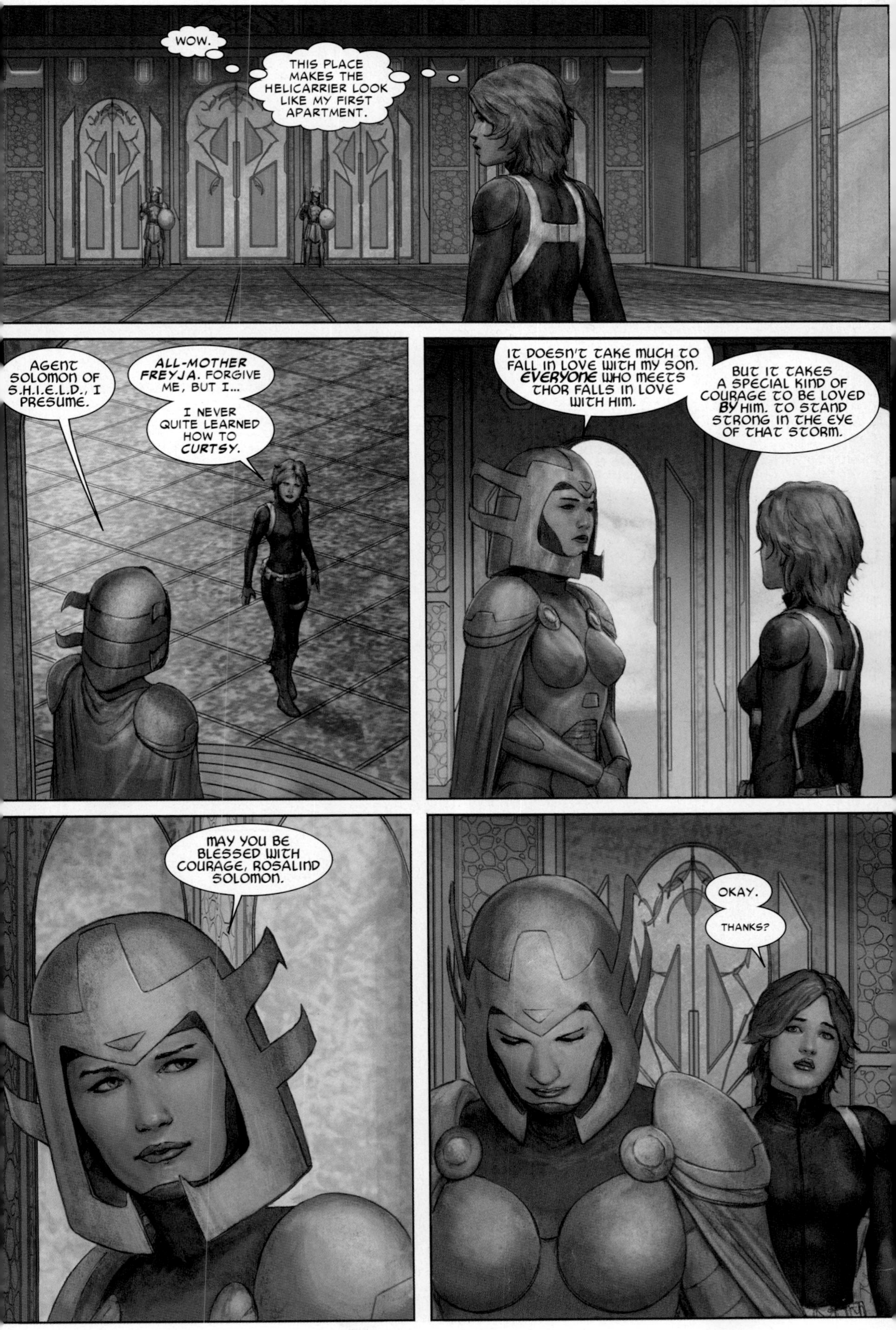

WOW.
THIS PLACE MAKES THE HELICARRIER LOOK LIKE MY FIRST APARTMENT.
AGENT SOLOMON OF S.H.I.E.L.D., I PRESUME.
ALL-MOTHER FREYJA. FORGIVE ME, BUT I...
I NEVER QUITE LEARNED HOW TO CURTSY.
IT DOESN'T TAKE MUCH TO FALL IN LOVE WITH MY SON. EVERYONE WHO MEETS THOR FALLS IN LOVE WITH HIM.
BUT IT TAKES A SPECIAL KIND OF COURAGE TO BE LOVED BY HIM. TO STAND STRONG IN THE EYE OF THAT STORM.
MAY YOU BE BLESSED WITH COURAGE, ROSALIND SOLOMON.
OKAY.
THANKS?

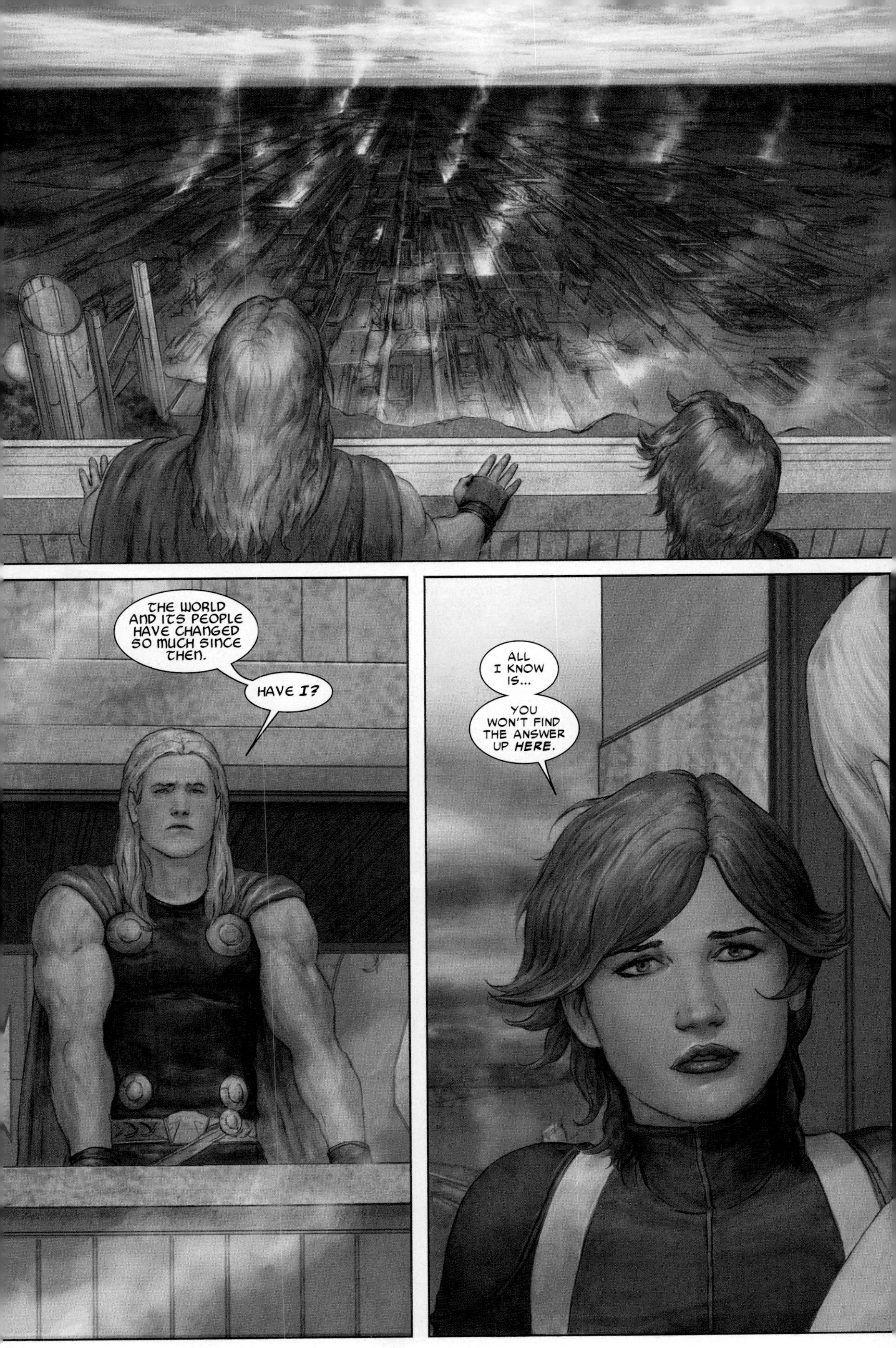
THE WORLD AND ITS PEOPLE HAVE CHANGED SO MUCH SINCE THEN.
HAVE I?
ALL I KNOW IS...
YOU WON'T FIND THE ANSWER UP HERE.

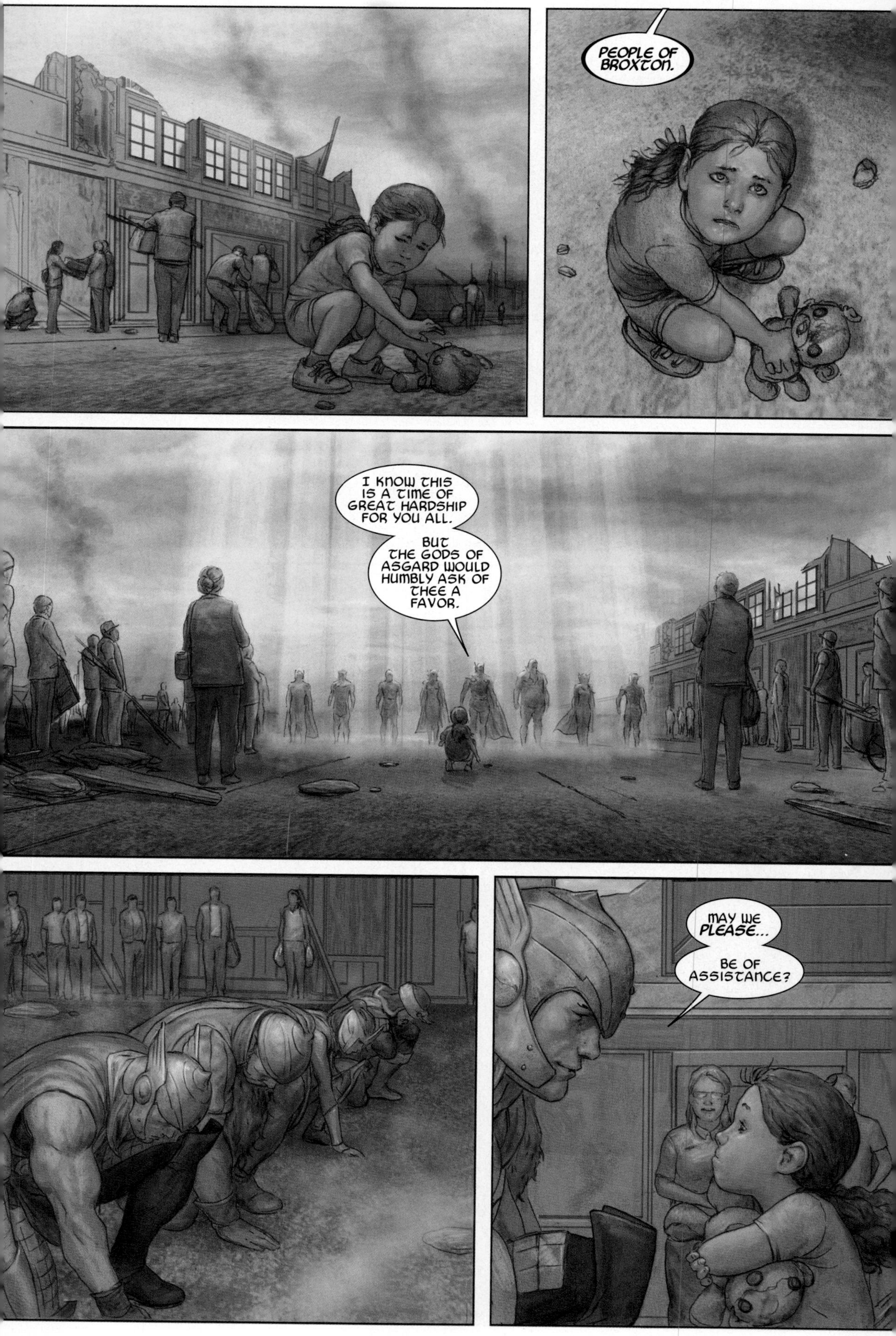

PEOPLE OF BROXTON.
I KNOW THIS IS A TIME OF GREAT HARDSHIP FOR YOU ALL.
BUT THE GODS OF ASGARD WOULD HUMBLY ASK OF THEE A FAVOR.
MAY WE PLEASE...
BE OF ASSISTANCE?

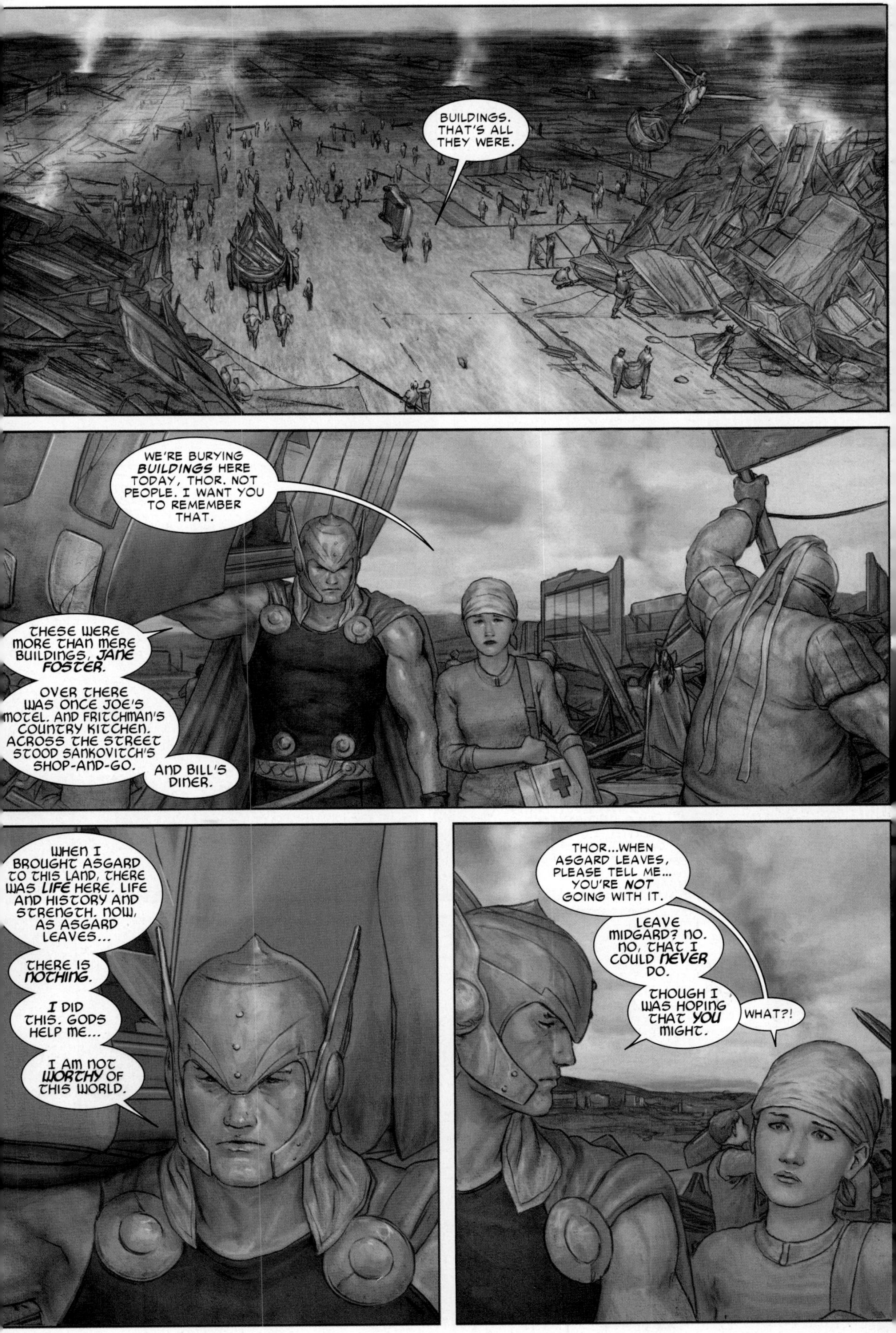
BUILDINGS. THAT'S ALL THEY WERE.
WE'RE BURYING *BUILDINGS* HERE TODAY, THOR. NOT PEOPLE. I WANT YOU TO REMEMBER THAT.
THESE WERE MORE THAN MERE BUILDINGS, *JANE FOSTER*.
OVER THERE WAS ONCE JOE'S MOTEL. AND FRITCHMAN'S COUNTRY KITCHEN. ACROSS THE STREET STOOD SANKOVITCH'S SHOP-AND-GO.
AND BILL'S DINER.
WHEN I BROUGHT ASGARD TO THIS LAND, THERE WAS *LIFE* HERE. LIFE AND HISTORY AND STRENGTH. NOW, AS ASGARD LEAVES...
THERE IS *NOTHING*.
I DID THIS. GODS HELP ME...
I AM NOT *WORTHY* OF THIS WORLD.
THOR...WHEN ASGARD LEAVES, PLEASE TELL ME... YOU'RE *NOT* GOING WITH IT.
LEAVE MIDGARD? NO. NO, THAT I COULD *NEVER* DO.
THOUGH I WAS HOPING THAT *YOU* MIGHT.
WHAT?!

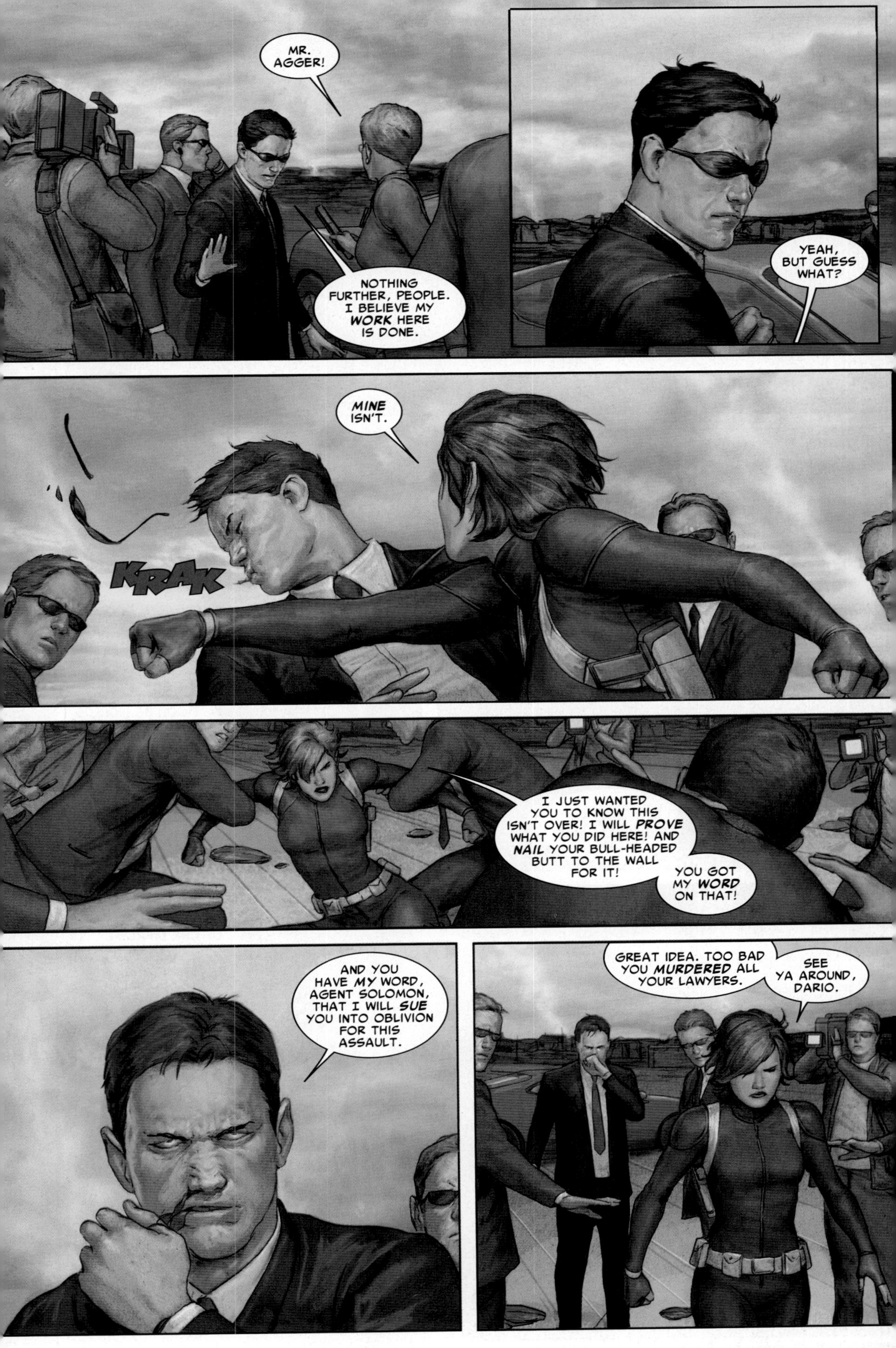
MR. AGGER!
NOTHING FURTHER, PEOPLE. I BELIEVE MY WORK HERE IS DONE.
YEAH, BUT GUESS WHAT?
MINE ISN'T.
KRAK
I JUST WANTED YOU TO KNOW THIS ISN'T OVER! I WILL PROVE WHAT YOU DID HERE! AND NAIL YOUR BULL-HEADED BUTT TO THE WALL FOR IT!
YOU GOT MY WORD ON THAT!
AND YOU HAVE MY WORD, AGENT SOLOMON, THAT I WILL SUE YOU INTO OBLIVION FOR THIS ASSAULT.
GREAT IDEA. TOO BAD YOU MURDERED ALL YOUR LAWYERS.
SEE YA AROUND, DARIO.

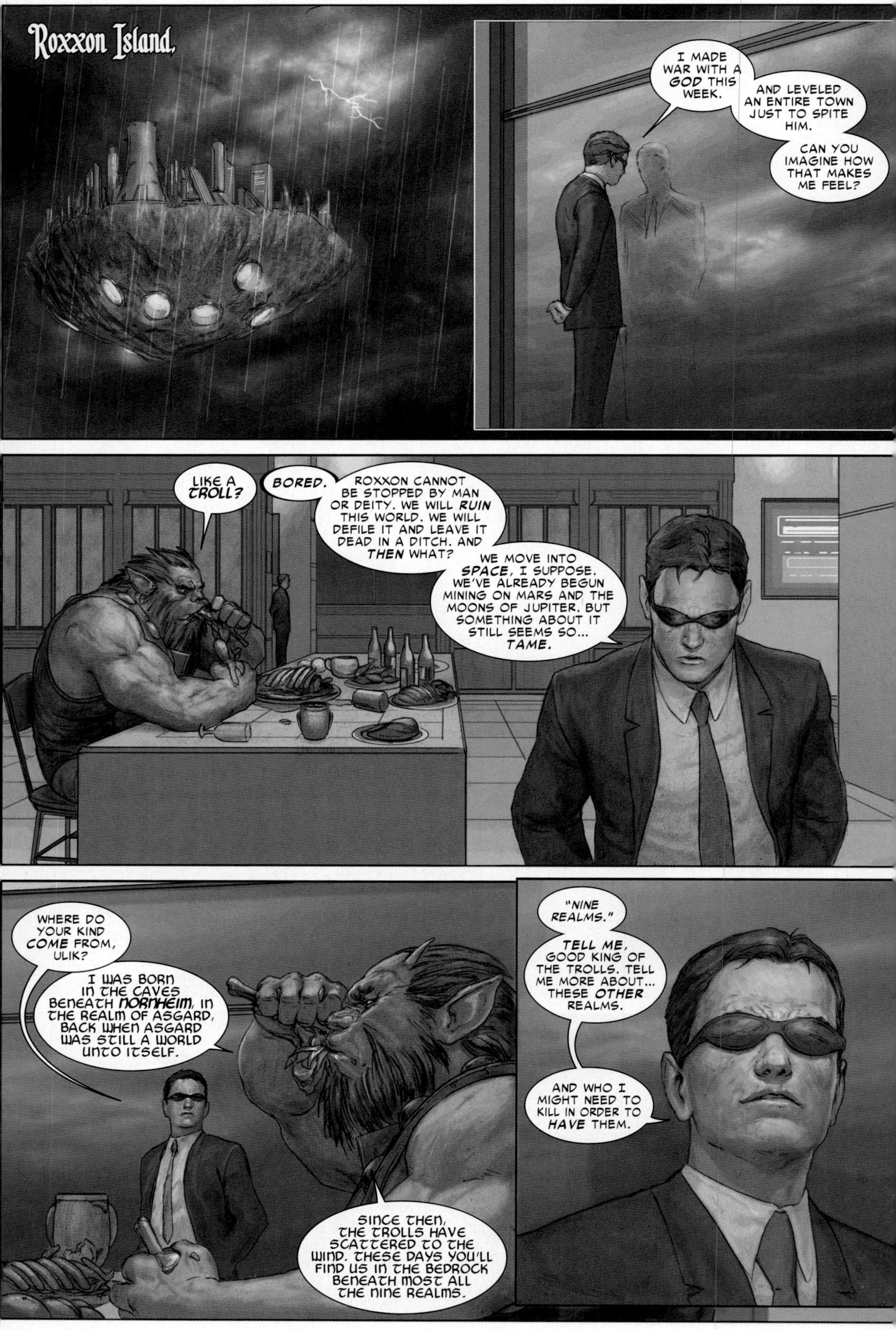

Roxxon Island.
I MADE WAR WITH A GOD THIS WEEK.
AND LEVELED AN ENTIRE TOWN JUST TO SPITE HIM.
CAN YOU IMAGINE HOW THAT MAKES ME FEEL?
LIKE A TROLL?
BORED.
ROXXON CANNOT BE STOPPED BY MAN OR DEITY. WE WILL RUIN THIS WORLD. WE WILL DEFILE IT AND LEAVE IT DEAD IN A DITCH. AND THEN WHAT?
WE MOVE INTO SPACE, I SUPPOSE. WE'VE ALREADY BEGUN MINING ON MARS AND THE MOONS OF JUPITER. BUT SOMETHING ABOUT IT STILL SEEMS SO... TAME.
WHERE DO YOUR KIND COME FROM, ULIK?
I WAS BORN IN THE CAVES BENEATH NORNHEIM, IN THE REALM OF ASGARD, BACK WHEN ASGARD WAS STILL A WORLD UNTO ITSELF.
SINCE THEN, THE TROLLS HAVE SCATTERED TO THE WIND. THESE DAYS YOU'LL FIND US IN THE BEDROCK BENEATH MOST ALL THE NINE REALMS.
"NINE REALMS."
TELL ME, GOOD KING OF THE TROLLS. TELL ME MORE ABOUT... THESE OTHER REALMS.
AND WHO I MIGHT NEED TO KILL IN ORDER TO HAVE THEM.

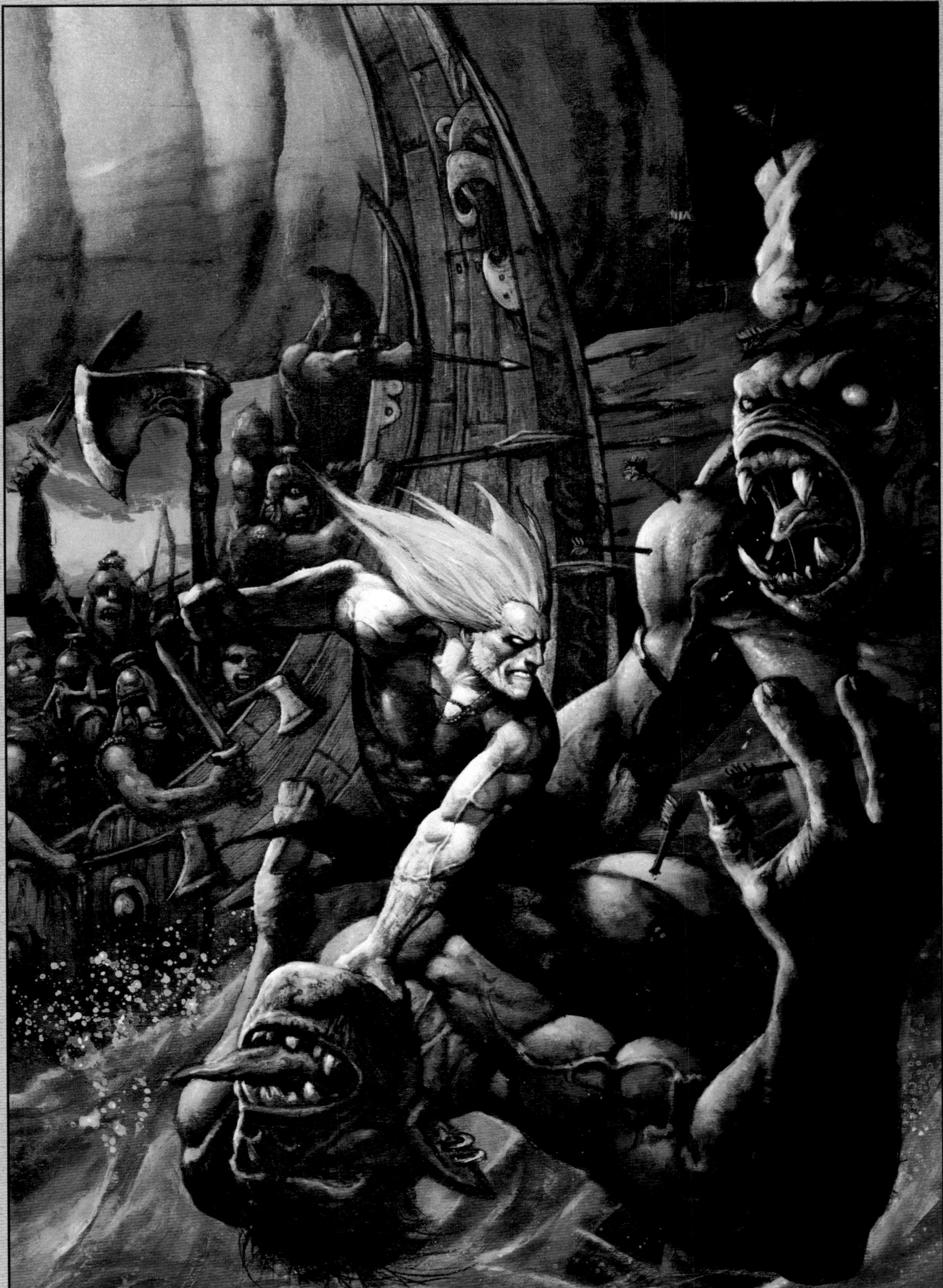
BISLEY 14.

#25 VARIANT
BY SIMON BISLEY

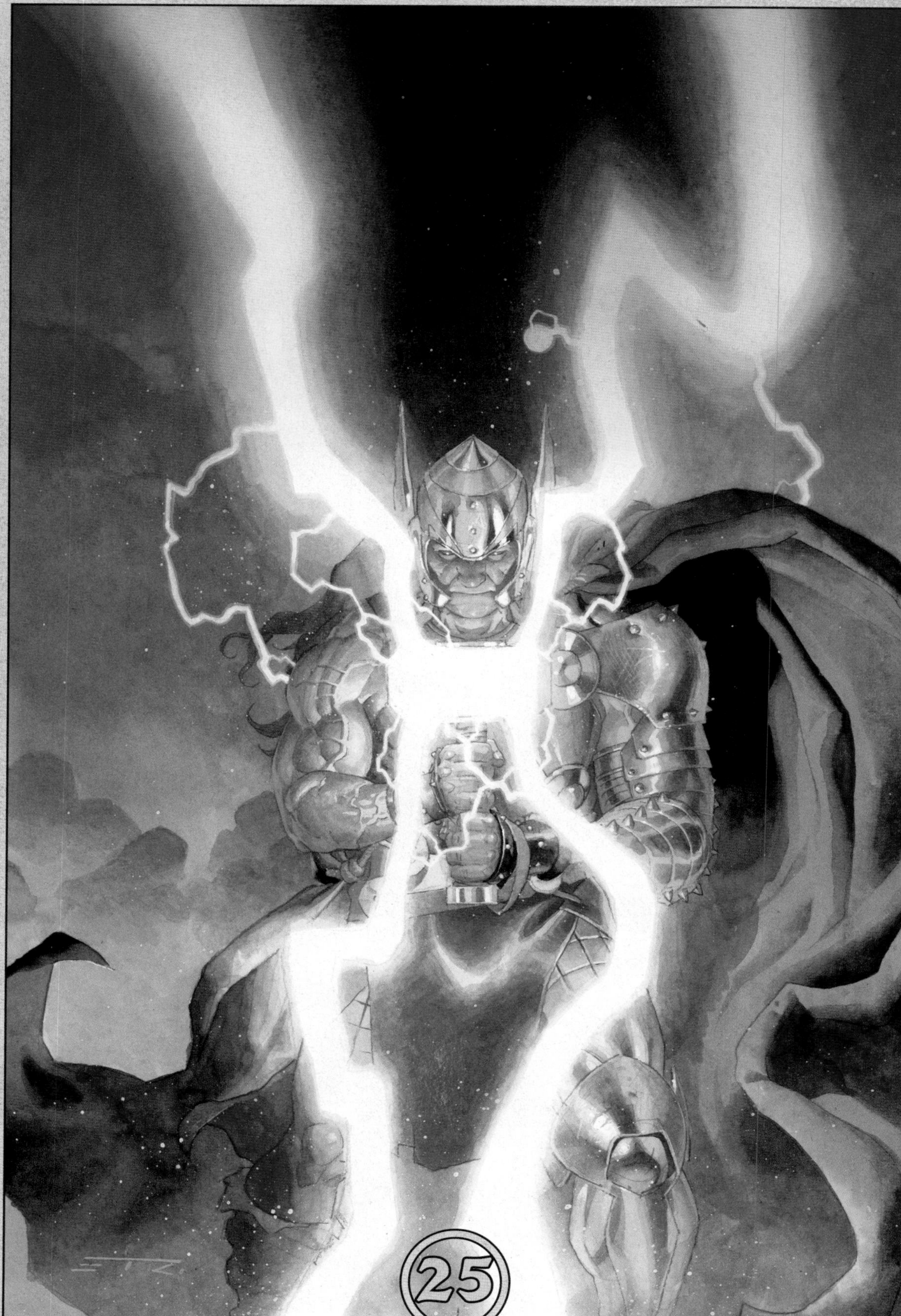
25

Tales of Thunder

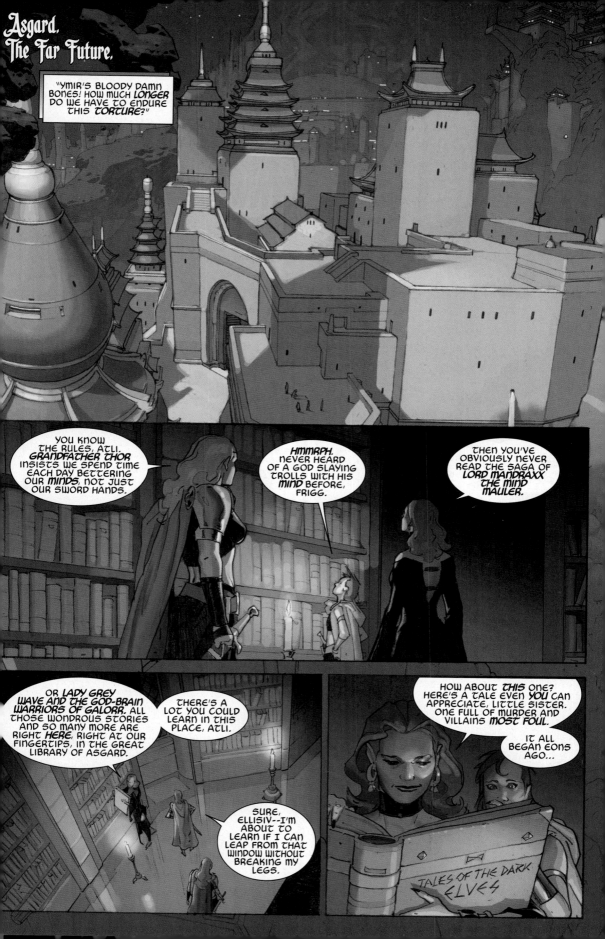

Asgard, The Far Future.

"YMIR'S BLOODY DAMN BONES! HOW MUCH *LONGER* DO WE HAVE TO ENDURE THIS *TORTURE?*"

YOU KNOW THE RULES, ATLI. *GRANDFATHER THOR* INSISTS WE SPEND TIME EACH DAY BETTERING OUR *MINDS,* NOT JUST OUR SWORD HANDS.

HMMRPH. NEVER HEARD OF A GOD SLAYING TROLLS WITH HIS *MIND* BEFORE, FRIGG.

THEN YOU'VE OBVIOUSLY NEVER READ THE SAGA OF *LORD MANDRAXX THE MIND MAULER.*

OR *LADY GREY WAVE AND THE GOD-BRAIN WARRIORS OF GALORR.* ALL THOSE WONDROUS STORIES AND SO MANY MORE ARE RIGHT *HERE,* RIGHT AT OUR FINGERTIPS, IN THE GREAT LIBRARY OF ASGARD.

THERE'S A LOT YOU COULD LEARN IN THIS PLACE, ATLI.

SURE, ELLISIV--I'M ABOUT TO LEARN IF I CAN LEAP FROM THAT WINDOW WITHOUT BREAKING MY LEGS.

HOW ABOUT *THIS* ONE? HERE'S A TALE EVEN *YOU* CAN APPRECIATE, LITTLE SISTER. ONE FULL OF MURDER AND VILLAINS *MOST FOUL.*

IT ALL BEGAN EONS AGO...

TALES OF THE DARK ELVES

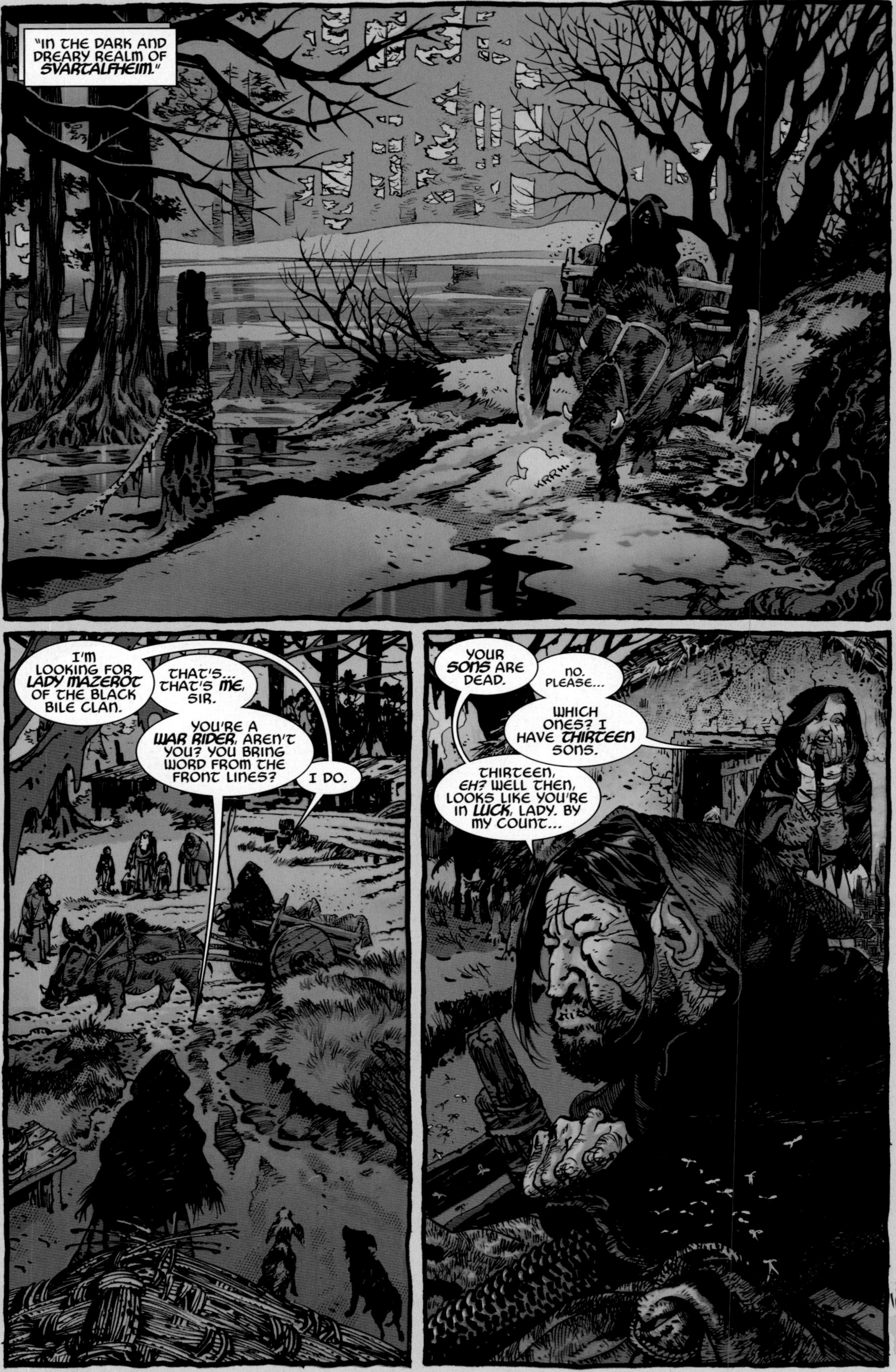
"IN THE DARK AND DREARY REALM OF SVARTALFHEIM."
KRRH.
I'M LOOKING FOR LADY MAZEROT OF THE BLACK BILE CLAN.
THAT'S... THAT'S ME, SIR.
YOU'RE A WAR RIDER, AREN'T YOU? YOU BRING WORD FROM THE FRONT LINES?
I DO.
YOUR SONS ARE DEAD.
NO. PLEASE...
WHICH ONES? I HAVE THIRTEEN SONS.
THIRTEEN, EH? WELL THEN, LOOKS LIKE YOU'RE IN LUCK, LADY. BY MY COUNT...

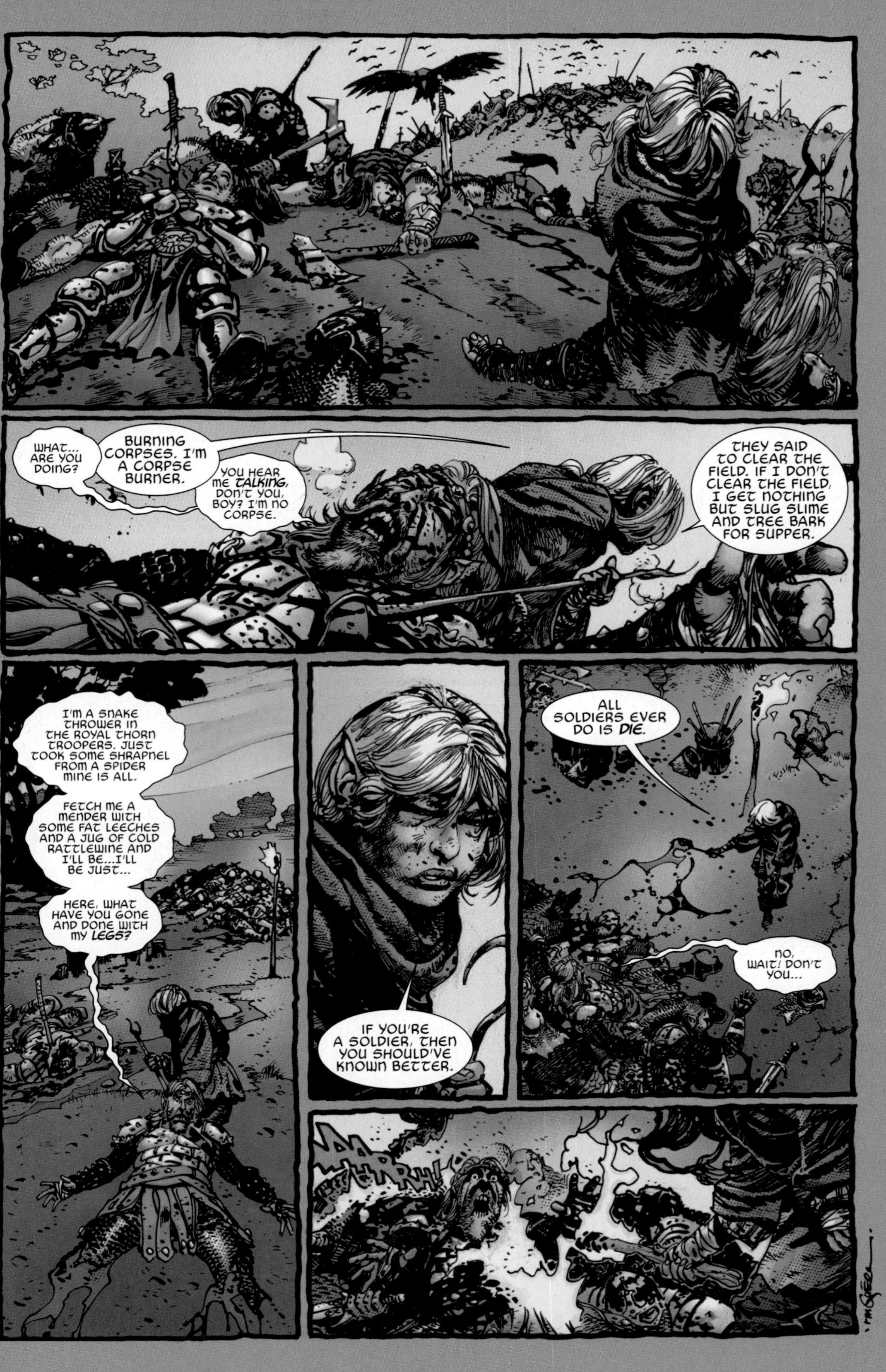
WHAT... ARE YOU DOING?
BURNING CORPSES. I'M A CORPSE BURNER.
YOU HEAR ME TALKING, DON'T YOU, BOY? I'M NO CORPSE.
THEY SAID TO CLEAR THE FIELD. IF I DON'T CLEAR THE FIELD, I GET NOTHING BUT SLUG SLIME AND TREE BARK FOR SUPPER.
I'M A SNAKE THROWER IN THE ROYAL THORN TROOPERS. JUST TOOK SOME SHRAPNEL FROM A SPIDER MINE IS ALL.
FETCH ME A MENDER WITH SOME FAT LEECHES AND A JUG OF COLD RATTLEWINE AND I'LL BE...I'LL BE JUST...
HERE, WHAT HAVE YOU GONE AND DONE WITH MY LEGS?
IF YOU'RE A SOLDIER, THEN YOU SHOULD'VE KNOWN BETTER.
ALL SOLDIERS EVER DO IS DIE.
NO, WAIT! DON'T YOU...

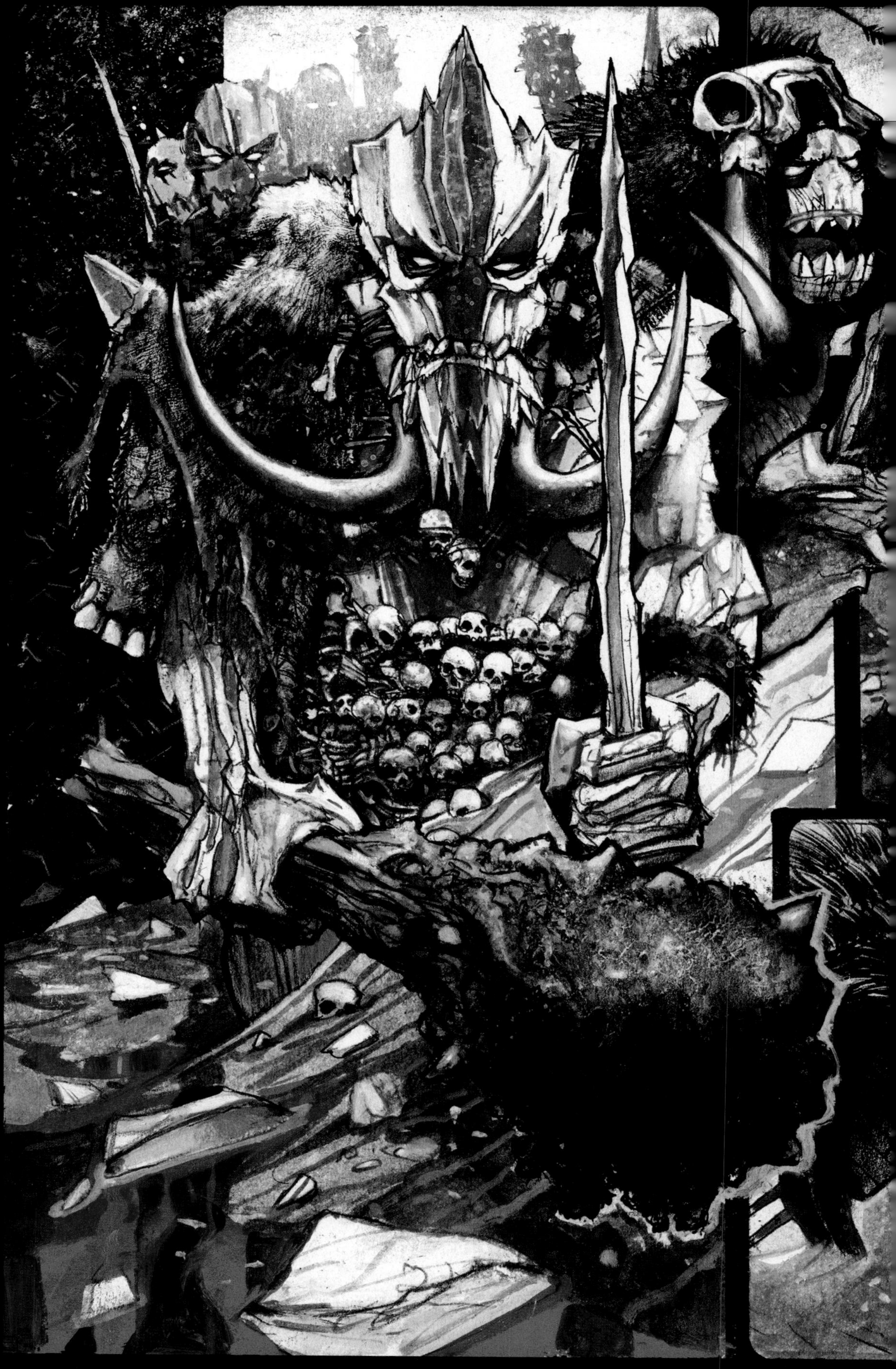

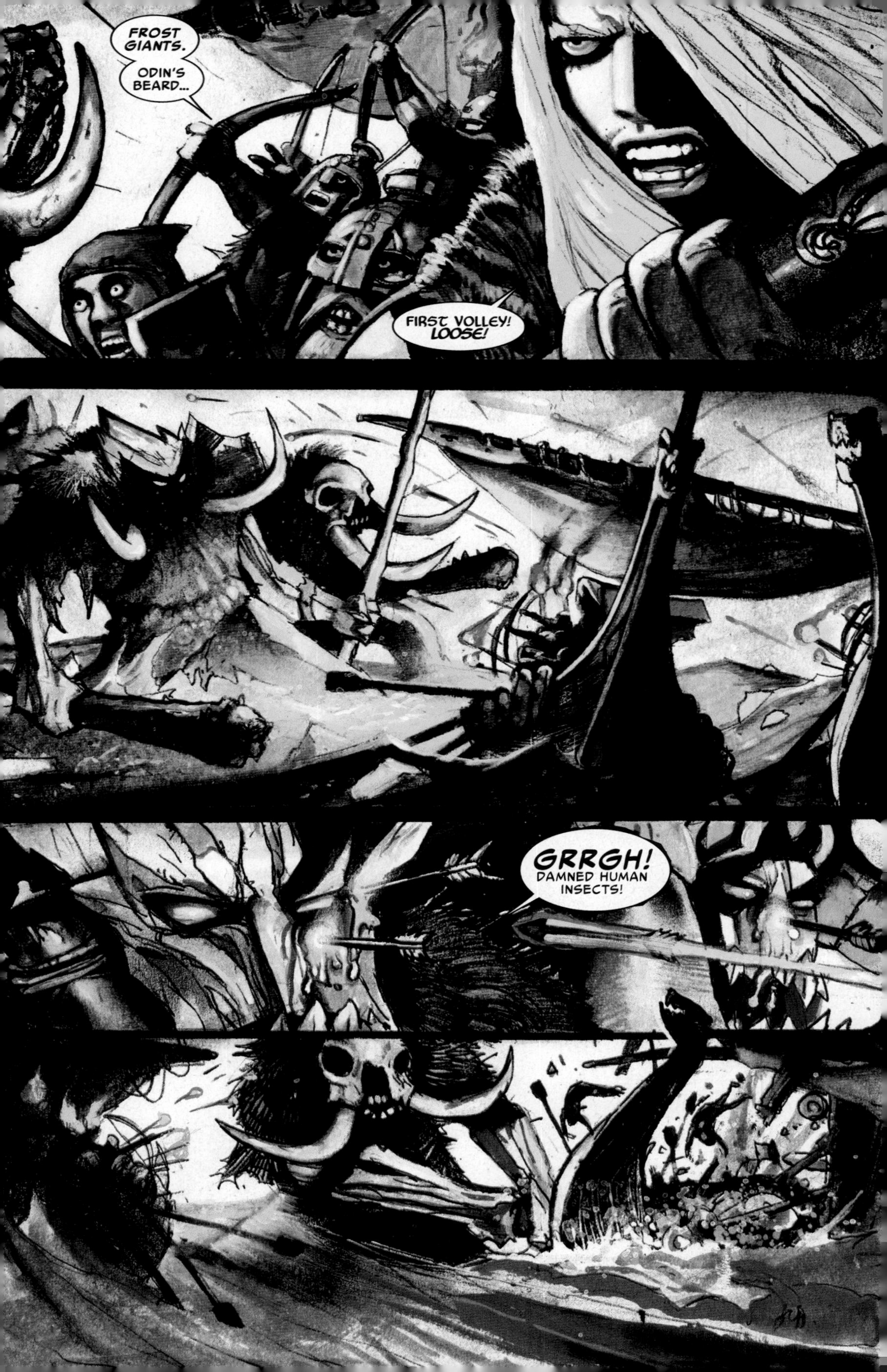
FROST GIANTS.
ODIN'S BEARD...
FIRST VOLLEY! LOOSE!
GRRGH! DAMNED HUMAN INSECTS!

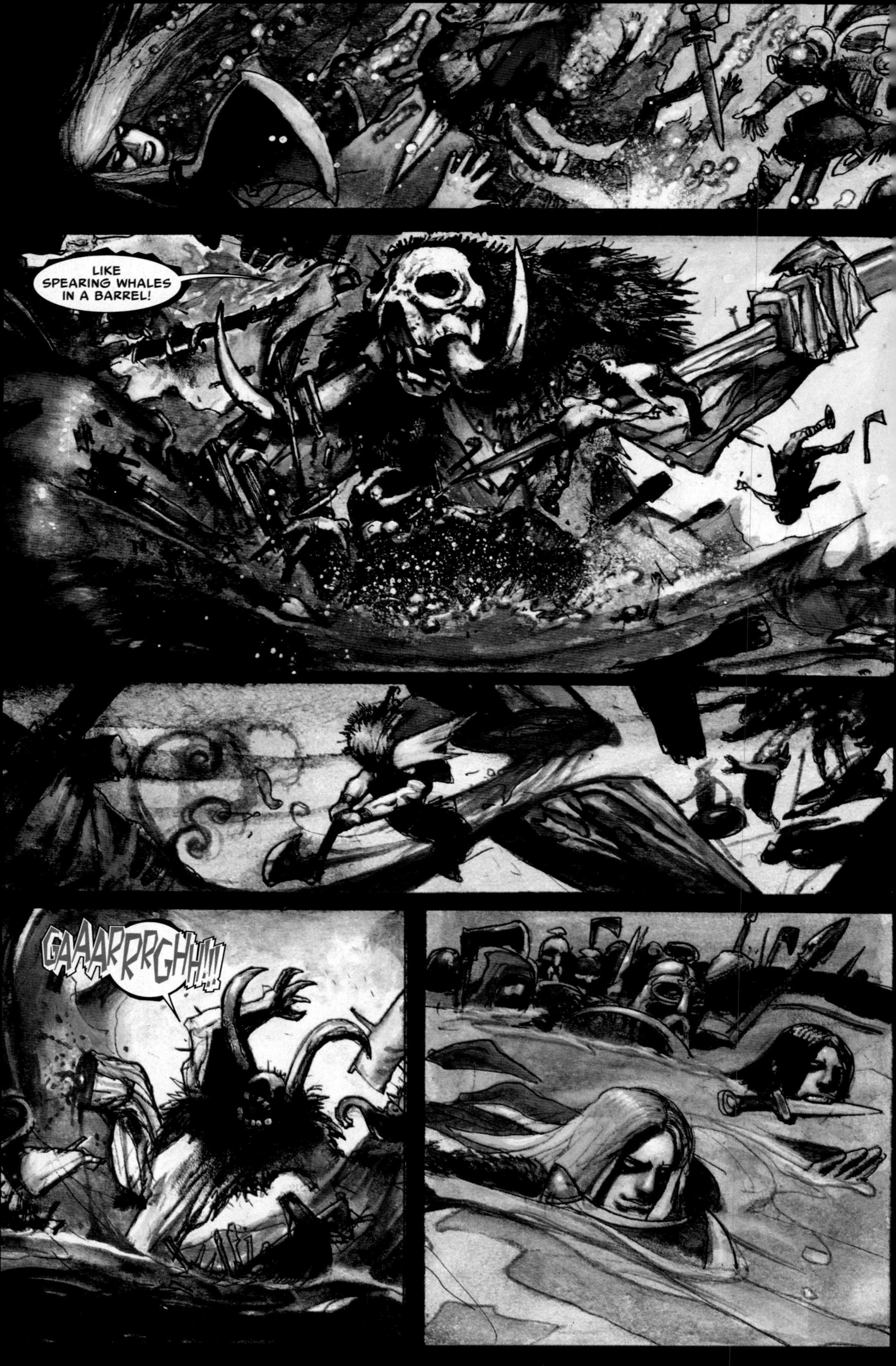
LIKE SPEARING WHALES IN A BARREL!
GAAARRRGHH!!!

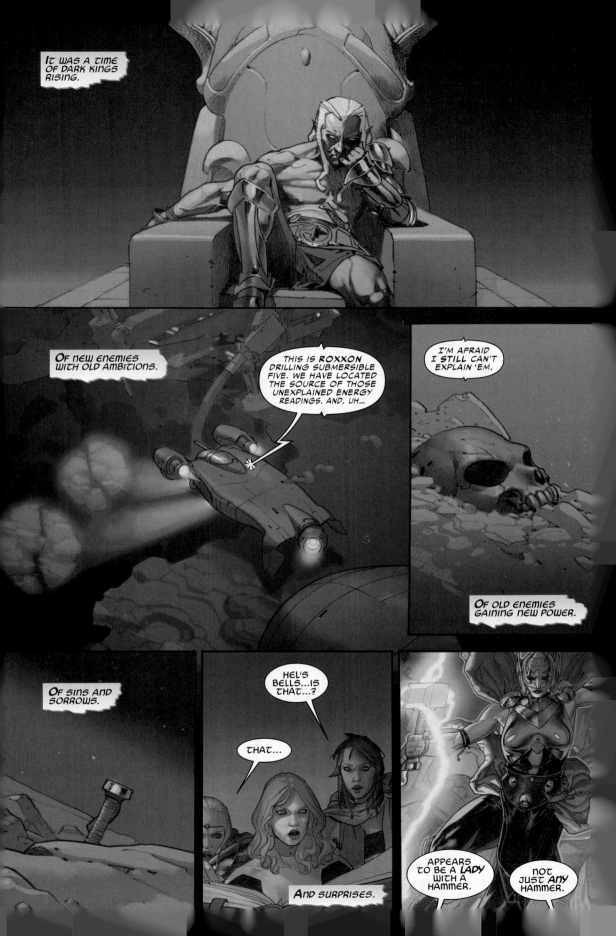

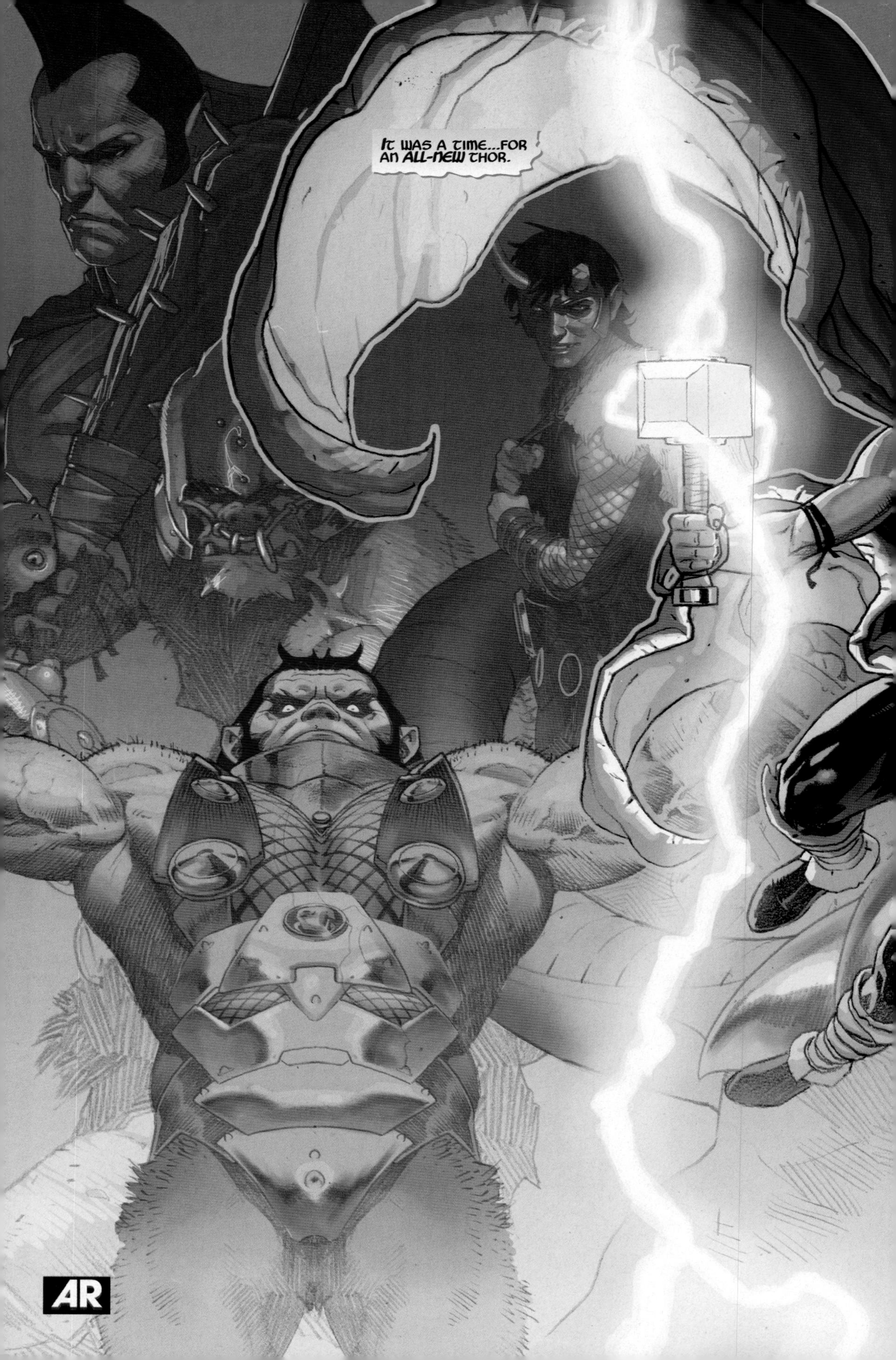
IT WAS A TIME...FOR AN ALL-NEW THOR.

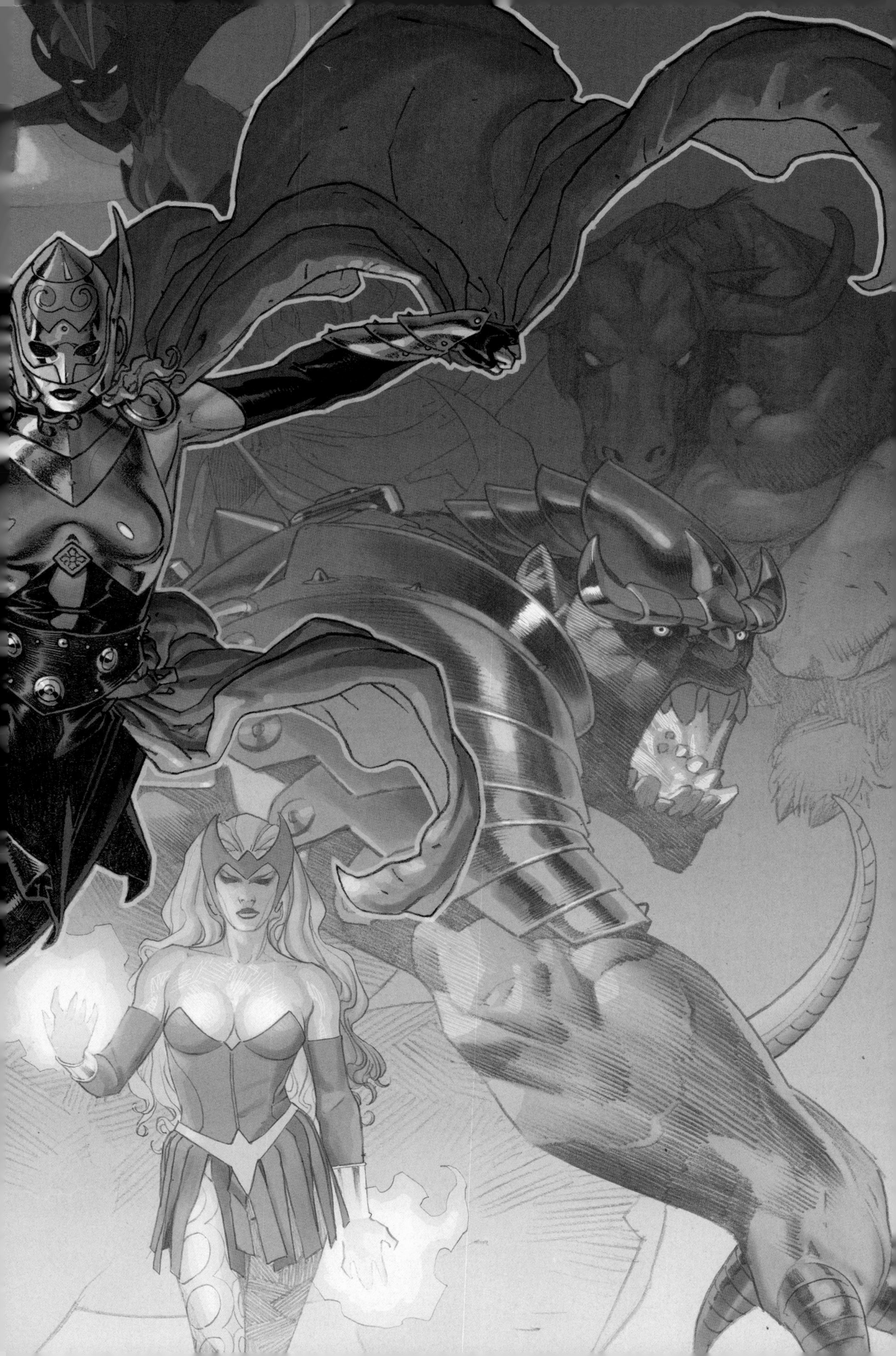

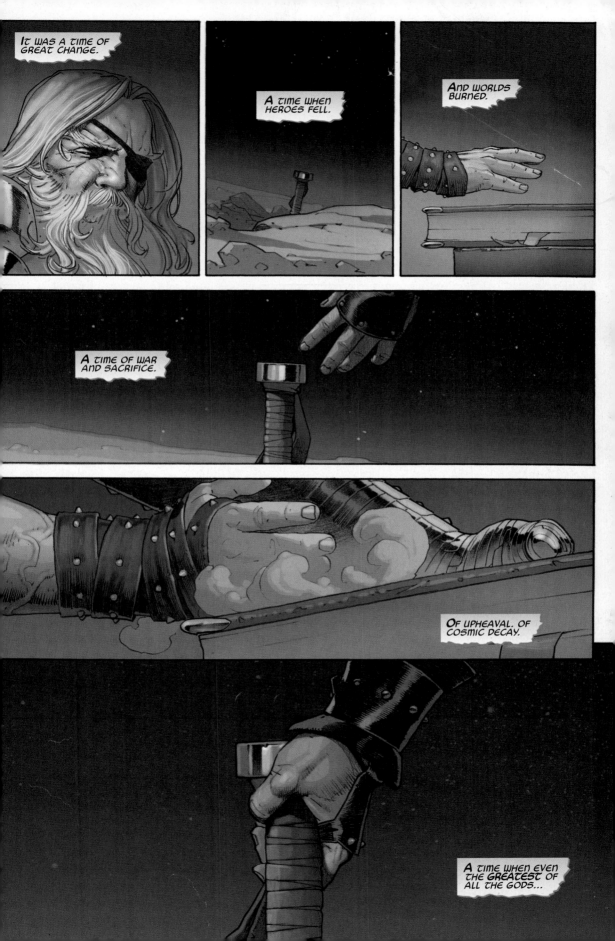

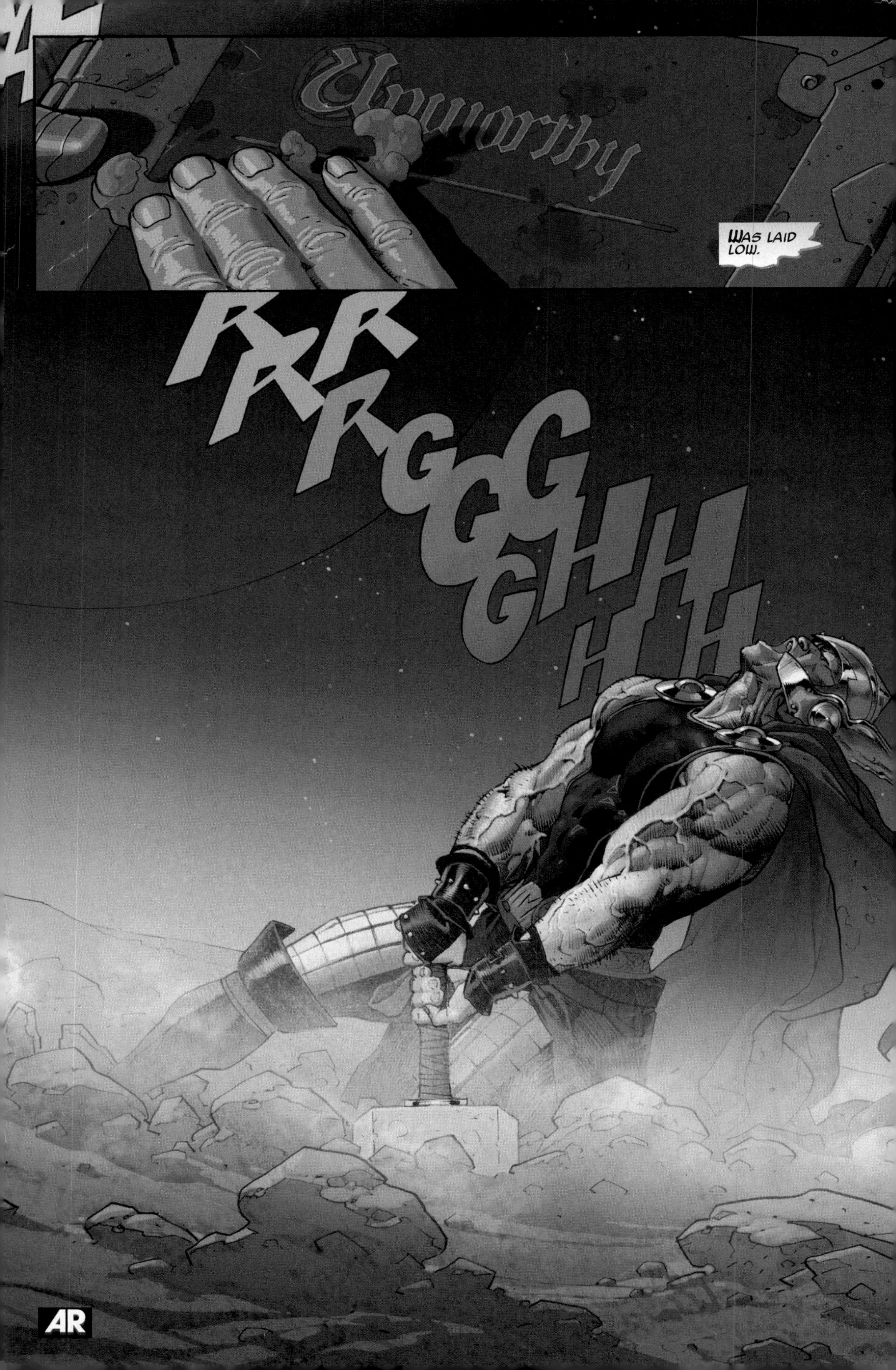
Unworthy
WAS LAID LOW.
RRRRGGGGHHHH
AR

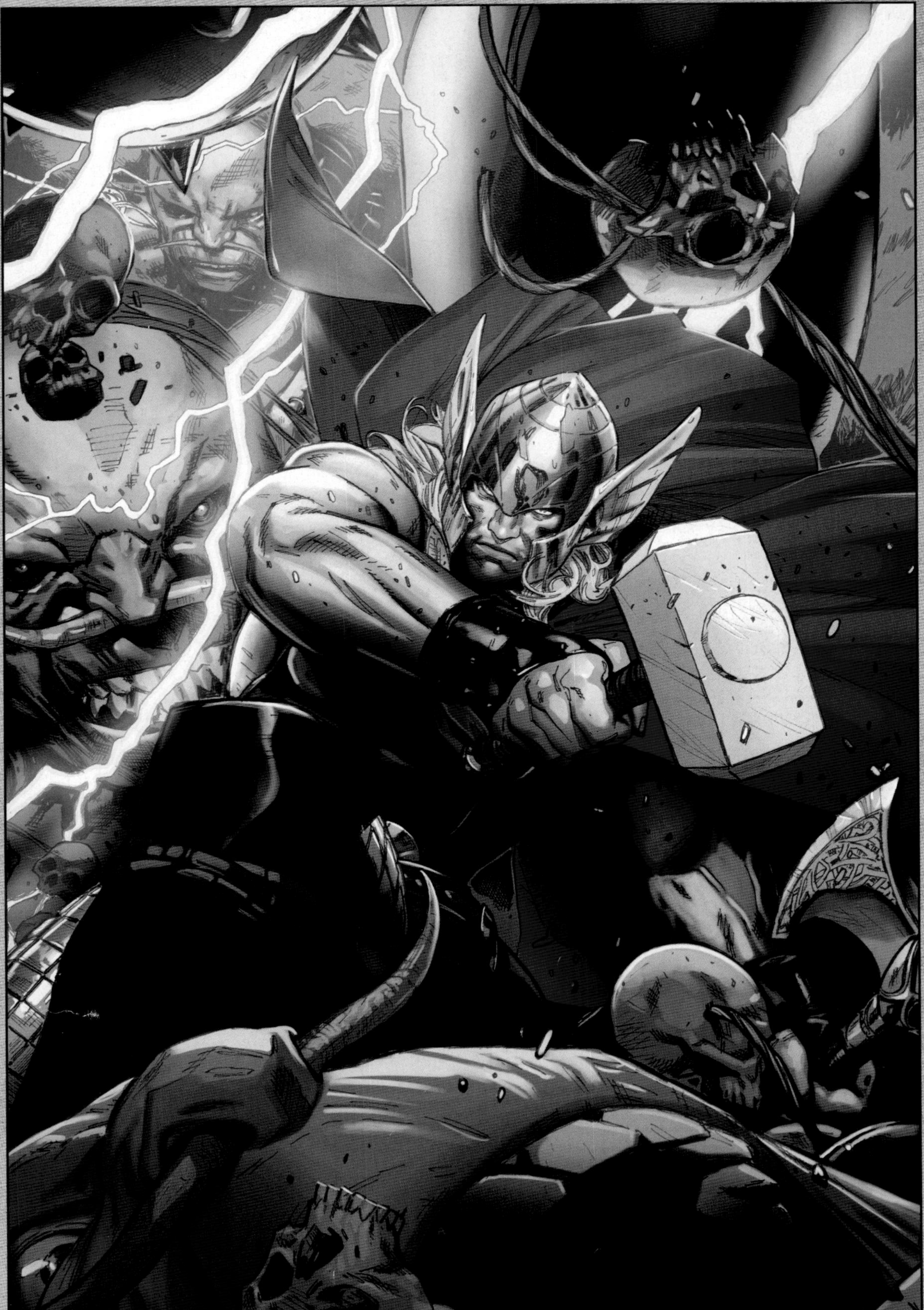

#19 VARIANT
BY CLAY MANN & IVE SVORCINA

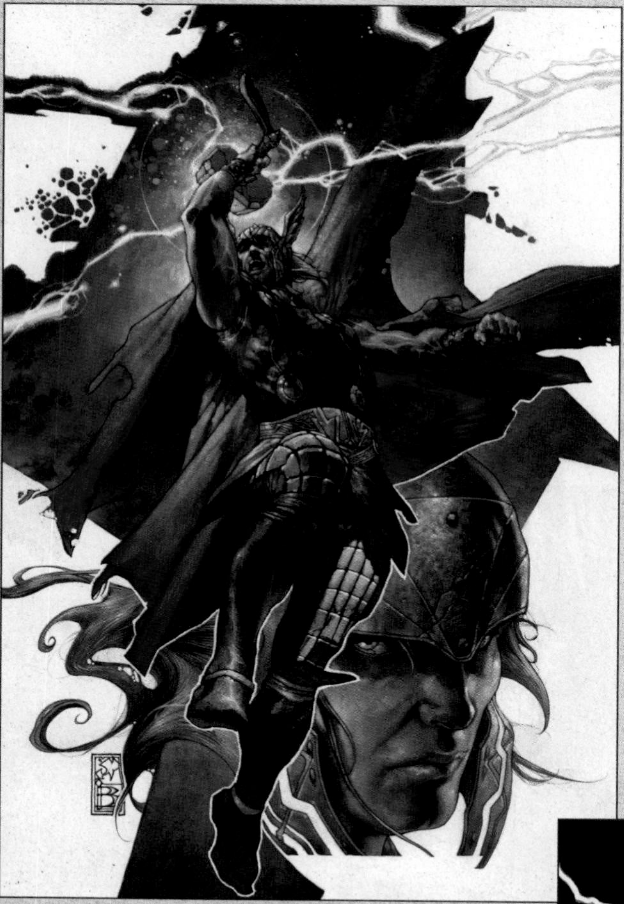

#19 VARIANT
BY SIMONE BIANCHI

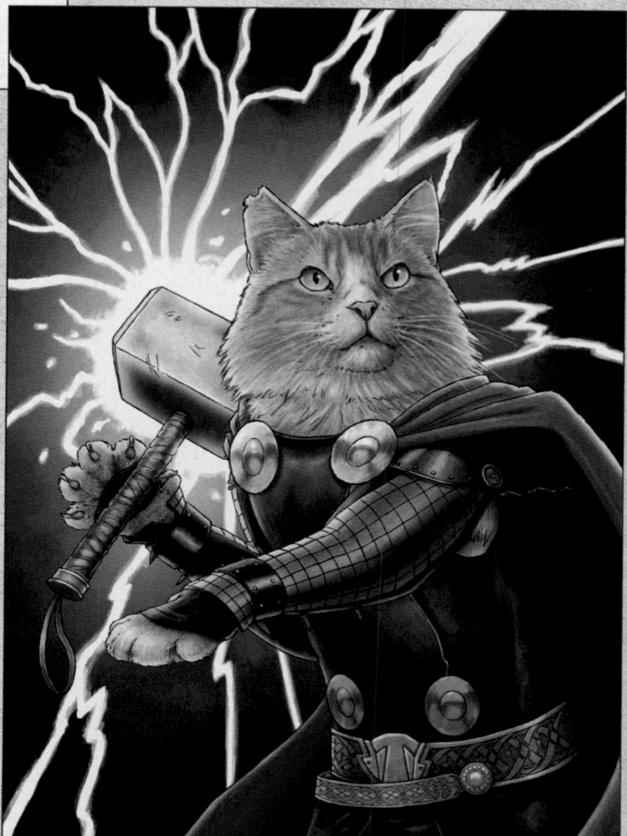

#19 ANIMAL VARIANT
BY JENNY PARKS

#20 VARIANT
BY NIC KLEIN

#21 VARIANT
BY RON GARNEY

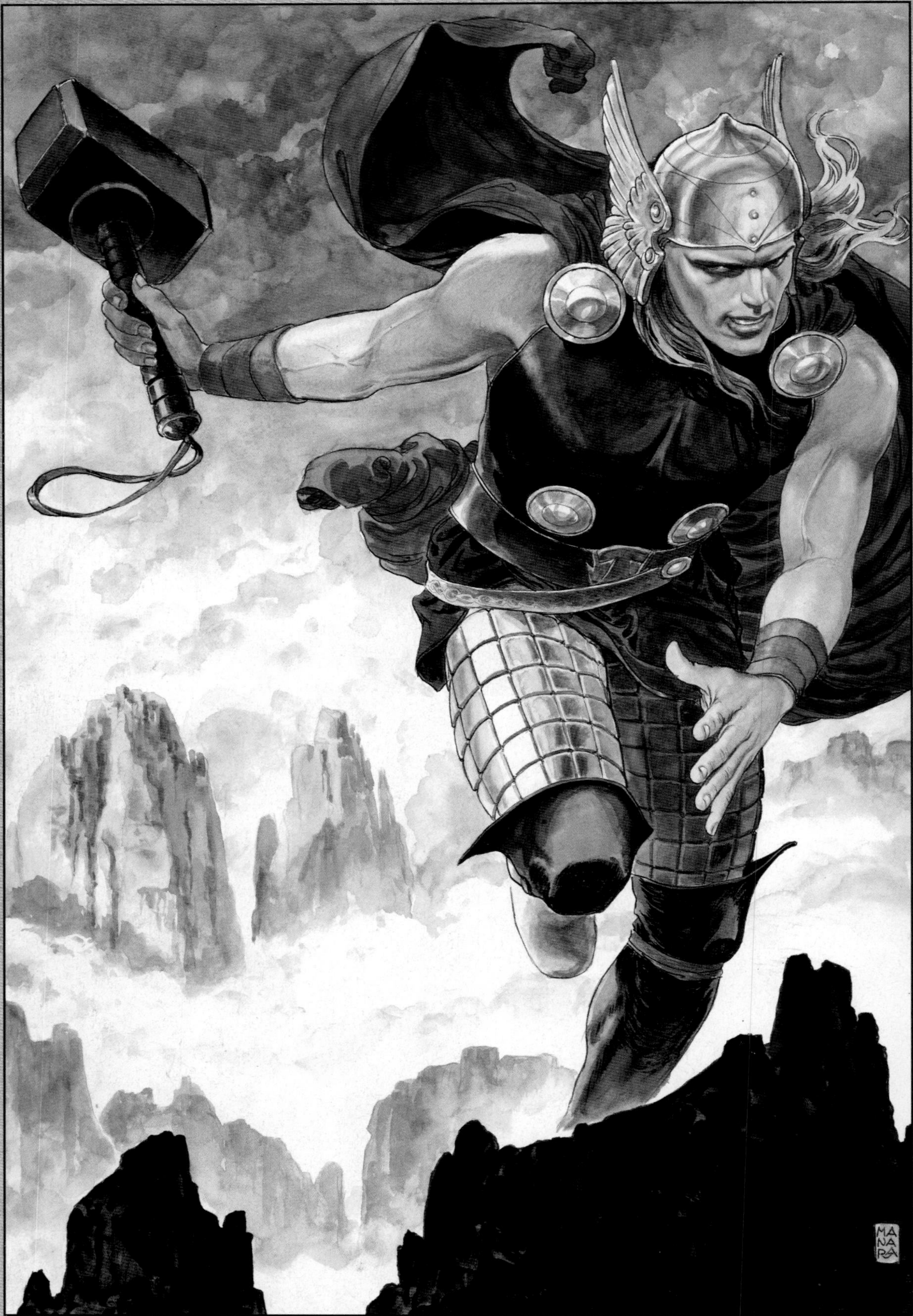
MANARA

#25 VARIANT
BY MILO MANARA

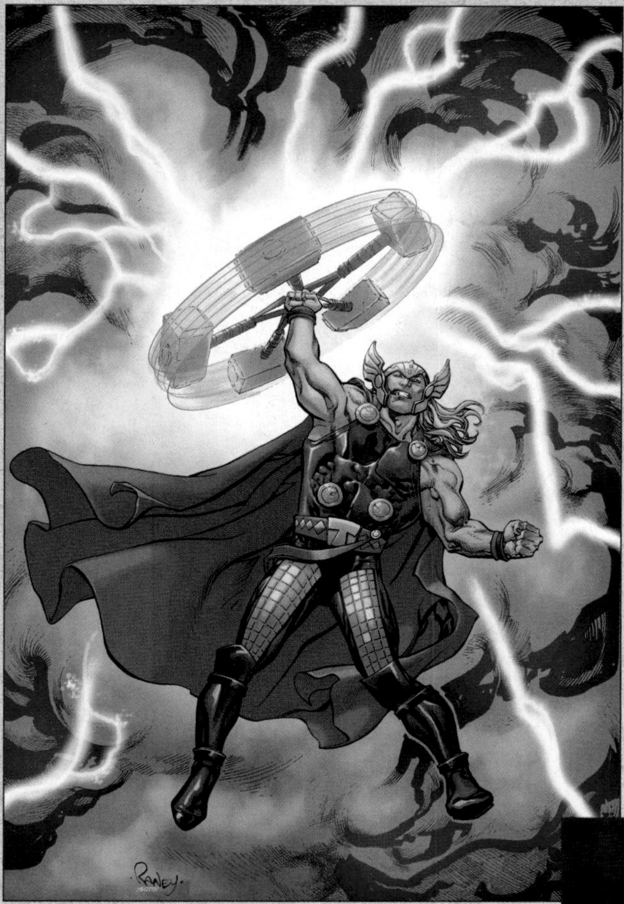
RANEY

#25 VARIANT
BY TOM RANEY
& CHRIS SOTOMAYOR

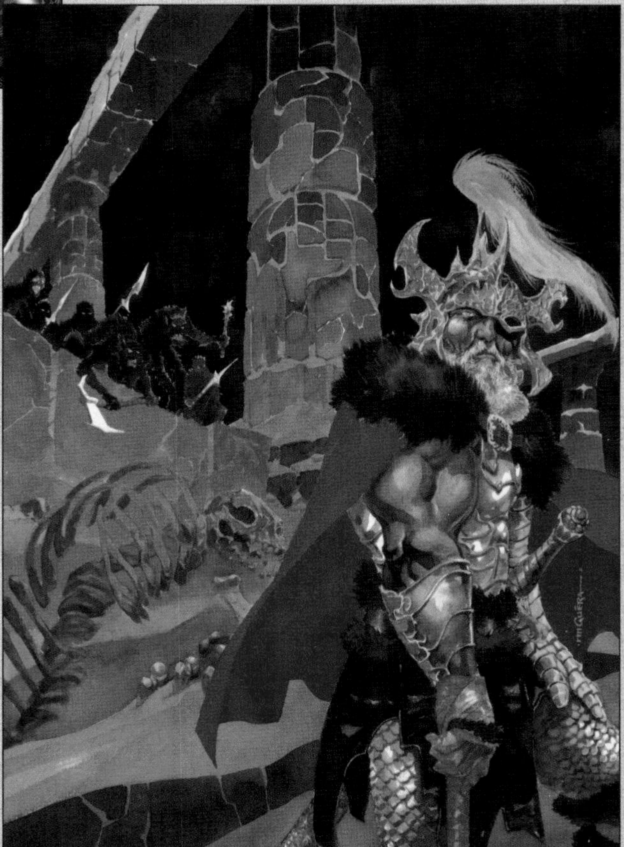

#25 VARIANT
BY R.M. GUERA

MARVEL AUGMENTED REALITY (AR) ENHANCES AND CHANGES THE WAY YOU EXPERIENCE COMICS!

TO ACCESS THE FREE MARVEL AR CONTENT IN THIS BOOK*:

1. **Locate the AR logo within the comic.**
2. **Go to Marvel.com/AR in your web browser.**
3. **Search by series title to find the corresponding AR.**
4. **Enjoy Marvel AR!**

*All AR content that appears in this book has been archived and will be available only at Marvel.com/AR – no longer in the Marvel AR App. Content subject to change and availability.

THOR GOD OF THUNDER AR INDEX

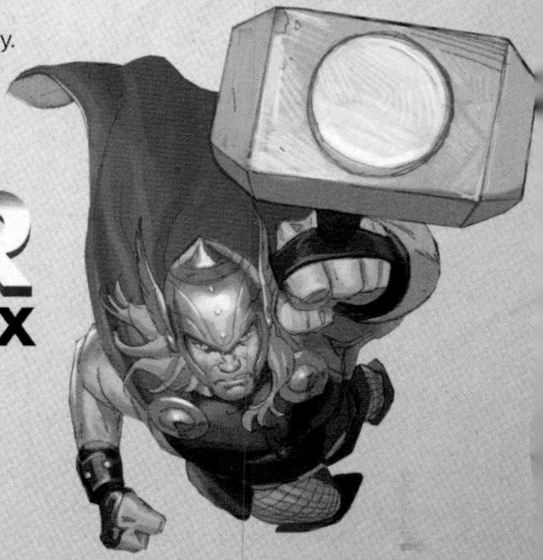